Peter Cave teaches philosoph and City University in Londo broadcaster, having scripted th for BBC Radio 4. His previous publications include the best-selling *Can a Robot be Human?* and *What's Wrong with Eating People?* He lives in London.

HOW TO OUTWIT ARISTOTLE

And 34 Other Really Interesting Uses of PHILOSOPHY

PETER CAVE

Typeset by Ellipsis Digital Limited, Glasgow

Printed and bound in Great Britain by Clays Ltd, St Ives plc

Quercus

This paperback edition published in Great Britain in 2012 by

Quercus
55 Baker Street
7th Floor, South Block
London
W1U 8EW

Illustrated edition originally published 2011, as *How to Think Like a Bat*.

A CIP catalogue record for this book is available
from the British Library

ISBN 978 0 85738 832 2

Pr

CONTENTS

INTRODUCTION

A woman was advising her anguished friend, 'Be philosophical – then you won't need to think about it.'

Well, being philosophical is sometimes taken to mean that you should adopt a resigned attitude to the world. The study that is Western philosophy, starting with the ancient Greeks and continuing today in universities, bars and cafés – even bedrooms – is, though, far from quiet and unthinking. Philosophers think – but not just that, for they think about thinking and they think about how we think about the world, about how we conceive of ourselves, about how we possess a sense of right and wrong, about how we find meaning in life (if we do).

What philosophers think about is, largely, what we already know or think we know. But in thinking they bring out tensions in our thinking, in our understanding of the world. They sense those bumps of intellectual dust lurking under, or within, our conceptual carpet – and they try to find ways of smoothing them out. They may be successful in their smoothing, only to find, though, that they have moved the bumps, the dusty conceptual dubieties, to elsewhere under the carpet. Here is a simple example.

We often explain what people do in terms of the end in view. Joanna jogs for her health: health is the aim. Yet how can health be the explanation of Joanna's jogging? After all, the anticipated health is in the future; how can something in the future cause something to happen, the jogging, right now? Worse is to come. The health may never be realized – she may collapse with exhaustion – so how can something non-existent (for she failed in her health quest) explain Joanna's current jogging? Well, we can smooth over that intellectual bump. We may insist that, really, it is Joanna's *desire* for good health – and it is that desire that precedes and causes the jogging. So, we may breathe easily, contented now, in that there is no problem with explanations in terms of ends after all. But then a philosophical whisper is heard, 'Ah, but Joanna desires good health; yet how can she desire something that may not exist?' Now we are finding a bump in the belief area of our intellectual carpet.

When reflecting philosophically on the topics in this book, we should keep in mind certain elements, certain distinctions, that often arise and can help to clarify. Let me hasten to add, though, that even these distinctions give rise to controversy. Still, let us note some important ones straightaway.

One is the distinction between what must be so and what merely happens to be so. Obama happens to be President of the USA in 2012, but he might not have been. It is a contingent fact that he is President. Obama might have gone in for pig farming, instead of politics. (We assume there is a distinction.) In contrast, it is surely a necessary truth – and not a contingent truth – that the number seven is an odd number. Obviously the word 'seven' might have meant 'six', but we are talking of the number seven, not of the word 'seven'.

Another related distinction is that between *a posteriori* knowledge and *a priori* knowledge. The distinction is relevant when wondering quite how we came to know or believe something. Much of our knowledge and many beliefs derive from the world around us, the empirical world of tables and chairs, fields and fish, newspapers and forest walks. We go out and investigate or, at least, laze in front of the television and soak up. Such knowledge – knowledge that can only be derived through our experiences of the empirical world – is *a posteriori* knowledge. There is, though, another sort of knowledge – *a priori* knowledge – that we can arrive at independently of experience. Assuming that we have the concepts of multiplication and number, we can, in principle, work out that $9 \times 7 = 63$. In contrast, even if we understand what it is to be a president of the USA and what it is to be the elected democratic candidate, we cannot work out by reason alone that in

2012 they are one and the same individual. We need experience of election results to know that.

An important concern of philosophers is the avoidance of contradictions. A contradiction cannot possibly be true: it is a necessary falsehood. It cannot be true that this sentence is in English and not in English. The sentence is either in English – or not. That either/or statement just made is a necessary truth, one that must be true. To be consistent, we must avoid contradictions. After all, if we hold contradictory beliefs, one of our beliefs is bound to be false.

A mistaken quip is that there are no right or wrong answers in philosophy. Philosophers are able to point to mistakes in arguments – inconsistencies, impossible pictures of how things are or could be. But, having said that, it is true that philosophers still offer different pictures of how we are to understand the world – of free will, the self, the groundings of morality, and so forth. Philosophy is a living subject. Paradoxically it can breathe life as much through re-considering the thoughts of great philosophers in the past, such as the ancient Greeks Socrates, Plato and Aristotle, as through thinking hard about new and refreshing ways of approaching philosophical problems – indeed, new and refreshing ways to live.

CHAPTER 1

How to know that you exist . . .

'I just think I do'

Your existence is known to you – well, so it seems. You are reading this – or at least you think you are – and maybe sipping a drink and yawning, with eyes closing. Therefore, you exist. The basic idea is the well-known maxim 'I think, therefore I am', most famously associated with the 17th-century French philosopher René Descartes. Descartes tried to doubt everything. In thinking about these things, doubting about this and that – even drunkenly seeing pink elephants – he must surely be existing. Well, so he reasoned.

'I think, therefore I am'

These words – 'I think, therefore I am', or *cogito ergo sum* in Latin – are probably the most well-known words of any philosopher. Mind you, that is not altogether accurate, for numerous philosophers have doubtless often said 'I'm so tired' or 'I need another drink' – and such words are more familiar to most people.

The basic idea of the *cogito* – '*cogito*' is the shorthand used for 'I think, therefore I am' – is to prove that you exist from the fact that you are thinking. It needs to be undertaken in the first person, using 'I'. I know I exist because I know that I am thinking; and that I am thinking is taken to be self-evident, obviously true – well, it is when I am thinking. Even if this works and even if I am thereby certain that I exist – and Descartes is right in being certain that he exists; and you are right in being certain that you exist – it still leaves open the question of what is this 'I' that is thinking and is therefore existing. Some discussion of the I, of the self, occurs in later chapters. We have enough problems here in sorting out what is right and wrong about the *cogito*, but in doing this, we shall still have to say a little something about the I, the self.

The *cogito* has a simple argument form. The first premise is 'I think'. The conclusion is 'I exist'. That looks like an inference, our moving from the premise to the conclusion. Let us consider it in that way, though there is much debate whether Descartes meant it to be so taken.

If I know that the premise is true and if I can see that the conclusion follows, then I ought to know that I exist. I should be able to see that the conclusion follows for it is self-evident, it may be claimed, that thinking necessarily requires existing. In fact, in Descartes' famous *Meditations on First Philosophy*, where he meditates, thinking through what he can know for certain, he does not use the exact *cogito*. "'I am", "I exist"', he writes, 'is necessarily true each time that I pronounce it, or that I mentally conceive it.'

The *cogito* version is first given in an earlier work which, in part, sets the scene for his *Meditations*. Let us stick with the *cogito* version – and return to the *Meditations* later. We need to see whether the premise is known. Well, do I know that I am thinking?

The thinking

> But I observed that, while I was thus resolved to feign that everything was false, I who thought must of necessity be somewhat; and remarking this truth – I think, therefore I am – was so firm and so assured that all the most extravagant suppositions of the sceptics were unable to shake it, I judged that I could unhesitatingly accept it as the first principle of the philosophy I was seeking.

Descartes uses the concept of 'thinking' in a very wide sense – to cover experiencing, having feelings. Why can we not make the *cogito* argument even more general? After all, I am typing, therefore I exist; I am drinking wine, therefore I exist; and I am surrounded by adoring women, therefore I exist.

7

All right, the last is a fantasy; but it reminds us that we have fantasies and wrong perceptions, and that we make mistakes. Therefore, if we are seeking absolute certainty, those arguments do not work: we may be wrong about the premises. In other words, we can *doubt* whether we are typing, wine-imbibing, and being surrounded by members of the opposite sex. I might be dreaming all those things.

What I cannot be mistaken about – surely – is that it *seems to me as if* I am typing, *as if* I am drinking wine, *as if* there are the adoring and adorable women. I cannot be mistaken about how my experiences strike me – just as I cannot be mistaken about whether I am in pain. And so, when thinking about these matters, surely I know that I am thinking – and can rightly conclude that I exist.

Some may say, though, that I need to know another premise – one that Descartes' argument hides – namely, the premise, 'Whatever thinks exists'. Well, can we be sure of that?

Arguably, we can. If something is thinking, then it exists. There are, though, two puzzles here. One derives from the fact that, in works of fiction, characters think. Jane Eyre did a lot of thinking, as did Oliver Twist, as did Shylock and Sherlock Holmes – yet they did not exist. May not Shylock have thought, 'I think, therefore I exist'? The answer is yes; but we need to preface the remark by the words 'in the play'. There is no Shylock in real life, as described by Shakespeare, having experiences of thinking. But that leads to the second puzzle: what is this 'I', this something, that is thinking 'in real life'? Indeed, is there something at all? Have we not been too casual in accepting the 'I' in 'I think'?

Thinking in the rain

A glib criticism of the *cogito* is raised by noting that we may speak of its raining, without being committed to an 'it' that does the raining. So, Descartes was only entitled to spot that thinking was going on – not that he, or any subject, was doing the thinking. His premise should be, 'There is thinking going on', not 'I am thinking'.

The raining analogy initially appears poor. What is rain? Droplets of water. The droplets have properties such as being wet, being roughly spherical. So, even with the rain example, we do think of properties, such as being wet, or being spherical, as needing a subject. From 'there is thinking going on' it seems that we can infer something is thinking. We can so infer because just as it makes no sense to suppose green or round could exist without an item being green or round, so it makes no sense, it seems, of there being thinking without something doing the thinking.

The raining analogy may gain strength, though, once we reflect on what is involved in the thinking. Just as rain is a collection of droplets, thinking is a collection of thoughts – and maybe we could make sense of thoughts as individual entities with properties, yet without a 'something' having them all, holding them all together as a unity.

We may, though, still insist that there needs to be a subject – a thinker for each thought – but that is miles away from being committed to the existence of one and the same thinker, persisting through time, having the different thoughts such as 'I think', 'I exist', 'what a clever French philosopher I am' – and so on. In Chapter 2 we shall encounter the problem of what constitutes a persistent self through time. Indeed, a hundred years after Descartes, David Hume was challenging the existence of the self, writing:

> . . . when I enter most intimately into what I call myself, I always stumble on some particular perception or other . . . I can never catch myself at any time without a perception, and never can observe any thing but the perception.

Let us proceed, assuming that we can move from 'There is thinking' to there is a thing that thinks which is being referred to by the first person pronoun 'I'. Now, I think of myself as an item that persists through time; but, from the fact that I am thinking now, nothing can be concluded about my existing in the past or the future. So, at best Descartes' argument shows only that I can argue to my existence now, for this moment. That is not very impressive, for, of course, we all think of ourselves as having a past and a (dwindling) future. Still, let us see what more Descartes draws forth from his *cogito*.

Descartes' bath-time mistake

I am thinking, and, according to Descartes' reasoning, I can conclude that thinking is essential to my existence. That is, were I not thinking, I should not be existing. Immediately there is the hint – nay, the loud shout – of paradox. Do I not exist when I am sound asleep and not dreaming? Descartes seems to assume that, in such cases, really we are conscious, dreaming, but it is just that, on waking, we have forgotten that we dreamt.

Descartes' argument to show that thinking is his essence appears to rest on a simple mistake. Whenever Descartes thinks about these things, he notices that he is thinking – but that is hardly surprising. Just because he may notice that he is thinking, when he is thinking – and hence can argue that he is existing at such times – it does not follow that he does not exist when he is not thinking. Obviously, he does not notice that he exists when he is not thinking about matters: in order to notice, he would need to be thinking.

11

Descartes' mistake is akin to arguing in the following way. Suppose you only thought about philosophical matters when in the bath. When thinking about those matters, you may notice that you were always wet when you existed. But it would be crazy to conclude that being wet was essential to your existence. Still, let us grant that thinking is essential to me. Descartes goes further still. Not merely is thought essential, but it is my whole essence. That is, no other properties are essential to me in order for me to exist. I am wholly a thinking thing. True, as it happens, I am a thinking thing connected to a biological body; but the body is not essential to me.

Descartes reaches his 'whole essence' conclusion by another mistaken move – well, so it appears. He argues from the fact that the only thing he notices about his essence, when pretending that he may be dreaming or being deceived, is that he is thinking. But from the fact that the only thing I notice about my essence is thinking, it does not follow that thinking is the only thing to be noticed about my essence. I may have overlooked many other things that are essential to me.

A lesson about necessity

People who know a little about Descartes' argument sometimes say that Descartes proved that he must exist – that he necessarily exists. God alone, though, is a necessarily existent being (if he exists); so, Descartes cannot have meant that existence is necessary to him in that divine way. (Descartes was French, but he was not that conceited.) What presumably is meant – and can mislead – is that when Descartes existed, he must have existed. Let us lead into the misleading. 'If I am thinking, then I must exist' is ambiguous. The correct understanding is: 'If I am thinking, then it necessarily follows that I exist.' That is very different from saying, 'If I am thinking, then it necessarily follows that I necessarily exist.' What is the source of that second 'necessarily'? Nothing justifies popping in the extra 'necessity'. Although I do exist, it does not follow that I must exist. I might not have existed. My parents might never have met, might never have engaged in funny things with their bodies. My existence – your existence, Descartes' existence – they are all contingencies: they happen to be, but not necessarily so.

When Descartes writes in the *Meditations*, '"I am", "I exist", is necessarily true each time . . . I mentally conceive it,' he does not mean that he must exist. Rather, 'I exist', when thought, conceived or uttered, is self-verifying. That is why Descartes' *cogito* need not even be judged as an inference; rather Descartes is presenting 'I exist' as a distinctive and basic self-verifying thought – just as, if you shout out 'Someone is shouting' what you say is bound to be true; and, in reverse, if you shout out 'No one is shouting', you ensure that what you shouted is false.

Did Descartes steal the *cogito*?

Descartes is regarded as the father of modern philosophy because he sought to understand the world afresh, without reference to previous philosophers, or to the Bible. It has been pointed out that St Augustine also presented the *cogito* in his fifth-century writings. How much Descartes was stimulated by St Augustine is not known; but it was drawn to his attention. Descartes, though, used the *cogito* in a radical way – as the basis of his search for certainty and truth. His search has been influential in philosophy – and also among comedians. How often, I wonder, have waiters suffered drunken philosophers saying 'I drink, therefore I am'?

CHAPTER 2

How to awake as a gigantic insect
. . . *yet still be you, or who?*

When you wake up, you rarely have to wonder who you are – well, not for long. You remember your past – well, some of it – and usually can tell whether it was you or someone else whose doings you remember. Right now, you have no worry that it may not be you who reads these words. You make plans for the future, too. Yet what sense is there that it is you continuing through time into a future? What makes you the same person as that person in the future, drawing your pension – and that person in the past, trekking to school?

Transformed into a gigantic insect

'As Gregor Samsa awoke one morning from uneasy dreams, he found himself transformed into a gigantic insect. "What has happened to me?" he thought.'

Although the tale *Metamorphosis* by Franz Kafka is fictional, the above seems to make sense, as do many other tales – be they fairy, mythical or science fictional – of people undergoing radical changes in body, sometimes even exchanging bodies. There appears to be nothing contradictory in the idea of your having a different body, even a different brain – yet remaining you, the same self. In fiction, princes can turn into frogs; in reality, all the atoms composing your body, including your brain, are replaced by other atoms, yet you continue being the same individual. Furthermore, many religious believers anticipate continuing to exist without embodiment to the tiniest degree.

Just because we can imagine, picture or dream certain changes, it does not follow that what we imagine, picture or dream really is logically possible. The Dutch artist M. C. Escher drew pictures that seemed to show steps continuously rising ever higher, even though they formed a closed figure; yet such a series of steps is impossible. Some fairy tales may have the prince transformed into a stone and then back again; but it surely does not make sense – is not possible – for a person, even a prince, really to be a stone.

Identity does not, of course, demand lack of any change; but there are limits. This mangle that I own is still the same mangle that I stared at years ago, even though the rollers are worn. Yet if, where the mangle stood a moment ago, there is now a bowl of flowers, we ought not to conclude that maybe the mangle is now a bowl of flowers: that would be to assert a contradiction. So, we need to be careful in drawing conclusions about what logically could be so – without contradiction – from what we can picture, imagine or dream.

Here is another 'be careful' warning. Let us not confuse how we tell whether someone is the same person with what constitutes someone being the same person. The way in which we currently tell whether Kerry is the same person as the one I met last week is by physical appearance – or fingerprints or DNA – but we do not think that what constitutes Kerry being one and the same person over time are those features. It is surely logically possible for me to find myself with different fingerprints, different DNA, different looks – that could be a relief – and in a strange location, yet still be me.

Forgetting her self

With the above 'be careful' warnings to the fore, we may yet reasonably insist that there is nothing contradictory in the supposition that we wake up one morning and find ourselves differently embodied – and, furthermore, in a radically different location. If there is nothing contradictory in that, then how we continue to be the same individuals into the future – how I have a future – must rest, at least in such circumstances, on some continuity in the psychology, rather than continuity of body.

The gigantic insect is Gregor Samsa, we take it, because it possesses awareness of itself as Samsa, having Samsa's memories, recalling from within what it did on previous days, and feeling surprise now to find an insect's body where the human used to be, and so forth. That is how psychological continuity can be seen as the essence of personal identity; yet such an approach quickly hits problems. One problem concerns replications of psychology; but, first, let us review another problem, one that concerns the degree of psychological continuity. Quite how 'thick' should the continuity be?

For me to continue as me, it is suggested, I need memories of what I did, of my hopes and feelings – but only to some degree and extent. After all, I fail to recall everything about my past; and I may remember some childhood incidents, yet have many gaps in my memory of recent events. We need to picture continuity of my memories over the years, as if they were the overlapping strands that constitute a rope. We need also to make sense of my having those memories – of what I did – from within, not as a spectator, yet having those memories without making essential reference to 'me'. If what makes me *me* is my having memories of what *I* did, then we have a circular explanation and so no good explanation at all. Let us assume that we can avoid circularity; let us also assume some grip on how the overlapping of the psychological continuity works.

Many people, at some stage, suffer from amnesia – to varying degrees. Suppose our beloved Aunt Agatha now no longer knows who she is, has no memories and is very changed in character. Perhaps she has even lost all language ability. Somewhere along the line of those losses as they developed, we may be inclined to insist that Aunt Agatha is no longer with us; only the husk lives on. And that inclination is in harmony with personal identity being constituted by psychological continuity. True, we may still respect the house and other assets as belonging to our aunt, but that would be akin to respecting the requests in her will after her death.

Forgetting my self

We considered Aunt Agatha from our external position – we spoke of her in the third person 'she' – but let us think about our own futures, were we to suffer amnesia. Let us look at matters from an internal position, from the first person, from 'I'. Here are two approaches.

On the one hand, suppose an accident leaves me without memories, without any sense of being Peter Cave. Would the surviving conscious entity still be me? Well, this biological entity – this chunk of flesh – prior to the accident would be continuous with the chunk afterwards, yet that would seem insufficient for the entity to be me. The body exchange tales showed us how 'same body' is not necessary for my continuing to be me. The amnesia tale suggests that 'same body' is insufficient – not enough – for me to be me.

On the other hand, perhaps we have been too quick in rejecting the amnesiac as me – and in rejecting Aunt Agatha as still with us, albeit with extreme amnesia. Consider the following possibility.

Tomorrow this body – 'my' body – will be treated in such a way that there is no one there, so to speak. My memories will be wiped, and some painful torture will then be applied. Can I not still make sense of how it would be me, experiencing the severe pain, right here in this body – even having lost my mind? That torture, it seems, would not be causing pain in someone else; it does not strike me as if 'I' would not be experiencing the pain. Better still – well, for the argument, though not the victim – suppose that it is prior to any memory loss that the torture begins, so that it would surely be me suffering the pain. But, as the pain continues, the torturer gradually makes me forget all the things that I have ever done, makes me forget my name, forget all my hopes and plans. Would not I – *I* – still be feeling the pain? And would not I still be feeling the pain, even if some odd false 'memories' washed onto the brain in this body, so that I thought I was a king with great powers? After all, returning to Kafka's tale, he speaks of Gregor Samsa awaking as an insect, but might it be that an insect awakes, mistakenly believing itself to have been a human called 'Gregor Samsa'? What is the distinction, and how can it be established, between finding myself with a different body and having the same body but with mistaken memories?

In two minds – or two thousand and two

Psychological continuity as essential to personal identity suddenly is not what it is cracked up to be. Because of the torture example, what makes you you would now appear to hang on what happens to this, your body. Here is another problem with psychological continuity.

You awake in unusual surroundings. Well, to stress the 'first person' importance, let us speak of 'I' and 'me'; but do put yourself in my shoes.

I awake in unusual surroundings, my body feeling strange (stranger than usual), a little 'newer' maybe. 'Where am I?' A Professor Zag – well, so his name badge says – peers over me, asks me my name and information about myself. I give all the correct answers – for I am, of course, Peter Cave. 'Ah, so it has worked – splendid,' says the professor. 'Your old body was over the hill, on the verge of death; so we quickly copied all your memories and plans and awareness over onto this duplicate body – just in time.'

> *'That's decent of you,' I reply, glad to be alive, feeling much better than usual. I am about to leave, when I note someone else also waking up, in a body very similar to mine. 'Who's that?' I ask. 'Oh, that's another copy from you yesterday. We thought we'd better do two, in case something went wrong with one. Fortunately, nothing has gone wrong.'*

Fortunately? *Fortunately*? What am I now to make of things? That other Peter Cave is peering at me, equally baffled. 'But I'm Peter Cave,' he says. Once we envisage copying memories, character traits – as if akin to software programs playing on different hardware – we must live with the puzzle of seemingly more than one 'me'. Indeed, we need not stop at just two; there could be two thousand and two. For simplicity's sake, we remain with two. 'Two' is sufficient to manifest the problem.

Suppose I, Peter Cave, were to be told what would happen before the Zag operation – namely that my old body (including brain) was at death's door, but that I should not worry as my 'mind', well, my psychological states as manifested by the neural structures – would be played on a new brain. Were that to be done, with no duplication, I may well think that the resultant person would be me. After all, I – *I*? – wake up, saying that I am Peter Cave and how pleased I am that the operation worked. But how should I anticipate the future when two individuals, because two copies have been made, have the same claim to be me? If I am identical with both resultant individuals, then they must surely be identical with each other: they must be numerically one and the same person; but that seems nonsense. Maybe I remain just one person spread across two similar bodies; but what sense can I make of controlling two bodies, with, presumably, two very different viewpoints – with each individual seeming to think itself different from the other?

Survival

We become entangled, wondering, 'Will it be me?' when encountering the crazy thought experiments outlined above. There are many, many more such experiments, with variations on replications, splitting brains, tele-transportation of bodies – and even of psychological streams fusing together rather than dividing. One response is to ignore such crazy cases; but if they are possible, then we can surely assess now how our concepts apply to them, if at all, instead of waiting to see what we would then say.

With regard to such examples, we could despairingly insist that we do not know what to say about whether a given resultant individual will be me. Perhaps, though, we are held captive by a picture, the picture being that, with regard to any resultant individual, either it must be me or not me. Perhaps, though, the 'black or white' insistence is the error. After all, we have no sharp dividing line with regard to when a person – when you, when I – began. A fertilized egg, embryo, foetus, baby gradually developed into you, the fully-fledged person. Must there then be a sharp dividing line that determines whether I am the same person as a resultant individual after some bizarre experiments? Maybe the correct answer is 'No'.

My brain is to be divided – or replications of me are to be created – so that by tomorrow, my original body will have been destroyed, but two separate individuals wake up, with all my memories and beliefs. What then happens is that one will be tortured for the rest of his life; the other will be given all the fun that he desires. How should I view my future? No future at all because I shall be dead, or as a future of pain, or as a future of pleasure? Perhaps the correct approach is to recognize that I should be surviving partially as someone undergoing considerable pain and partially as someone undergoing great pleasure. Perhaps I ought to be in 'two minds' about the future. And when those two individuals look back, they will each correctly think, 'I am to a large extent the same person as that Peter Cave yesterday'.

CHAPTER 3

How to fire the neurons in your head ...

without even trying

Actors act by pretending to be what they are not. For philosophers, there is the seemingly simple question of what counts as performing an action. What do we do when we do anything – and how do we do whatever it is that we do? We walk and talk, we move arms and legs. How do those things get done by us? And how do they differ from things that just get done? Quick answers make reference to desires, decisions or intentions as mental events or states. But as we shall see, what we do, when we do, can be something of a mystery.

Little willings

The Cambridge philosopher Ludwig Wittgenstein asked us to suppose that a man's arm goes up. Now, if the man raised his arm – was responsible for doing so – surely there is more to it than simply the arm having gone up. After all, the arm may simply have gone up, after being pressed against the wall, as an automatic reaction, the man having, so to speak, nothing to do with it. Or the arm could have been lifted by others, the man also then having no control over its movement. Were the arm lifted by others, or just moving after pressure, the man would be passive; if the man raised it himself, he was the agent. So, quite what does an agent do when he does? In Wittgenstein's own words:

> When 'I raise my arm', my arm goes up. And the problem arises: what is left over if I subtract the fact that my arm goes up from the fact that I raise my arm?

Here is one suggestion. The man was the cause of his arm's rising – and he wanted his arm so to rise. That suggestion, though, does not work as it stands. Maybe the man did indeed want his arm to go up – yet, because it was paralysed, he caused others to lift the arm for him. In such a case, he was not himself directly lifting his arm. Another suggestion is that the man wanted his arm to go up – and that want *directly* caused the arm to move. That also, though, carries an inaccuracy: we may choose to do things; but we cannot choose our wants. You can decide to lift your arm; but you can no more decide to want to lift your arm than decide to fancy eating the stale bread or decide to want to drink the horrible medicine.

Because of the problems above, we may insist that when the man (directly) lifts his arm, and not with pulleys and strings, there must be a mental event – a decision, a little willing, a trying – that causes the arm to go up. The man, in some way or other, wills the arm to rise – and that act of willing causes the arm to rise. The act of will is the instrument whereby the arm gets moved.

Understanding actions as essentially requiring some mental events, such as willings, that precede and cause the bodily movements, hits many problems. For a start, just consider our everyday experiences. Think of all the things that we do in a day: make some coffee; run for the bus; drive a car; stop at the lights; switch on the computer; telephone a friend; turn the corner; hide the parcel; caress a lover; remove some clothes; set the alarm clock. Did each action require a willing, a mental event – some sort of internal trying – to occur, to make each one into an action? And how many? Does telephoning a friend require one willing – or separate willings for lifting the receiver, dialling the number, pressing the 'connect' button – and so forth? Going on our everyday experience, in many of those cases just mentioned, no little willings would have occurred at all.

Supporters of willings sometimes argue that some such mental events must have occurred for actions to have occurred. Perhaps the mental events went unnoticed; perhaps they were subconsciously undertaken. Our response to the supporters is by way of question: why posit such mental events for which there is no evidence? The supporters' answer spins us back to the original question: the supporters may answer that there must be some such events – to mark the distinction between things just happening and an agent doing those things. The response should be: why assume that there *must* be some such events to mark the distinction? No doubt there are many physical – neurological – events that precede the bodily movements, but before people knew about them, they could mark the distinction between mere happenings and agents' actions. Further, ignoring the tiny local difficulty that 'willing' events often seems absent, such events pose philosophical perplexities even when they do occur. Some perplexities are forthcoming.

Go on – will that feather to rise!

The appeal to willings – to some sort of mental tryings or decidings – is to mark out bodily movements as being actions for which the agent is responsible. One puzzle is the status of those willings. A natural expression is 'an act of will': willings are what we do. They are actions. We became involved in all of this, though, through insisting that for actions, such as raising the arm, to be actions there must be willings involved. So, if willings are also actions, then each willing itself requires a willing – and that leads us along the path of an endless regress. That is one puzzle. Another puzzle is quite what is it that we are supposed to be willing or deciding, if such events are required for our moving our limbs and performing other actions. Let us consider three key possibilities, continuing to use the simple example of arm raising.

Perhaps, when you raise your arm, you will that you raise your arm. That answer, though, gets us nowhere: we are trying to understand what is involved in someone raising his arm. So we still need to know what it is that you will.

Perhaps certain neural firings in your head cause the required electro-chemical changes in the muscles that cause your arm to go up. But the only way that you know how to bring those changes about is by raising your arm. By raising your arm, those neural changes must have occurred a little beforehand. Once again, then, that does not help us in understanding what it is that you will when you raise your arm. No one wills electro-chemical changes to occur – when they move their limbs.

Perhaps you, in some way, can simply will this chunk of flesh, your arm right here, to go up in the air. Well, to get a grip on that proposal, focus your attention on anything in your surroundings – a book, the table, the chair. Or, if they seem too heavy, pop a feather or a sheet of paper on the floor. Let us suppose that you have the feather on the floor a few feet away from you. Now, focus your attention on it – and will, just *will*, that feather to rise up in the air. Come on – it is a light feather.

Presumably you are failing to lift the feather by willing: we assume you lack Uri Geller-type 'powers'. Still, maybe things are different with your arm: after all, you are attached to it. So, now, place your arm out before you and, by focusing on it – in the same way as you focused on the feather – will your arm to rise. If all you are doing is indeed focusing on the arm, willing it as you did the feather, then it fails to move (I trust).

The wrong picture

The above three attempts at understanding what we will when we move our limbs have all failed. Maybe we should simply accept that we have been captivated by a mistaken picture. In the normal course of events, we simply move our limbs, without any willings, be they little or large. True, there are abnormal cases: after an accident, we may need to try hard to move an arm. But the standard cases in which we do things do not involve tryings or willings.

Of course, much of what we do, we perform intentionally. Some things we decide to do. Some things we are motivated to do. Some things we do on purpose. Many things we do without being forced to do – and so forth. Such talk of intentions and decisions and motives may again lead us to think that there must be certain mental events or states, of which we are conscious, that cause the bodily changes – the movement of limbs, the run for the bus. Yet we often acknowledge that we acted in certain ways – intentionally, deliberately, not compelled by others – even though unaware of any intention or deliberation occurring before the actions: before the arm goes up; before we dash for the bus.

The picture that we need to resist is that which marks the difference between intentionally raising your arm and accidentally raising your arm (or with someone raising it for you) as the existence of a mental event, prior to the bodily movement, being present in the intentional case. What picture may we deploy instead?

The picture should be composed of how people do take responsibility for what they do – what, for example, they are disposed sincerely to say, if asked. To raise your arm intentionally does not require a prior mental event. To raise your arm intentionally is, in normal circumstances, often to be able to give reasons, to be able to answer the question, 'Why did you do that?'

The answer may be: 'to make a philosophical point' or 'to attract attention'. The answer may sometimes even be, 'I just did it.' Contrast those with the answer you would give, if someone asked you, 'Why did you push the man into the river? 'I didn't,' you say, 'the wind blew me against him.'

There is a story highlighted by Elizabeth Anscombe (an eminent pupil of Wittgenstein) of a soldier undergoing an army medical; he is becoming somewhat irritated by the doctor. The doctor asks him to clench his teeth. Calmly, the soldier removes his false teeth and suggests that the doctor clench them for him. With the comments above in mind, we may see how the soldier is passing the responsibility for the clenching onto someone else: the soldier is not doing the clenching; the clenching is not his responsibility, not an action of his.

What are you doing?

Our focus has been on a simple example of arm raising, but we do many things that take us way beyond bodily movements – or so it seems. With the arm raising, we may be waving – or we may be drowning. We may be stroking the squirrels, reaching for a gun, or poisoning the pigeons in the park – and we may say that we are doing such things. In doing those things, we may also be doing, and say that we are doing, things such as upsetting the neighbours, realizing the best solution for our life, or annoying the park warden.

The examples above may lead us, though, to insist that what we directly do are some basic actions which then cause other events to occur – other events at which we aim. What I do directly is raise my arm, but only indirectly do I poison the pigeons and annoy the wardens, even though the poisoning may be my intention.

The thought behind the direct and indirect classification is that the 'direct' marks out that over which I have some special control and knowledge. Surely, *I* know if I am raising my arm – but things may go wrong with my action, resulting in a poisoning or an annoyance. Maybe I have fed the pigeons the wrong grain; maybe the wardens are unconcerned.

We should, though, question the value of the direct/ indirect classification. After all, I can, in certain circumstances, make mistakes about the movement of my limbs. People experience phantom limbs – and, with suitable mirrors, I may be misled about the location of my legs. Such thoughts threaten to return us to the idea that what we directly do are the acts of will; but we have already seen through those. Perhaps we should simply accept that the actions that we perform are indeed the ones that we say we do – when the things happen that we intend to happen.

Were you poisoning the pigeons? Well, yes you were – if you intended to and if they are poisoned as a result. There are, though, many nuances; so we end with an example from the 20th-century Oxford linguistic philosopher John Langshaw Austin. Austin possessed wit; witness, in view of his name, his lecture title *Sense and Sensibilia*. The following is from his paper 'Three Ways of Spilling Ink':

The notice says 'do not feed the penguins'. I, however, feed them peanuts. Now peanuts happen to be, and these prove, fatal to these birds. Did I feed them peanuts intentionally? Beyond a doubt. I am no casual peanut shedder. But deliberately? Well, that seems perhaps to raise the question, 'Had I read the notice?' Why does it? Or did I feed them 'on purpose'? That seems to insinuate that I knew what fatal results would ensue.

CHAPTER 4

How to be free . . .

and neither chimp nor wanton be

People often reflect on how what we do appears to be causally determined, be it by our genes, diet or latest drugs of design. Of course, we may choose our lifestyles; but what determines the choices? The answer is: our experiences, our character, our predispositions – but those, too, are grounded in our brain states, processes and events. Those states, processes and events result from prior causes over which we have no control, no free choice. Did we choose how our brains would develop? Clearly not. So, what hope is there for our acting freely?

Dear kindly Sergeant Krupke

When in front of Sergeant Krupke, then later the judge – and seeking to evade responsibility for misdeeds – the loutish teenagers argue, 'It's our upbringing that gets us out of hand; we can't help it, you need to understand.' They might have added that their genes, brain structures and environment also contributed to their bad behaviour, for those factors are also way outside their control. And, with such causes, the louts cannot be morally responsible for the results. Wise judges could respond that they are terribly sorry, but given their judgemental upbringing and brain circuits, they cannot help but sentence the defendants before them to ten years in jail – and to hard labour.

Whether we act freely or not is a key factor in whether we are morally responsible for our deeds. Once we reflect on factors that affect our choices and hence our actions we can see how, if all that we do is caused in those various ways, then we surely cannot be acting freely. The chains of causes may carry back as far as the primeval slime, and we certainly had no control over that. Closer to our actions today, whatever the proportions between nature and nurture, we result from the combination, a combination concerning which we lacked all choice. How can we make ourselves free? The answer would seem to be: we cannot.

If the above is right, dire consequences flow. If we never make *free* choices and hence are never acting freely, how can it ever be right to blame or praise us? After all, we cannot help what we do. Determinism and free will – and hence determinism and moral responsibility – are incompatible, or so it seems. If the world is deterministic, then free will is an illusion and so is moral responsibility.

What a fine mess!

The above sketches the deep philosophical problem of free will and determinism – determinism understood as a scientific determinism whereby events are caused by prior events through certain laws of nature. As Friedrich Nietzsche, famous for announcing the death of God, writes:

The one who acts certainly labours under the illusion of voluntariness; if the world's wheel were to stand still for a moment and an all-knowing, calculating reason were there to make use of this pause, it could foretell the future of every creature to the remotest times, and mark out every track upon which that wheel would continue to roll.

Of course, the world may not be deterministic. Paradoxically, that fails to come to the rescue of devotees of free will. If our behaviour is not determined, then it must be random, and we cannot be held responsible for what happens randomly. So, a 'solution' to the problem that some propose – namely, that at the micro level of quantum mechanics an indeterminism reigns (well, so it is currently thought) – is no solution at all. Further, it is no solution to speak of our actions being partially determined, for what is the remaining partial portion? Presumably, that portion is undetermined and we are cast back into the random problem. Some claim not to grasp what determinism is. To respond that it is simply the claim that every event has a cause raises the puzzle of the nature of causation. What counts as one thing causing a change in another? Let us, though, pinpoint our problem with a particular example. I assume that you freely chose to be reading this book. No one, I hope, is forcing you with whips or chains. Now, let us reflect.

To be freely reading this book implies, it seems, that you could have chosen otherwise. In the circumstances in which you decided 'I'll try out this chapter instead of going skating', you could have gone skating (or whatever). Yet your decision to read this chapter is surely grounded in neural events that caused electrical changes in your muscles that caused your hand to grip the book – and so forth. And those neural events were caused by other neural events, associated with thoughts such as 'maybe a little philosophy will be good for me' – and those other neural events, too, are presumably caused. Whatever the chain of causes – or, if you prefer, replace 'cause' with 'random happenings' – there is no room for your free choice understood as *your* being able to do otherwise. In fact, things are worse because – as explored in Chapter 2, *How to awake as a gigantic insect* – there appears no place for you – for the *I* – at all in such a deterministic explanation. What a fine mess philosophers have got us into.

Escaping the mess – or changing the subject?

The general line of a solution, offered by many philosophers, is compatibilism. It is most famously associated with the 18th-century Scottish philosopher and man of good heart and humour, David Hume. Free will and determinism are not in conflict: they are compatible. We should add, for completeness, that the line can also reconcile free will and indeterminism. How is reconciliation achieved?

It is achieved by sleight of hand, say some. By careful understanding of what it is to act freely, say others. The incompatibility between free will and determinism arises because we understand the former in terms of agents, in particular circumstances, being able to do otherwise than they do. Perhaps that understanding is mistaken. Compatibilists argue that your freely reading this book hangs on whether you are doing what you want to do. If you are doing what you want, then – with some caveats (next section) – you are acting freely. A causal explanation of your reading does not undermine your reading freely. To be caused is not to be coerced. Further, for there to exist a scientific understanding such that the causes of your action occurred randomly does not undermine your reading freely – if you are doing what you want to do.

The oft-given and immediate objection to compatibilism is that we cannot choose our wants, desires and characters. We just find ourselves with them. The sensible response is to challenge the objectors, 'Quite what, dear objectors, are you seeking?'

Objectors, it seems, seek an impossibility. They seek a subject, an agent, a chooser, to be a subject with no features at all that lead to a choice, for, once a feature is given, the objection is, 'Ah, but the subject did not choose to have that feature.' Once we recognize that the deep metaphysical problem of free will is founded in that nonsense, the focus may shift to that of what is involved in your getting what you want – and that is a problem which may be given a political polish.

From chimps to people

With compatibilism adopted, we may readily see how whether we are choosing and acting freely comes with qualifications. If a gunman holds the gun at your head, ready to fire, in case you resist purchase of this book, then, assuming you do not want to buy, you are not acting freely in your purchase. Mind you, of the options available, you have a preference for book purchase with head intact over money saved and head with bullet. Free choice and action depend on your wants and also options available. Actions are restricted – certain wants cannot be satisfied – when external authorities block the way. The blocks come in different strengths – from outright bans and prison sentences for possession of drugs to high charges for visas to enter a country. Laws, police and costs can stop us from, or slow down, our getting what we want. Those are external blocks; but there are also internal blocks. A chimp, we may judge, lacks internal blocks; she simply acts on her desires. True, she may be tempted by the bananas on the left and male chimp on her right. Which she goes for is not a matter of reflection, but simply that of which desire is the stronger.

Now, consider Humphrey, a person, no chimp. Humphrey frequently wants to loiter in lingerie departments and he acts on those wants. He gets what he wants. Is he acting freely? Well, as it stands, maybe 'Yes'. Suppose, though, that Humphrey also has the desire to be a non-loiterer: he wants to quit the habit and focus attention on reading Plato. If so, our assessment of his lingerie loitering activities changes. Although he is getting what he wants in that his first-level desire to loiter is satisfied, he fails to satisfy his desire not to loiter. Humphrey has a second-order desire to quell the first-order desires or, at least, to resist yielding to them. In as far as Humphrey cannot prevent himself from succumbing to his first-order desires, he is no free agent. He has internal obstacles to his satisfying his second-order desires; and he treats those second-order desires as what he truly wants.

'Forced to be free'

Once we have the idea of different orders of desires – and of how we may be prevented from what we truly want to do by our own more basic desires – there is scope for external help, but also external dangers. With the recognition that people may truly want to be better educated, stop smoking and live longer lives, governments may impose compulsory learning projects, ban cigarettes, and enforce screening programmes. Now, those particular policies may well benefit people and give them what they truly want. There are, though, dangers. Governmental actions could go much further, the actions justified as those which people *would* want, if only they understood the best way to health, even the best way to live. People, it has been said, are then being forced to be free – the expression comes from the 18th-century French philosopher Jean-Jacques Rousseau. This, though, is a curious notion of people acting freely, for they may be opposed to what they are having to do and unaware that really, deep inside, they (allegedly) want to do it. Chapter 24, *How to tolerate the intolerable*, investigates this further, with J.S. Mill's Liberty Principle.

Rebels, wantons

Turning to the individual – using our Humphrey again – we can see how the idea of differently ordered desires may generate complex cases. Humphrey has his lingerie-loitering first-order desires; but because of a puritanical upbringing, he also has the second-order desire to be free of those first-order desires. Yet, he may – in his heart of hearts – yearn to rebel against his puritanical upbringing, desiring to be rid of his second-order desires and giving himself fully to the first-order desires and perhaps many more desires associated with those first-order ones, such as wearing the lingerie in public.

Thus it is that reflection can lead us to wonder about the satisfaction of which desires would be a manifestation of who we truly are. Thus it is that we confirm that different orders of desires distinguish human beings from non-human animals (or most of them). The chimp lacks reflections regarding desires about desires. Chimps, cats and dogs know nothing of fighting desires or rebelling against some. Young children are akin to the chimp: they are moved by whichever desires are strongest. A few adults are – at least at times – moved in the same way as the child or chimp, with no reflection, being simply motivated by the strongest of first-order desires. If we encounter such – and are unable to engage reason or reflection with them – we may consider them non-persons or persons with personhood suspended. They are wantons – just trying to do what they want. We could lapse into treating them as objects, as pebbles moved by the waves, as insects reacting to scents or thermostats to the heat. And thus we should be treating them as causally determined by desires and nothing more. But those are exceptional cases.

In everyday life, we treat individuals with whom we engage at least as if they are capable of reflecting on their desires and then making choices – even if the world is deterministic. Reflection on the competing desires to which compatibilism draws attention returns us to our treatment of others typically as often choosing which desires to seek to fulfil, however mythical that be – with their being held responsible for those choices. And that is how we must treat ourselves.

Suppose you firmly believe that all your wants, decisions and actions are causally explained by previous states of which you are unaware and over which you lack control. Under such a supposition, you still have to choose what to do next – whether to read on or go for a drink, or face the skating. However deterministic or indeterministic the world, we have to treat ourselves and others as, in the main, morally responsible for what we do. If we did not, what then could we choose to do? And so, for much of the time, we cannot help but treat ourselves as free – and that is just what it is to be free. Well, arguably, that's the best we can make of it.

CHAPTER 5

How to outwit Aristotle . . .
and be a bit of a logician

> Mention logic to people and it can cause a stampede for
> the door. Although many of us approve of a logical
> argument, people often avoid those who are thought to be
> logical: after all, if logical, then they must be cold fish,
> devoid of emotion. That is wrong. Logic is simply the
> science of good argument – and knowing how to argue
> well is no bad thing. Here, take my hand – no, fin.

Deductive logic

The father of logic – the first logician – was the ancient
Greek philosopher Aristotle. He investigated the syllogism, which is a particular form of deductive
argument that consists of a major premise, a minor
premise and a conclusion. Premises and conclusions
are just sentences, statements, propositions or beliefs
that so and so is such and such. There are important
distinctions to be made. For example, sentences consist of the words on the page; propositions are what

sentences express. For the introductory logical purposes here, however, we may ignore such distinctions. Here is an example of one form of a syllogism (more on forms occurs later on):

Premise 1	All cats are animals.
Premise 2	All animals have legs.
Conclusion	All cats have legs.

Deductive arguments are seeking to show how moving from some propositions – some beliefs, some assertions – certain conclusions must flow. Given the premises about cats, animals and legs, it must follow that the conclusion, that all cats have legs, is true. Deductive arguments, though, do not need to possess a syllogistic form such as the one above; deductive arguments do not need to have just two premises. Here is another type of argument, though – for simplicity – still with two premises.

Premise 1	If Lucy is smiling, then she is drinking whisky.
Premise 2	Lucy is smiling.
Conclusion	Therefore she is drinking whisky.

This type of argument is frequently used by us. It has its own name: *modus ponendo ponens*, often shortened to '*modus ponens*'. In our everyday lives, we often think in that way. 'If she takes the job, I'll see less of her – ah, she is going to take the job; so, I'll see less of her.' 'If I have another drink, I'll be tired tomorrow. Oops, I'm succumbing; I'm having another drink – so, I'll be tired tomorrow.' Both arguments above – and the forms of those arguments – are valid. 'Validity' has a special meaning here. Whether an argument is valid or not can be worked out in a simple way. Suppose all the premises are true. Then ask whether, on that supposition, the conclusion would also have to be true. If the answer is 'yes', then the argument is valid. That is, in a **valid argument** the conclusion logically follows from the premises.

One key point is that you can therefore have valid arguments – arguments in which the conclusions follow from the premises – even if all or some of the premises are false. In such cases, the conclusions may be true, or they may be false. If you have a valid argument, though, the one combination that cannot exist is that of all the premises being true and the conclusion false. A valid argument does not permit you to move from truth to falsehood.

Here is one last piece of common English that is used technically by logicians. An argument is **sound**, if it is both valid and the premises are true. If both those conditions hold, then the conclusion will also be true.

Inductive logic

With deductive arguments – if they are valid – the premises logically entail the conclusion. Many of our arguments, though, are not deductive, but may be inductive. In good inductive arguments, the premises provide good evidence for the conclusions, but they are not designed logically to entail the conclusions. For example, we may enumerate a lot of true premises as we run through a vast number of ravens:

> Raven #1 is black.
> Raven #2 is black,
> and so on – to
> Raven #1,000,000 is black.

and we may conclude that therefore all ravens are black. The one million ravens being black may be good evidence for this conclusion, but the argument is not deductively valid. We cannot logically deduce that all ravens are black from sighting the million black ravens – unless we have an additional premise that the million ravens are all the ravens that exist.

Non-deductive reasoning can take other forms. For example, we have some evidence – and so we reason and conclude to what we think is the best explanation for that evidence. Robinson Crusoe sees what he takes to be footprints in the sand. The best explanation is the existence of another person on the island, but, of course, the existence of that other person is not guaranteed. After all, maybe the tidal waves just happened to form those shapes, or maybe they were Crusoe's own footprints – and so forth. Chapter 10, *How to tell the future*, discusses how inductive reasoning can be justified, if it can; here we merely make the point that such reasoning differs from deductive reasoning. The rest of this chapter looks at deductive reasoning.

Good and bad deductions

We saw above how, in the argument about Lucy, we have a simple valid argument. Well, we could replace the sentences and parts about Lucy and whisky by letters of the alphabet: so, the argument *form* becomes

> If p, then q
>
> p
>
> Therefore, q

The 'p's and 'q's are to be replaced by declarative sentences – whichever ones you are considering. Whichever they are, if following that format, your argument would be valid – even if, in some cases, appearing to be bizarre. If there's an eclipse, the pigs will squeal; there is an eclipse; so, the pigs will squeal. If she pays back the money, pigs will fly; she will pay back the money; so pigs will fly. Both of those arguments are valid. We may easily point to forms of bad argument, though, that must always be invalid:

If it rains, the guests will get wet.
The guests will get wet.
Therefore, it will rain.

That is invalid: after all, suppose that the two premises are true: does it follow that it will rain? Well, no. Maybe it is true that the guests will get wet because the host plans to pour water over them as a joke. We could set out the form of that **invalid** argument as

If p, then q
q
Therefore, p

This form of argument has a name – the fallacy of affirming the consequent. The consequent is the 'q', the segment after the 'then'. The 'p', the segment after the 'if', is the antecedent. Here is another example of that fallacy:

If Ben is happy, then Beth is happy; Beth is happy; therefore, Ben is happy.

That is invalid because, even if the premises are true, the conclusion does not have to be true. Maybe Beth is indeed happy when Ben is happy; but perhaps she is also happy when Basil is happy – and, in those circumstances, Ben may well not be happy.

Let us return to Aristotle's syllogism. Here is a syllogism. Is it valid?

> Some happy mammals live on farms.
> Some pigs are happy mammals.
> Therefore, some pigs live on farms.

Well, the possibility lurking in the syllogism shows that the conclusion does not have to be true, if the premises are true. After all, the pigs that are happy mammals may be just those who do not live on farms.

All the nice girls love a sailor

The forms discussed above are fine for showing some good and some bad arguments. But we need to take a step further – a step into 'quantification' – if we are to expose how other mistakes in reasoning may occur. Let us display an example where we need to be aware of ambiguities. A famous example is, 'All the nice girls love a sailor'. Now, think how differently that may be understood. In order to simplify, suppose we have just three nice girls, Amadea, Amelia and Anthea – and three sailors, Sam, Sid and Stan. How may we understand 'All the nice girls love a sailor'?

Amadea loves just one sailor, say Sam; Amelia loves another, say Sid; and Anthea loves one, maybe Stan. That is, they may love different sailors. An alternative reading, though, could be that there is just one lucky sailor, Sam, say, who is loved by all the girls. There is, of course, a third possibility that all the nice girls love each and every sailor. It was Gottlob Frege, a German logician in the late 19th century, who clearly saw how to set out forms of argument in order to manifest such differences. In 1879 he published his *Begriffsschrift* – 'concept writing' – where he proposed a certain type of notation. Symbolism in logic can frighten people, but it can be of considerable value in making differences transparent. Transparency is important. We may casually say, 'Everyone seeks happiness,' and wrongly conclude that therefore there is just the one happy state that everyone seeks. It is 'the girls and sailor' error. Every child has a mother – but it does not follow that there is just one mother who has conceived every child. Aristotle opened his highly influential work *Nicomachean Ethics* with:

> *Every art and every inquiry, and similarly every action and choice, is thought to aim at some good; and for this reason the good has rightly been declared to be that at which all things aim.*

That looks as if it also commits the 'mother/child' error just mentioned.

Quantifiers

How do logicians illuminate the errors above so that more elusive errors may be exposed? Well, let us return to our three nice girls and sailors and let us consider the proposition that Amelia loves Sam. We rightly think of Amelia, an individual, standing in a loving relation to Sam, another individual. But when we speak of someone or everyone loving Sam, we ought not to think of 'someone' or 'everyone' as a subject, a strange individual. Rather, we need to think of an activity, an operation, whereby we are scanning the girls to see if the description '— loves Sam' applies to some, none or all.

Our scanning equipment may register some loving of Sam and some non-loving, but may fail to show us which girls love and which do not. So, we cannot fill in the gap '— loves Sam' with a name; we need to register what is going on in a different way; and this is where logicians use quantifiers. They would write, using the quantifier, '$(\exists x)$ (x loves Sam)' to show that there exists someone or ones that love Sam: for some x, x loves Sam. If the scanning equipment registered loving everywhere for Sam, then we should use the universal quantifier to say that for all x, x loves Sam: $(\forall x)$ (x loves Sam).

The above notation saves us from the risk of thinking that 'someone' or 'everyone' or 'no one' should be treated in the same way as names such as 'Amelia'. Continuing with our example, we may also consider the incomplete sentence with two gaps '— loves —' where we may scan for whether there is any loving going on – both with regard to who does the loving and who is loved. This is where it becomes important which scanning occurs first. We may discover, for example, that there is one sailor loved by all the nice girls or that each sailor has just one girl loving him. We may discover that nobody loves any sailor – and that can lead us into wondering how we can talk about nobody or even *about* any individual such as Aristotle (see Chapter 13, *How to know what we are talking about*).

A great twentieth-century American logician with a wonderful name, Willard van Orman Quine – a 'moveable van' – wrote, with Frege in mind, 'Logic is an old subject, and since 1879, it has been a great subject.' Well, Aristotle was a great pioneer in the early attempts at logical regimentation, but since Frege – and the work of twentieth-century philosophers such as Bertrand Russell – arguments can be regimented in ways undreamt by Aristotle, and in ways that might have bedazzled and even outwitted that master – that master who centuries ago was referred to as *'The Philosopher'*.

CHAPTER 6

How to know what knowledge is
. . . some know-how required

When questions of knowledge arise, people can easily become philosophers. After a little reflection they announce, 'Well, of course, we cannot know what the future is. We don't even know what the present is: right now we may be dreaming.' This chapter rests on the simple truth that, before we can pronounce on knowledge, we need to know what knowledge is. Before we can decide whether we do know this or that, we need to know the nature of knowledge.

Necessary and sufficient conditions

To explain what a rectangle is, we could set the scene by saying that it is a closed figure with four straight sides. That gives one necessary condition for a rectangle. For anything to be a rectangle, it had better have four sides; but having four sides is not enough. The figure needs also to have internal angles that are right angles.

Those necessary conditions taken together are sufficient for a figure to be rectangular.

As shown with the geometrical example, we can sometimes explain what something is by providing necessary conditions that, taken jointly, are sufficient. Note: we may overkill; we may go too far. All squares are rectangles. Having a square figure is sufficient for an item being a rectangle, but its being a square is not necessary for something to be a rectangle: it is not necessary that rectangles should have equal sides.

Let us try the above approach on knowledge. We have a typical individual, albeit with an untypical name – Erskin. What is it for Erskin to know that the Earth orbits the Sun or that Riga is Latvia's capital? To save us from repeatedly giving such examples, think in terms of what it is for Erskin to know that p – where p can be replaced by any such propositions. Choose whichever ones you fancy. Well, one necessary condition is surely that p be true. If Erskin knows that Riga is Latvia's capital, then it had better be true that Riga is the capital. Were Riga not the capital, then, while Erskin could think he knows, he would not in fact know.

Of course, that p is true is not sufficient for Erskin to know that p. There are millions of truths unknown by Erskin – unknown, indeed, by all of us. So, at the very least we need a condition concerning Erskin's psychological state: Erskin needs, in some way, to assent to that p. This is a necessary condition that is often presented in terms of Erskin's being certain or believing that p. 'Believes' here, by the way, does not imply that Erskin lacks knowledge because he believes or claims only that he believes.

We now have Erskin with a true belief that p. Is that sufficient for his knowing that p? Well, he may have his true belief by luck. He may wake up one morning, simply convinced that Khartoum is the capital of Sudan and that Lady Jane will win the 2.30 horse race. Let us assume that he is right. Still, if he lacks any form of justification, he surely lacks knowledge.

Our latest consideration above suggests to many philosophers that knowledge is typically to be grasped as true *justified* belief. Mind you, considerable work is needed on this. For a start, some knowledge arguably is self-evident, without any further justification. Justifications have to come to an end. And if we insist that any appropriate justification needs to guarantee the truth of what it justifies, then we should rule out most things that we claim to know as being knowledge. We are, though, trying to secure a grip on how we deploy the concept of knowledge ordinarily. So, its possibility ought not to be ruled out before we get started.

Sophie and Plato

Some have argued that neither belief nor justification is necessary for an Erskin to possess knowledge. Some have also argued that even if an Erskin has true justified belief, it does not follow that he has knowledge: true justified belief is not always sufficient for knowledge. Let us focus, first, on the doubt about the belief condition – and then on whether the true justified belief analysis is sufficient for knowledge. That will lead us into focus on the justification condition.

Sophie, a clever but sensitive student, attends an interview for a place on a university's philosophy course. Before the interview she is familiar with the basic philosophers, including Plato. She used to read him for an hour every day. Yet, when she is asked whether Plato wrote the *Republic*, she gets tongue-tied. She lacks belief and certainty about even Plato's existence let alone about what he wrote. Once out of the interview and calmed down, she can again speak eloquently about the Greek philosophers.

We could, indeed, make the Sophie case vivid: before the interview, her headmaster happens to ask her to run through the major works of Plato, as he drives her to the station – and she gets everything right. Similarly, she gets everything right about Plato when he picks her up on her return. During the interview, she seemed to lack belief; yet do we want to say that she lacked the knowledge? If she lacked the knowledge, how did it suddenly pop back in, after the interview?

The above example suggests that belief is not essential to knowing. There can be cases in which you know that p, yet do not believe that p. Sophie knew that Plato wrote the *Republic* even during the interview, but lacked belief that he did.

There are many nuances to such examples, but the underlying thought is that you may be unable to express what you know, yet what you believe is more available to you and hence can be readily expressed by you. The quick challenge, therefore, is to point out that you may well have beliefs that, because of the surrounding conditions, you are unable to express or even recognize. Emotional turmoil – nervousness, depression, love's anguishes – might distort your awareness of your beliefs as much as your awareness of your knowledge. After all, when you are fast asleep, you are in a position to announce neither what you know, nor what you believe – yet a sleeping person surely does not lack knowledge and belief. Possession of knowledge and belief is a disposition – relating to what you are disposed to do and announce when in a variety of circumstances.

Sophie with drink in hand

You are at a party. You can see Sophie in the corner,

drink in hand, chatting to Suzie who seems to have no drink. You know Sophie well. Sophie, at a party, drink in hand – well, given the colour, she is bound to be drinking some red wine. And that is what you believe. You are, though, a bit of a logician. You know that from the judgement that Sophie, in the corner, is drinking red wine it follows that someone in the corner is drinking red wine. So, your belief that someone in the corner is drinking red wine is justified by your belief that Sophie is drinking red wine – and that latter belief is justified by you on the basis of what you can see. Hence, you have a justified belief – and, allow us to add, it is true. There really is someone in the corner drinking red wine.

There really is someone in the corner drinking red wine, but it is not Sophie. It is Suzie. Suzie's wine glass is hidden from view. Sophie is drinking some obnoxious soft drink; she is unwell. In this case, it seems incorrect to say that you know that someone in the corner is drinking red wine. Examples such as that one show that the simple traditional analysis of knowledge as true justified belief is inadequate – at least, unless some explaining is done about the nature of the justification. Of course, in the example there is a step in the reasoning that, as it transpires, is false – namely, the step that Sophie is drinking red wine. Various attempts have been made to understand justification in such a way that it must be adequate; and then it is argued that it is bound to be inadequate if including a false step. That approach, though, generates its own difficulties. After all, you may actually have reasoned straight to the truth that someone is drinking red wine without forming the belief that Sophie is the drinker. Let us return to this particular 'justification' problem – after looking at one that solely concerns whether justification is always necessary for knowledge.

Sophie predicting the weather

If Sophie knows that p, does she need a justification for her belief that p? Suppose that she reliably gets things right – for example, predicting the weather – but she has no idea how she does it. Her predictions come to her in a flash. Of course, later on, Sophie's repeated predictive successes arguably justify the belief that her next predictions are right. But perhaps her continual reliability indicates that those first successes were no flashes in the pan: maybe they, too, were instances of knowledge.

The above example leads to the thought that Sophie – as knower – need have no justification. What makes Sophie a knower is the existence of an appropriate link between her beliefs and what makes those beliefs true. The obvious link is a causal connection. Beliefs about the world constitute knowledge when what makes the beliefs true has brought about the beliefs. If Sophie knows that she visited Istanbul three years ago, presumably a causal connection exists in some way between the Istanbul visit and that memory.

Knowledge of the future would seem to raise a problem for the causal analysis. What makes Sophie's belief true that it will rain tomorrow is rain tomorrow; yet how can rain tomorrow cause what it is that Sophie believes today? It cannot. But the clouds today that cause Sophie's belief in rain tomorrow are the very clouds that cause the rain tomorrow. Sophie's belief and what makes the belief true have a cause in common. Perhaps that establishes that Sophie knows that it will rain tomorrow.

Sophie in Sofia?

The causal thought given draws us away from a justification analysis – 'justification' in the sense that the knower must be able to provide a justification. Rather, the suggestion goes, a justification needs to be available in the sense that, in principle, a causal explanation could be given for knowledge to be present. And this latter approach, the causal approach, handles well the 'Sophie with drink in hand' problem.

In the problem, you truly believe that someone is drinking red wine – and you are able to provide a justification – but even though you have a true justified belief, our intuitions tell us that you do not really know that someone is drinking red wine. And now – arguably – we can see why. The causal explanation of your belief involves reference to Sophie's glass of obnoxious juice – and not reference to Suzie's glass of red wine which accounts for the truth of your belief. Should we announce 'three cheers' for the causal approach to knowledge? Well, the cheers would be premature. Consider the following – on which we end.

You have a true justified belief that Sophie is in Bulgaria, in Sofia in fact. You know she wanted a holiday there; you saw her board the right flight. You can provide a justification for your belief. Furthermore, there is the correct causal link between your belief and what makes your belief true. On the doormat, though, is a postcard from Sophie. You have not read it yet. It says, in Sophie's hand, 'Hi, I had to change planes in Prague – so I decided to try out Prague, not Sofia.' The postcard is appropriately dated and postmarked: it has been posted in Prague. Once you read the postcard, you will certainly no longer believe that Sophie is in Sofia. In fact, though, she is in Sofia, but some weeks earlier, as a jape, she arranged for a friend in Prague to mail you the misleading postcard she had written. Now, before you read the postcard, you have a true and justified belief that Sophie is in Sofia. Once you read the card, you will change your mind. Some suggest that if you really know that Sophie is in Sofia, your belief that she is should not be so easily changed. For you to have knowledge, your belief requires some stability in the face of misleading evidence.

The stability requirement now raises the awkward question of how misleading and how close the misleading evidence needs to be to you for it to undermine your apparent knowledge. After all, if the sheer *possibility* that you could be being misled is sufficient to undermine your claim to knowledge, well, we have rolled into the arms of the sceptic who lives in the following chapter.

CHAPTER 7

How to stop worrying about the evil genius . . .

and about being a brain in a vat

You are flying high across forests and oceans, then the alarm clock sounds and, sure enough, it was a dream. Yet, right now, you are certain that this is no dream: here and now, you embrace reality. But what if your reality is no reality at all? What if an evil genius has your brain in a vat and is pumping it with simulations, illusions. The mere possibility of there being a deceitful genius shows, it may appear, that we never truly know anything for sure.

Sceptics

The sceptic is often no more than a philosophical device, a figure who doubts whether we possess the knowledge that we claim. After all, we do all make mistakes. Our senses sometimes deceive us – maybe because of excess whisky – and events can mislead us. Even well-attested scientific theories come and go – and, if they stay, they may undergo radical revision.

Some areas of alleged knowledge readily generate a sceptical attitude: they give rise to local scepticisms – that is, scepticisms confined to certain intellectual localities. Many people today, in the West, are sceptical of the possibility of religious, ethical and aesthetic knowledge. Such subject areas are submerged in doubt. Some would readily see economics and sociology drowning in the same sceptical seas. After all, insist such sceptics, there are no reliable sources for predictions concerning economic and social activities – and people frequently disagree about whether there is a god, which are the true moral values and what is good art. Centuries ago, though, many thinkers expressed no doubts about the existence of God, about the need to worship him, and about the moral law – yet they would question the very possibility of a scientific understanding of the Universe. The world depended on the ways of God – and those ways were mysterious.

Philosophers may adopt sceptical stances because they think that there are no objective facts to be known in the particular locales. Perhaps, for example, there are no moral facts. They may, though, recognize that there could well be objective facts of the matter: they simply doubt that we could ever have knowledge of them. Perhaps there is a fact of the matter with regard to whether God exists; but our human understanding is too impoverished to find out – one way or the other. In his first two *Meditations*, Descartes famously put forward a line of argument – a thought experiment – to generate as much doubt as possible. It is his method of systematic doubt. It gives rise to a global scepticism, though Descartes' ultimate aim was to overcome such scepticism through proof of his own existence and then of God's existence and of God's non-deceptive nature.

Towards the global

Descartes notes that we often make mistakes about what we see, hear, touch – and so forth. The tower appears rectangular from a distance; yet, near to, we see that it is round. The stick appears bent when immersed in water – yet we pull it out and discover it is straight.

That the senses sometimes deceive us in such ways provides no good justification for the belief that we are always deceived. We have used the senses to spot the deceptions. When we stroke the stick submerged in water, it feels straight; out of the water, it looks straight. Indeed, just because we sometimes make mistakes on the basis of what we see, it does not follow that it is possible that we always do. Some coins are counterfeit; but for that to be so, there must be, or at least have been, some non-counterfeit ones. So, too, when Descartes later makes the point that we have often been taken in by our dreams, the point carries the implication that some non-dreaming experiences also occur.

The above cases of error provide no good reason to think that all our experiences may be deceptive – be it because of sensory mistakes or because we dream. What the above cases may show is that, with regard to any particular experience, we cannot know whether it is deceptive – or not. The problem with this latter claim is that it appears to be false. On the basis of further investigation, we discovered the stick that appeared bent to be straight. On the basis of the alarm clock going off, we wake up and realize that the flying over forest and oceans had been but a dream.

A problem with the quick responses just given of 'on further investigation' is that they may need reiteration. Yes, the alarm clock wakes you up – or does it? Maybe you have just dreamt the alarming sound and, in a few minutes, a radio alarm will go off, making you realize that the earlier awakening was just in your dream. A little reflection should show that whichever features we may promote as distinctive of reality as opposed to dreams – perhaps reality possesses features of coherence, vivacity, interaction with other people – it remains possible that we are dreaming such features to be present. That still fails to establish the possibility that we are *always* dreaming. It shows that, on any given occasion, we may be making a mistake.

If to know something demands the impossibility of any mistake by the 'knowers', then we have no knowledge at all of things other than our experiences. That Euclidean triangles have three sides is a necessary truth – it has to be true – but we could make a mistake about such matters. We may be so tipsy that we start arguing that triangles have four sides. To revert to a matter from Chapter 1, *How to know that you exist*, if I am thinking, it follows that I exist; but ply me with whisky and I may sincerely think that I lack all existence.

The evil genius

The above considerations recognize that, on any particular occasion, we may make a mistake about certain matters, but not mistakes thereby on all occasions, though it remains open that no occasion exists such that we could not be mistaken. The hypothesis of the evil genius – and it is merely the logical possibility of the genius – is designed to show that it is logically possible that on virtually all occasions we are being deceived.

The genius is deemed evil because he is out to deceive. There is, it seems, no contradiction in the idea of an evil genius deceiving us. Assuming that we cannot rule out such a possibility, it follows that we cannot be certain that there are trees and turnips, tables and treacle. Maybe an evil genius pumps us with the experiences of our familiar world, but no such world exists. The evil genius is all there is 'out there'. That possibility, it seems, suffices to establish that we ought to be sceptical about ever gaining knowledge of the world. As Descartes proposes:

> Some evil genius no less powerful than deceitful, has employed his whole energies in deceiving me; I shall consider that the heavens, the earth, colours, figures, sound, and all other external things are nought but illusions of which this genius has availed himself in order to lay traps for my credulity.

The background story runs like this. To have knowledge of the world, we take it that the world (in some appropriate way) causes our experiences which lead to our beliefs about the world. Perhaps we believe that the cat is asleep in front of us. Our belief results from our visual experiences of the cat – and those visual experiences have been caused by neurological changes that have been caused by stimulation of the optic nerve that has been caused by streams of photons caused by the cat that snoozes. That is, there is a causal transmission from the world to our brain which in some way generates the experiences.

The evil genius hypothesis relies on the seeming fact that the particular causal transmission is not essential to our experience: the very same experience could be directly caused by some external power, a power which is nothing like a cat. All our experiences – well, those that we relate to the world outside our experiences – could be caused by the disembodied genius and hence would be deceptive. Our beliefs about injuries to our limbs, about our limbs' existence, about even the existence of brains, may also be deceptive. True – Descartes would claim – I have the experience of pain as if in my leg, but there may be no injury to the leg. In fact, there may be no leg. True, I have beliefs about brains – and may even have had experiences as if seeing brains – but the evil genius could be the cause of those experiences.

Too much of a good thing

The evil genius is evil; and he is remarkably good at deceiving. Indeed, he is so remarkably good that maybe he is too good. Let us consider what constitutes deception by taking some gentle steps. Suppose I am setting out to deceive Esmeralda. I tell her that I have bought her a fine yacht, *Miss Chief*, in which to go sailing, and that it is moored in the local harbour. Esmeralda is very excited, races down to the harbour – and finds no yacht. I deceived her; but she has quickly discovered the deception. Suppose I want to achieve a more robust deception.

In this second version, she races down to the harbour, sees, it seems, a yacht named *Miss Chief*. She is thrilled, smothers me with kisses, yet as she starts to step towards it, she realizes that it is but a hologram. My deception has lasted a bit – but she still has found out.

We may propose more successful versions of deception. Perhaps in a third version there really is a physical yacht there, but as she steps aboard, she discovers it to be made out of paper. Perhaps in a fourth version, she can even walk safely onto it, but then realizes that she is trespassing: it is not ours. Perhaps in a fifth version, she can step onto it and we really do own it; but when she investigates further, she realizes that it is not seaworthy, hopeless as a yacht – and is more like a decoy yacht.

In the above cases, my deceptions are becoming more and more successful; but each deception can still eventually be discovered. That is a mark of deception: that it is uncoverable – even though it may never be uncovered. Now, that mark should expose the defect of the evil genius and his deception. His 'deception' is too successful – and, paradoxically, is no success at all. His 'deception' is too successful because, it seems, there is no possible way of telling that we are being deceived. The evil genius has the world exactly as it appears. It is as if I proudly announce that I really have deceived Esmeralda this time – because the yacht is owned by us, is brand new, can be successfully sailed, has all the right equipment and so on. And, I laugh to myself, that now Esmeralda will never discover the deception. And indeed she will not: this is because there is no deception to discover. No wheels are turned by the hypothesis that she is deceived.

When not to worry

We may pop the hypotheses considered – the dreaming, the evil genius and indeed being just a brain in vat – in the same sinking sceptical boat, when wondering about our knowledge.

Here, though, is a simple valid argument, one in which the conclusion follows from the premises:

1. If you know that there is a book in front of you, then you know that you are not being deceived into thinking that there is such a book.
2. You do not know that you are not being deceived (after all, you could be dreaming, or in a vat, or misled by the evil genius).
3. Therefore, you do not know that there is a book in front of you.

Of course, the 'book' example could be replaced by any alleged knowledge about the world. Does the argument show that we lack knowledge about such matters? By way of answer, we need to consider whether we have any good reason to think that we are being deceived. Arguably, Premise 1 is too strong. A premise that we may be prepared to accept is the following:

> If you know something, then you have no good reason to believe that you are being deceived about that something.

We have no good reason to believe we are deceived by the evil genius, for that appears to be no deception at all. The dreaming hypothesis also does not damage our knowledge. Right now we have no good reason to think that we are dreaming. If it turns out that we have been dreaming – well, that shows that we did not then know what we thought we knew. As for the 'brain in vat' hypothesis, again, we have no good reason to believe that we are in a vat. After all, have we ever encountered a brain in a vat being fed misleading experiences?

Maybe the evil genius could deceive us by having everything in the world made out of treacle. But our lives and activities, loves and ambitions, all continue in the same way: the genius ensures that we never discover the treacle truth. That is a magnificent deception – until we realize we have no good reason to believe it; indeed, we have no good reason to believe that it even makes sense. It is no deception at all.

CHAPTER 8

How to be a ghost in the machine

. . . *or is that impossible?*

We often speak of the mind and the body as two separate items – and, if we are religious, we may think it possible that we could exist in an afterlife, without a body. Afterlives or not, certainly our consciousness and our experiences seem very different from physical items, from blobs of biology. Yet many people – including many scientists who work on the brain – think of our conscious experiences as occurring in the brain. The brain is where the mind is. Is that right? What is the relationship between mind and body – and, in particular, between the mind and the brain?

Dualisms

Once again, Descartes deserves to be placed at the beginning of the scene. He and many philosophers over the centuries have offered a dualism when it comes to understanding what people essentially are – 'essentially', that is, what *must* be true of us. Human beings and any particular human being can exist without their eyes being blue; but many would argue that human beings can exist only if they have living brains. Common sense tells us that we are minds and bodies. 'Body' is taken to include the brain. More accurately, and according to Descartes, I am essentially my mind and my mind is a totally different thing, a different substance, from my body. This sort of dualism fits in readily with the beliefs of many religious believers, because at least, if true, it shows that it is logically possible to exist disembodied in an afterlife, even if such existence is unlikely.

Descartes' dualism – known as 'Cartesian dualism' – sees minds as essentially conscious entities without any material or physical properties. 'Matter' was the term used, thinking of tables and chairs, and mountains and marmalade, as constituted by extended material or moving atoms. In view of scientists' current understanding of material bodies, in terms of electrons and other subatomic particles and charges, it is arguably better to see Descartes' dualism as being opposed to physicalism. Physicalism is the position whereby minds ultimately, in some way, need to be understood solely in physical concepts, though who knows what concepts physics may be deploying in the next century. Hereafter, we may use 'materialism' and 'physicalism' interchangeably, without risk.

For Descartes, minds are not in space; they do not have length or breadth or physical location. When someone is thinking about her holidays, we cannot really make sense of that holiday thought occurring, for example, two inches in from her left ear. In contrast, bodies do have size and shape and physical location; but bodies lack consciousness. We cannot make sense of a pebble or a table or a glass of water having thoughts, having experiences. We cannot make sense of a lump of flesh – of a liver, a kidney, even a brain – thinking. That is Descartes' position with regard to what is essential concerning minds and bodies. Descartes argues for his dualism. Here is what seems to be his basic argument:

1. My body can be pretended by me not to exist.
2. I cannot be pretended by me not to exist.
3. Therefore, I am not identical with my body.

This is intended to show that he is something different from his body (including brain); and, as we have seen in Chapter 1, *How to know that you exist*, he argues further that he is a thing that essentially is conscious – in other words, a mind. We have spoken of 'pretend', but Descartes would also stress how we may doubt the existence of the body simply because of the dreaming or evil genius possibilities. We may be deceived about the existence of bodies, but we should still need to exist – in order to be deceived.

Even if we accept premise 1, we may challenge premise 2. Can I not pretend that I am not existing? After all, I might not have been born. Descartes' reply must be that I need to exist to do any pretending, so there would be some inconsistency in my pretending not to exist when pretending – whereas there is no inconsistency in my pretending to have no body when pretending.

Psychological attitudes

Assuming that we accept the premises to be true, must we accept the conclusion? Remember, it is a remarkable conclusion. If the argument is sound, then we really are saying that we are distinct from bodies, from brains, from anything physical. We may still be linked to brains, to bodies, but what we essentially are is completely different from them; and the properties of being conscious, of experiences, are completely different from physical properties. Now, in the argument, Descartes is claiming that something holds true of *my body* – namely what can be pretended about it. He is also saying that what is true of my body is not true of me, of 'I'. So, surely my body and I must be different. After all, if Melissa is in London and Miranda is in Los Angeles (and hence not in London), then Melissa and Miranda cannot be one and the same individual (unless stretched remarkably across ocean and continent).

Soon after Descartes, the German philosopher Gottfried Leibniz promoted a principle known as 'the identity of indiscernibles'. Descartes' argument seems to be relying on a related Leibrizian principle: the indiscernibility of identicals. If two seemingly different items are really one and the same item, then everything true of one must be true of the seeming other. If Melissa and Miranda are identical, then if Melissa is in London, then so must be Miranda. Descartes' argument is making a similar appeal. If I and my body are identical, then whatever is true of my body must be true of me, of 'I'; yet Descartes has pointed to one feature, admittedly complex, that holds of my body yet not of me, the feature being: what I can pretend about the item.

There is just one small problem with Descartes' use of Leibniz's principle. The problem is that the principle can quickly be shown not to apply when we have features including reference to, for example, pretending, imagining, hoping, believing – that is, to psychological attitudes. We can unwittingly hold conflicting psychological attitudes to one and the same identical item.

Maybe I admire Melissa who lives next door. She is kind and gracious; she looks charming and I delight in her. I read in the newspapers, though, about Miranda who looks dreadful in the identikit picture: she is wanted by the police for embezzlement and suspected murder. I think she is mean and nasty and deserves to be caught. I certainly lack adoration for Miranda. Yet Melissa and

Miranda may be one and the same person. I came to my understanding and attitudes towards one and same person via different routes. They were presented differently to me. Hence, unwittingly I am admiring that woman who is Miranda and whom I expressly do not adore, do not admire. As we shall see in Chapter 13, *How to know what we are talking about*, the two names for the individual possess different senses or intensions.

The Melissa/Miranda embezzler example may, though, be a poor analogy for Descartes' argument. Descartes may insist that he possesses an immediate awareness of himself, not mediated by newspaper descriptions or any other descriptions, and that he is aware of all that is essentially true of his self. Of course, we may wonder how he can be so sure of that.

Intimate connections: more than a pilot in a ship

Whatever the particular strength of Descartes' arguments, the dualistic picture of how things are with human beings may still be accurate. Well, it may seem accurate – until we reflect further on some puzzles that the picture generates. Here are some.

My experience of myself – of how I move around the world and do things – seems far removed from my being distinct from my body and my using my body as an instrument to do things. I may ride a bicycle, drive a car, or use a hammer; but I do not use my arms and legs in such ways – in such 'detached' ways. When an injury occurs to my leg, I do not usually experience it in an intellectual way; rather, I immediately feel pain. Descartes, to his credit, recognizes all that. Descartes makes the point that I do not stand in relationship to my body in the way that a pilot stands to his ship. I am far more intermingled with my body. I frequently have access to what is going on with my body 'from within'. I often know, from within, the position of my limbs. Descartes' dualistic picture, though, makes it difficult to understand quite how that special intimate relationship holds.

That intermingling of mind and body is a particular problem for Descartes, but, more generally, he has often been attacked for making it mysterious how the mind can affect the body – and the body the mind – even without the problem of the special intimacy. If the mind really is a distinct substance, different stuff, from the brain, then a causal connection seems impossible.

Of course, mind and body do interact. Well, they do in that, when I want a drink, I may well stretch out my hand. When I think about certain situations, I may begin to blush. My mind, because of the psychological changes, has affected my body. And when car alarms go off, I may well experience a headache and have some nasty thoughts about the owners. That is, interaction occurs by way of my acting – my mental events seem to cause changes in my body – and by way of my perceiving, when the world impinges on me. And there are more dramatic interactions. Inject me with enough morphine and, the evidence suggests, my psychological life will cease.

Interaction: a puzzle?

Descartes sought to solve the interaction puzzle by speaking of the interaction occurring at a particular point in the head – at the pineal gland at the centre of the brain. The gland is, of course, physical; so we still have the problem of how something non-physical can cause changes in the physical. The pineal gland 'solution' is no solution at all. The interaction problem, though, is only a problem if we accept one or both of two further positions. There should be no problem in accepting that psychological changes may bring about physical changes – and vice versa – unless causation between two events demands that they are, in some way, of the same type. After all, magnetic fields cause compass pointers to move; yet they seem pretty dissimilar. That consideration to one side, we may be convinced that all the actions of humans are caused by neurological events which are themselves caused by other neurological events and so forth. If that is so, then there is no space, so to speak, for psychological events to have any causal powers (the position of epiphenomenalism touched on in the next chapter). Again, though, we may wonder whether we have sufficient knowledge of the brain to be sure that every neurological change must have a physical cause.

The ghost in the machine

We have casually accepted talk of the mind as a substance, an entity. It is modelled on the body or the brain, except that it is mysteriously non-physical and not in space. Indeed, Descartes identified it with the soul. Now, we do possess an understanding of physical properties. We can deploy various concepts that apply to the physical world, conduct experiments and make successful predictions. We use concepts of force and mass and acceleration, for example, and we understand the workings of electricity. The mind, on the dualistic view, is totally different from the workings mentioned above. We are bound to feel at a loss, then, about what the mind is. Other than deeming the mind to be immaterial stuff, we seem to have little more to say with regard to any laws that science has uncovered concerning the immaterial stuff. We cannot experiment on it or test it directly. Yes, we have some psychological theories, but they are always mediated by physical behaviour.

Perhaps Descartes' picture is radically mistaken. Perhaps we ought not to think of the mind as an entity, a thing, at all. Perhaps talk of the mind is just 'short talk' for the set of psychological states that human beings undergo. As mentioned, even Descartes could not avoid acknowledging the unity of a person. In his words:

> Nature teaches me by the sensations of pain, hunger, thirst, etc., that I am not merely lodged in my body as a pilot in a ship, but that I am so closely united to it that I seem to compose with it one whole . . .

Indeed, with the mind as distinct entity in mind, Gilbert Ryle, a 20th-century British philosopher, mocked it as 'a ghost in the machine'. Even if we do, though, move away from thinking of the mind as a thing, we still have the question of what the psychological states – the intentions, the sensations, the thoughts – are. In the next chapter we shall see how well the brain fares in comparison with the ghost.

CHAPTER 9

How not to have feelings or beliefs
. . . or anything psychological at all

Our brains – well, those neurological happenings within our heads – affect our consciousness, our experiences and what we think and do. There can be no dispute about that. Wine causes changes in the brain and sufficient wine can lead us into feelings of joy, then to staggering and sickness. We all have experiences, yet when scientists examine our brains – operate on them, scan them – they are confronted by nerve cells, not by the kaleidoscope of our experiences. Yet, how can our experiences really, possibly, be just some changes in cells of the brain?

Mental states just are brain states

The previous chapter explored dualism, whereby mind and brain are distinct. Dualism was found to be mysterious. The obvious and popular alternative is the mind-brain identity theory. The theory presents in different guises but, at heart, it maintains that psychological states and events – conscious experiences, beliefs and desires – are nothing but brain states and events. The theory is sometimes known as 'materialism', 'physicalism' or 'central state theory'. Materialism has a long history, tracing back to ancient Greek philosophers, such as, for example, the atomist Democritus – known as the laughing philosopher. Laughing, no doubt, would be explained, as would all experiences, by Democritus in terms of material atoms in motion. One attraction of identity theories is methodological: theorists make use of a principle, namely, Ockham's Razor. William of Ockham was a medieval English philosopher. The razor is the principle: entities should not be multiplied beyond necessity.

The razor is used to shave off references to unnecessary entities, any beards or whiskers, in explaining how things work. Increasingly it seems likely that neurological science – investigations into the brain – will be able to explain people's behaviour. Well, that is the article of faith. In as far as that is so, it would be bizarre to be stuck with psychological states and events, as if they were somehow 'over and above' the physical states of the brain, in some weird way, dangling impotently from those states. What role could they play in explaining behaviour? None. They would form but powerless sideshows, unable to affect or effect anything. Indeed, such a view – known as 'epiphenomenalism' – has been held.

According to epiphenomenalism, psychological events are over and above the causal networks of the physical world. Neurological events cause behaviour and also, as a side effect, cause experiences; but the experiences lack all causal powers with regard to the physical world. An oft-used analogy is that of the steam engine: the steam moves the pistons and a side effect is the whistle; but the whistle has nothing to do with causing the pistons' movements. Think of the moving parts of a turbine, generating electricity; the movements may also cause shadows to change, but the shadows have no causal efficacy with regard to the electricity being generated.

Identity theorists challenge the need for such epiphenomenal experiences. They would be unnecessary entities; they should fall under the razor. Now, some related theorists would shave accordingly and say no more; they are eliminativists (to whom we shall return). Traditional identity theorists, though, merely shave experiences off, *if* taken as events distinct from brain events. Identity theorists typically recognize that psychological states and events – conscious experiences – obviously do exist; but they are strictly identical with the states and changes in the brain. Well, even here caveats are required.

Logical behaviourism

Here is the first caveat. When we speak of people being in pain, planning for holidays or being angry, we have in mind how they are behaving or are disposed to behave. Logical behaviourists would understand psychological states as consisting solely in such behaviour and behavioural dispositions. The theory gives rise to the cartoon of a couple in bed after sex, with one saying to the other, 'Well, it was good for you. How was it for me?'

The behaviourist model is that of salt being soluble: that salt is soluble amounts to the fact that, were it to be placed in water, it would dissolve. However, that analysis sounds inadequate; better is to come – and here it comes. Salt has a certain molecular structure in virtue of which, if it is placed in water, it dissolves. The molecular structure is the categorical base of the disposition. Identity theorists view psychological states as the brain states that are the categorical bases of certain behaviour. The man experiencing a headache, or a lost love, is in a certain neurological state – that is his experiencing – and it is in virtue of that state that he is likely to clasp his head, sound grumpy and take some aspirin.

Here is the second caveat. A particular type of mental state – for example, being in pain – may be realized in very different types of brain. Pains are multiply realizable. Octopuses, cats and chimps, maybe hypothetical Martians as well as humans, can all experience pain – yet their brains are pretty different. The brain states all count as pains because they play the same causal role – have similar functions – in the creatures with regard to other psychological states and behaviour. This line of thinking leads us into functionalism, which is often associated with versions of the mind-brain identity theory; let us, though, retain focus on the latter.

Lightning

Experiencing a visual sensation, feeling a tickle, having a thought, are just identical with certain neurological states and changes – according to the identity theory. Of course, if A is identical with B, then B is identical with A; so, as expressed, the identity theorist could equally well be claiming that many brain states are just psychological states. The identity claim, though, has attitude – directional attitude. That is, the theorist argues that psychological states are reducible to, are nothing but, brain states. The correct understanding of them is in terms of the concepts and laws of the neurological sciences.

Can there be any evidence for the claim that, for example, having certain sensations just is having certain neural changes? One proposed analogy draws on the discovery by the American polymath Benjamin Franklin that lightning is nothing but electrical discharge. How may we have shown that the white flash of lightning high in the sky was just electrical discharge? One simple answer is that the white flash occurred at the same time and in the same place as the electrical discharge. If one came after the other, we should not assert identity, but rather that the earlier event perhaps caused the later.

With the lightning discovery in mind, how could we show that a sensation or thought is nothing but a particular set of neural signals or transmissions? Well, we could have our human guinea-pig wired up appropriately; we may then measure when and where the relevant neural signalling occurs. But to show that the signalling is identical with the sensation, we need to know whether the sensation occurs at the same time and place as the signalling. Naturally, we ask our guinea-pig when the sensation occurs. Yet, unless already committed to the identity theory, it is often difficult to know what to say about the location of a sensation or thought; and, when it is easy, the location is rarely said to be in the brain. If the ache is in the foot, the identity theorist has to move into claiming, 'Ah, but perhaps the *having* of the ache is in the brain.' My thought about the holiday is – well, is it really three inches in from the left ear?

Perhaps we have simply to rely on Ockham's Razor to justify accepting the identity theory – but if we accept the theory, we meet some tricky problems. There are many features of psychological states that are not easily grasped as belonging to neurons, to cells of the brain. I have, for example, privileged access to many of my states. I have a pain in my arm; yet if having the pain is just a particular neurological happening – in principle, open to all to see – what becomes of my privileged access? It is also difficult to escape from the thought that the 'feel' of sensations is nothing like electrochemical activity in the brain, though we may wonder what that would feel like 'from within' – perhaps like our sensations after all? Further, think about beliefs, intentions and desires: they are directed onto objects, some of them non-existent – yet can we make sense of neurons being directed onto objects? We yearn to visit Damascus with Davinia: how can neural activity account for that directedness towards Damascus and Davinia?

There is a vast array of features of the psychological that do not seem to hold of neural activities; but if neural activities really are identical with sensations, intentions, thoughts and so forth, then what is true of one should be true of the other. We met the underlying principle here, the indiscernibility of identicals, in Chapter 8, *How to be a ghost in the machine*. What is to be done? Well, what is to be done here is to tell a tale.

Little red demons

We visit a remote tribe and learn that, when individuals fall ill, witch doctors are called. They perform various dances round the sick person, call on the spirits, eat of the sacred mushroom – and may then announce that they see little red demons running amok over the sick individual. The witch doctors alone can see the demons. The demons need to be placated. So, the witch doctors set off to the sacred forest, select various berries, make a stew which they pour over the patient: the little red demons eat well and cause no more trouble. And, as a matter of fact, often the patient does recover.

We are suspicious of the red demon theory. We gradually work out that the witch doctors have hallucinations, resulting from the sacred mushroom; and the berry stew applied to the sick individuals has some antibiotic properties. We can account for what happens in terms of familiar scientific concepts that have wide-ranging successful application. We discard the witch doctors' theory of red demons; and, in so doing, we do not anguish about how to fit little red demons in our medical theory. We do not insist that our Western theories cannot be satisfactory because they cannot account for red demons needing to be placated. We simply dump the demons – part of a rotten theory.

On that basis, some philosophers – eliminativists – argue that we should have the same approach to our concepts of desires, beliefs, sensations and so forth. They belong to our commonsense theory – folk psychology – that we have used for centuries to explain behaviour; but neuroscience will give us better theories. We need not worry how to translate concepts from folk psychology into the new theories. We just go with the new. Eliminativists have, then, a 'disappearance theory of the mind'. Their argument assumes that the concepts we deploy every day – intentions, desires, beliefs, sensations – belong to a theory, and it is a theory that has poor explanatory and predictive value. We may, though, challenge the eliminativists' claim that our use of concepts such as intention, desire and belief has poor predictive value. We may also wonder what sense we can make of human beings and their relationships, if our common concepts are fictional and akin to the 'little red demons'. Without concepts of intention, desire, belief, we should be unable to make promises, describe ideals and reassure lovers of our love.

Gilbert Ryle, as we saw in the previous chapter, dismissed the Cartesian mind, the soul, as but a ghost in the machine. That was done to direct our focus on what is involved in human beings having thoughts and sensations. That focus, for some, is then aimed at the brain; but it is extremely difficult to understand how brains can have such features. Eliminativists overcome that difficulty by jettisoning the thoughts and sensations and other psychological states, leaving us with just the brain, as understood by the neurological sciences, to explain behaviour. But what then remains of familiar human life, if our common psychological concepts lack sense and application?

Philosophical reasoning has to start somewhere, and maybe we are far more certain of our sensations and intentions, our beliefs and desires, than of the soundness of arguments to show that they do not exist. Perhaps we should remember that we are human beings with both psychological and physical features. Brains do not think; it is human beings who think. We should resist reducing ourselves 'really' to brains as much as we should resist reducing ourselves to immaterial souls – or even ghosts in machines.

CHAPTER 10

How to tell the future . . .

well, how it is possible so to do

You are trying to predict winners of the Kentucky Derby by studying the previous records of the horses. You are predicting on the basis of past happenings. Clarissa, however, predicts the winners by gazing into her crystal ball. You point out that reference to a horse's past form has been a more successful predictive method than a crystal ball. 'Ah,' Clarissa replies, 'but all that success is past success. We are concerned about the future.'

The problem of induction

We have outlined here the problem of induction, a problem not of pregnancy but of reasoning. It is usually oriented to time: just because things have regularly happened in the past, we have no good reason to infer that they will carry on happening in similar ways in the future. The spatial version is: just because things happen over here, we have no good reason to infer that they happen over there. Every day, we rely on inductive inferences yet it is remarkably difficult to see what, if anything, justifies them. There have been no observed instances of pigs flying; so, we feel justified in inferring that we shall see no flying pigs tomorrow. To date, all human beings, if alive, have needed to breathe; we infer that our children would be in a bad way if unable to breathe. And winners of horse races usually have manifested some good form; so we judge it likely that future winners will. The most general version of the problem of induction is a challenge to how we may move from

> All observed instances of F are G
> to
> All instances of F are G,

where, for example, 'F' is 'piggyness' and 'G' is 'non-fliers'. The challenge is most famously associated with an 18th-century Enlightenment figure, one already encountered, the splendid David Hume.

Of course, inductive reasoning does not guarantee that conclusions reached will be true. Even though there may have been overwhelming evidence to support the judgement that all swans are white (swans, at one stage, had been observed in many different locations and had always been white), as it turned out, some swans do lurk elsewhere and they are black.

In engaging in our inductions, in our inductive reasoning, we need to be aware of what happens in a range of diverse circumstances. After all, if I confine my evidence to human beings who are alive, I might foolishly conclude that human beings never die. We also need to be aware of likelihoods. I infer from past experience that when I turn on the tap, water is highly likely to flow, but occasionally these outcomes will not occur. Again, though, it is through our awareness of the past that we know things can go wrong – and, often, why they go wrong.

Clarissa the crystal ball gazer

In seeking to predict future winners based on past evidence – and, more mundanely, in expecting regularities to continue, be they about pigs, children or water supplies – we are surely more rational that those who rely on crystal balls. But how can we show that? Well, let us, briefly, reflect a little more on Clarissa and her crystal ball predictions of the Kentucky winners.

Clarissa may explain that the reason she is basing her predictions on the crystal ball is because it has been far more successful than other methods of predicting winners. If that is her justification, then she is not in dispute with us over the basic approach to prediction. We all agree that we should look to past regularities and, depending on conditions, project them into the

97

future. So, we would be in agreement that we should look at the evidence and see which method – crystal or horses' form – has a better past record of success.

Clarissa, though, may be in radical disagreement with us. Suppose we point out that crystal ball gazing has been unsuccessful in the past over predicting future winners. Clarissa agrees, but says that past failures are irrelevant. Maybe we suggest that Clarissa must therefore have an improved crystal; but Clarissa says that is 'not so' – same old crystal. She really is insisting that the past, with regard to winners, is no guide to the future. What can we say to her – or to anyone who challenges the relevance of past regularities for the future? Let us, indeed, consider the general problem, rather than focusing on the Kentucky. Kentucky is of specialist interest and was to capture attention, but what affects all of us are the mundane expectations of everyday life.

Justifications

To justify beliefs about the future based on the past, we cannot turn to the world around us and to what has happened, for we are then assuming that the past is relevant to beliefs about the future – but such is circular reasoning, for that is what we are trying to justify. Even the most successful ways of prediction have shown themselves to be successful only to date

– well, so Clarissa-minded individuals would insist. Turning to the empirical world for justification – that is, an *a posteriori* justification, via experience of the world – is, it would seem, hopeless.

But perhaps we have been too quick in our dismissal of the empirical world. After all, there must be laws of nature in operation – and we recognize how items have causal powers, how they can bring things about. Copper expands when heated. Because of gravity, apples – and people – fall to the ground; and alcohol causes people to stagger. Indeed, all that is true; but we now suffer the inductive problem arising in these particular cases. What justifies us in our belief that future copper will expand when heated and future apples will fall to the ground?

Sometimes we can justify things by reason alone – *a priori*, independently of experience. Just by reasoning alone, we can work out truths about triangles and numbers. Now, could a justification for our inductive reasoning be found *a priori*? Well, what principle could justify our move from all observed *F*s and *G*s to all *F*s are *G*s? Some philosophers have proposed a principle of the uniformity of nature. John Stuart Mill – the Victorian British thinker now best known for his political philosophy, but who wrote a highly important logic text – argued, for example, that inductive reasoning required the fundamental principle that nature is uniform. There are, of course, immediate questions: in quite what does the uniformity consist and whatever grounds do we have for holding that such a principle is true? We cannot simply say that the principle has worked in the past – for that again would be exposed to the charge of circularity.

The above points aside, what is curious about the suggested 'uniformity' principle is that if we initially accept it, we can surely quickly disprove it, by considering some inductive arguments making use of it. It looks as if we should be able to argue:

> All observed swans are white.
> Nature is uniform.
> Therefore, all swans are white.

We may know, though, that the first premise is true, yet the conclusion is false. So, we do not have a good argument with true premises and a true conclusion. Something is wrong in the argument – and we might reasonably conclude that nature is not uniform, well, not uniform in any simple way.

Sleights of hand

So far, we have failed to justify our practice of using inductive reasoning. It is worth mentioning here, though, how in this area of philosophical discussion, some moves are made that, once reflected upon, are clearly sleights of hand.

'For something to be glass,' someone may insist, 'it must break, if thrown forcefully at a brick wall. That is in the nature of glass. So, we do know what will happen to this typical wine glass in front of us – if thrown. That is how we have knowledge of the future.'

The above is but a handy sleight. Future responses of the material have been built into our understanding of the nature of glass. For something to be glass, it must smash when thrown forcibly against a hard surface. If we accept that – and let us accept it – then our inductive problem simply flips over to a new problem. Concerning this 'wine glass' in front of me, how can we be sure that it really is glass? We cannot – until we see whether it smashes when thrown against the brick wall. Our original inductive problem was: what justifies us in expecting that this glass will smash, if thrown? The problem has become: what justifies us in believing that what we have before us is made of glass?

Someone may reply that we should perform a chemical analysis on the wine glass to establish the true nature of its material. That is how we can tell whether it is glass. But the response to that reply is this: it just moves the problem along a stage, for how do we know that that material (which we discover it to be) will behave in the future as it did in the past?

Nothing in nature tells us that the underlying regularities we may have discovered must continue into the future. That leads some people to go outside nature. We live in an orderly world, they insist, and that requires explanation. The explanation is that our belief about the orderliness of the world can be justified by reference to a transcendent being, God, who designed the world to be orderly.

That is another misleading sleight. If the world's orderliness is a mystery that is in want of explanation, then the want is not satisfied by the orderliness being explained by a transcendent being outside of nature, namely God. Dissatisfaction should continue for we then have the mystery of how and why such a being interacts with this world – and what counts as orderliness for such a being and what his mysterious ways are.

What we do

There is no doubt that we do and should expect events in our future to resemble events in the past. We know what has typically happened when express trains have hit people on the tracks. So, if we want to avoid injury, we ought not to place ourselves in front of trains.

We know the effects of alcohol, starvation, lust – and much more.

Hume's approach to induction was to stress that we do just form expectations from repeated experiences. In his words:

'Tis not, therefore, reason which is the guide of life, but custom that alone determines the mind, in all instances, to suppose the future conformable to the past.

That we are guided by custom can be justified neither by reason nor by experience. It is the way that human beings are constituted. We may add that that, too, relies on an assumed uniformity in our human biology over time and space.

At this point, evolutionary theorists may pop their heads into the conversation. They may point to the fact that, as humans and similar creatures flourish, their tendency to base expectations on the past clearly possesses survival value, and shows that we often get things right by doing so – otherwise we should not survive. The evolutionary consideration, as with certain other considerations above, continues to miss the point. No doubt our projection of regularities into the future has served us well; but that still does not justify our belief that such projective tendencies will serve us well in the future. Maybe the Universe is such that up to this moment, regularities can be relied upon – and hence we have survived – but that thereafter chaos descends. Of course, we have no good reason to believe that; but then, it seems, we have no good reason to believe that regularities must continue into the future.

Although no good, non-circular reason can be given for our practice of making inductive inferences, within that practice certain past regularities may provide us with good reasons to expect similarities in the future. Observing the many cats in the house to be black does not provide a good reason for thinking that all cats are black; but observing ravens in a variety of places always as black provides good reason (though not conclusive) that all ravens are black. Further, changes in circumstances may rightly lead us to change beliefs and policies; as John Maynard Keynes quipped, 'when the facts change, I change my mind; what do you do, sir?'

The practice of inductive reasoning overall cannot be justified – even though it works. Mind you, our final chapter shows that deductive reasoning cannot be justified. Justifications have to come to an end.

CHAPTER 11

How to be a philosophical scientist
. . . *and a good one at that*

Philosophers are eager to investigate every discipline, and so naturally they philosophize about the sciences. Scientific progress has been a remarkable feature of the past 200 years. But how does science advance? As the previous chapter showed, there are problems in trying to justify knowledge of universal propositions, propositions that cover 'all' – including future cases. Yet science has with increasing success put forward many theories that work and continue to work. How is that possible?

Science and pseudo-science

When astrologers predict that you will meet difficulties in your life next week and astronomers predict a lunar eclipse at a certain future date and time, some may insist that both are basing their predictions on theories gleaned through evidence. And that the theories are indeed equally good may seem established when both predictions prove true. Yet, if we reflect further, the astronomical prediction was highly detailed, and more likely to go wrong, whereas the astrologers were running no risk at all. After all, whose life throughout a week does not encounter difficulties?

A scientific theory consists of certain concepts and general laws. The concepts are used to characterize features of the world, and the laws, using the concepts, allow us, given initial known conditions, to predict events and explain why they happened. Numerous laws have been discovered, often named accordingly – after, for example, Newton, Faraday and Einstein. Knowledge of the laws enables scientists' predictions to be successful, and enables engineers and technicians to build a whole range of devices that work – from electric kettles to brain scanners; from aircraft to laptops. Well, the latter usually work.

To be good scientists, which features should our theories (hereafter used to refer to the general laws) possess? The Austrian philosopher Karl Popper in the 20th century gave an influential answer. A theory is scientific if it is falsifiable.

In so far as a scientific statement speaks about reality, it must be falsifiable; and in so far as it is not falsifiable, it does not speak about reality.

A scientific theory should forbid certain states of affairs, given certain conditions; so, if those states of affairs arise, then the theory has been falsified. The point is simply that if we assert something substantial about the world, about the reality around us, we are asserting something that could turn out to be mistaken. No doubt we hope that we are not mistaken: we hope that the theory will not be refuted – but the possibility of its refutation must exist. If a theory logically cannot be refuted, then it says nothing about reality. It is vacuous.

The astronomical theory that gave rise to the eclipse prediction above was clearly highly scientific: it was very specific in its prediction and, no doubt, in many others. It ran the risk of being falsified, and, through future predictions, still runs that risk. The astrological theory, though, gave a prediction that was so vague that it was bound to come true. And, if astrological theories typically give such vague predictions, then the theories are protected from all possible refutation; so, to be told that astrology has not been refuted carries no weight. Astrology is a pseudo-science.

Psychoanalytic theories and Marxist theories of history have also been deemed pseudo-scientific by Popper. What predictions do they make that could be refuted? In the case of psychoanalysis, such theories are used to explain some aberrant behaviour

– perhaps by reference to the Oedipus Complex – once it has occurred. But we may wonder what evidence psychoanalysts would accept as refuting the theories. Commonly, adults seek to explain teenage behaviour. They may say knowingly, 'Ah, they are reacting against their oppressive parents', or 'Ah, they are just following their parents'. There is, though, as of yet no successful theory 'out there' predicting which individuals will react against upbringing and which will succumb. Which way is discovered, the theory 'predicts', so to speak, only after the events.

Popper's criterion for distinguishing between science and pseudo-science concerns empirical claims about the reality around us. We should note that, in contrast to scientific theories, there are many important and significant mathematical and logical theorems that cannot be refuted. They are not directly about the reality around us, but concern abstract relations. If, for example, something is a right-angled Euclidean triangle, then the square on its hypotenuse must be equal to the sum of the squares of the other two sides. That is a necessary truth – and can be proved by reason alone.

Making progress
Scientific theories should be open to refutation – but how do we acquire them in the first place? What

should we do? Well, we should make bold conjectures: they are our theories. We should then see how well they stand up to rigorous tests. We should, in other words, try to refute them. Our conjectures may, of course, be stimulated by particular observations; but because inductive reasoning, according to Popper, cannot be justified, we should not think of those observations as in any way supporting the truth of the conjectures. Once the theory is present, we seek to refute it. Even when a theory survives being tested many times, it remains a conjecture. If it fails, then good scientists reject the theory. Bad scientists, according to Popper, try to cling on to the theory, on to the wreckage. One clinging is by way of introducing an ad hoc modification, a modification fit solely for the purpose of protecting the theory. If a theory predicts the sighting of a planet, but no sighting is made by the scientists all of whom are operating in the Southern Hemisphere, the ad hoc revision may be that there is an exception to the sighting if done from that hemisphere on that day.

Making use of refuted theories, though, to suggest new conjectures is fine – if the new conjectures can give rise to predictions that are also falsifiable. The conjecture might have been that water boils at 100°C. It is falsified, but the conditions are then noticed to involve changes in atmospheric pressures. A new conjecture may then be suggested, one that takes into account such pressures.

The hypothetico-deductive method

Popper's approach relies on the fact that a universal proposition – for example, all ravens are black – cannot be verified. That is the problem of induction. However, the existence of a single non-black raven, it seems, can be verified and, if so, the universal proposition is falsified. Popper is deploying the hypo-thetico-deductive (HD) method in order to sidestep the problem of induction. The method tests the hypothesis, the conjecture, the theory, by putting it forward – 'all ravens are black' – as the universal premise of a deductive argument. It then adds a particular case, the 'initial conditions', for a second premise – 'this is a raven' – and so the conclusion that may be validly deduced is: 'this is black'. Hence, if the bird before us transpires not to be black, then the conjecture must be false. Well, so a crude under-standing of Popper's position suggests. However, we need refinement.

There are two elements involved in the attempted refutation. There is the theory and the set of initial conditions. So, in our example, if the bird is not black, that may be because the conjecture is false; but it may be because we are mistaken about the initial conditions.

Perhaps the bird is no raven at all. The moral to draw is that to reject a theory solely because a prediction has been falsified is not always rational. We have drawn attention to just one factor – the set of initial conditions – in addition to the conjecture. But things are far more complicated than that.

Planetary misbehaviour

Consider the splendid story of planetary misbehaviour told by the Hungarian philosopher Imre Lakatos. The tale starts with a physicist of the pre-Einsteinian era who takes Newton's mechanics and his law of gravitation, the accepted initial conditions, and calculates, with their help, the path of a newly discovered small planet, p. What then happens? Well, continues Lakatos, the planet deviates from the calculated path.

> Does our Newtonian physicist consider that the deviation was forbidden by Newton's theory and therefore that, once established, it refutes the theory? No. He suggests that there must be a hitherto unknown planet p' which perturbs the path of p. He calculates the mass, orbit, etc., of this hypothetical planet and then asks an experimental astronomer to test his hypothesis.

Lakatos now comments that the planet p' turns out to be so small that even the biggest available telescopes cannot possibly observe it: so, the experimental

111

astronomer applies for a research grant to build yet a bigger telescope. In three years' time, the new telescope is ready.

> Were the unknown planet p' to be discovered, it would be hailed as a new victory of Newtonian science. But it is not. Does our scientist abandon Newton's theory and his idea of the perturbing planet? No. He suggests that a cloud of cosmic dust hides the planet from us. He calculates the location and properties of this cloud and asks for a research grant to send up a satellite to test his calculations.

Now, continues Lakatos, if the satellite's instruments (possibly new ones, based on a little-tested theory) record the existence of the conjectural cloud, the result would be hailed as an outstanding victory for Newtonian science. But the cloud is not found.

> Does our scientist abandon Newton's theory, together with the idea of the perturbing planet and the idea of the cloud which hides it? No. He suggests that there is some magnetic field in that region of the universe which disturbed the instruments of the satellite. A new satellite is sent up. Were the magnetic field to be found, Newtonians would celebrate a sensational victory. But it is not. Is this regarded as a refutation of Newtonian science?

No, and Lakatos concludes that either yet another ingenious auxiliary hypothesis is proposed or the whole story is buried in the dusty volumes of periodicals and never mentioned again.

The point being made is not merely that auxiliary hypotheses may be brought into play – sometimes rightly, sometimes not – but that, in order to falsify the theory in question, we need to assume the general proposition that there are no intervening forces of other, possibly unknown kinds. Yet, of course, we may have more confidence in the theory that we are testing than in the belief that there are no such intervening forces; but how could that belief be falsified? How do we judge which to hold steadfast?

Paradigms

Popper's stress on conjectures and refutations ignores the fact that scientists conduct much of their investigation within a paradigm, a theory that is generally accepted and which forms the basis for research – a point stressed in Thomas Kuhn's writings on the history of science. The paradigm determines how matters are seen and is held firm, generating new research programmes, as outlined in the tale from Lakatos concerning Newtonian science. Depending on experiments and outcomes, anomalies may be spotted; but then, with suitable additional hypotheses, they are made to fit the paradigm. At some stage, though, the anomalies may become so great that there is a revolution: a new way of looking at the world, a new paradigm, comes into play. For centuries, the paradigm saw the Earth as centre of the world with planets embedded in epicycle spheres. More and more complexities – as in the Ptolemaic system – were introduced to fit new observations while retaining the paradigm. The system became so unwieldy, so the story goes, that a revolution was needed: as a result, the Sun was seen as the centre around which the planets moved – and that became the new paradigm against which normal science progressed.

Popper was certainly right to draw attention to how scientific theories must not be vacuous and must possess predictive power; but that means neither that scientists must always be trying to falsify theories nor, if the predictions are false, abandoning them. A host of factors needs to be taken into account – and a good scientist manages to judge their relative importance.

Popper sometimes wrote as if all scientific theories, unrefuted so far, were on a par: they were mere conjectures. But given the amazing predictive and explanatory success of many theories, we should surely view them as approaching the truth, saying how the world is. The word 'theory' may encourage the glib comment, 'it's just a theory', but let us remember that some theories are better, much better, than others. Some theories have survived considerable testing, intermeshing with other successful theories – whereas some theories are indeed 'just a theory'. The good scientist, the philosophical scientist, knows how to tell the difference.

CHAPTER 12

How to turn noise into meaning . . .

and not be like Humpty Dumpty

You are an English speaker – indeed, an English reader – and usually when you read these words, you immediately grasp their meaning. You see or hear straight through the media to the meaning. Unless new to English, it is astonishingly difficult to see these words as mere shapes on the page or to hear words spoken as but noises of the air. For us, English sentences are transparent. What is it that we see or hear – what is it that we grasp – when we understand the meaning of these English words and sentences?

Humpty Dumpty: the Egg trap

Lewis Carroll, in *Through the Looking Glass*, tells of Humpty Dumpty, the great wall-sitting Egg, who uses the word 'glory' when in conversation with Alice. Alice is baffled; she points out that she does not know what he means by that word. Egg smiles contemptuously. 'Of course you don't – till I tell you. I mean "there's a nice knock-down argument for you!"'

'But "glory" doesn't mean "a nice knock-down argument",' objects Alice. Egg responds, 'When I use a word, it means just what I choose it to mean – neither more nor less.'

Alice, of course, is doubtful whether we can make words mean different things and mean just what we want them to mean. Egg replies, 'The question is: which is to be master – that's all.'

In order to communicate, we need a common language, and Humpty Dumpty exploits our common language to explain his idiosyncratic meaning of 'glory'. Without the common language, Dumpty's meanings, if they could exist at all (see the last section of this chapter for doubts) would be unknown by others. Of course, there is no problem in giving odd or eccentric meanings to common words or special noises – spies, lovers, diaries frequently do so – and an individual could do so secretly, permitting no one else any access to those meanings. In principle, though, the meanings could be divulged.

We are masters of a common language. Curiously, in seeking to understand that mastery, certain philosophers have trapped themselves in a Humpty Dumpty position whereby we each start off mastering our own languages. The philosopher seemingly most notably entrapped was the 17th-century, highly influential English philosopher John Locke. Whether fairly or otherwise, let Locke be our stalking horse, Locke taken at face value.

When we use words and sentences – when we speak with others, using our common language, to describe, request, order – we place our ideas before the others. Our words, according to Locke, stand for ideas in the mind of him that uses them. The model is this: the meanings of my words are the ideas in my mind that I associate with them; and my ideas are private to me – until I communicate them to you. The insoluble problem becomes this: I cannot communicate my ideas to you until you know what my words mean – and that requires that you already know the ideas that I associate with my words. How a common language can exist becomes a complete mystery.

Wittgenstein's escape

Locke writes as if 'ideas' are images or representations of some kind. Let us use 'images' (be they visual, aural or other sense-based memories or experiences) for simplicity. The Lockean approach is valuable because it exposes some basic truths, truths that, apparently, Locke failed to appreciate – and truths that allow us to reject Locke's approach. They are truths very much brought to prominence by the Austrian Ludwig Wittgenstein in the 1930s and '40s, when he had returned to Cambridge and when his philosophy took a new direction – at least, seemingly so.

Think of all the words that we use: connectives such as 'and', 'or' and 'if . . ., then . . .'. Also, think of proper names such as 'Plato' and 'Socrates', 'Darwin'; general words such as 'sand', 'sea' and 'success'. When we use them, we rarely experience associated mental images. What could be the mental image of 'or' or even 'success' that gives those words meaning? Further, even when we do have mental images, fleeting by, they do not fix the meanings of what we say: indeed, they may be misleading. Some people, for example, have images of colour when hearing numbers mentioned.

'Go, get me some goats,' say I; but my mental image is of sheep. What I said was something about goats, not sheep. And what I meant to say, in the sense of 'intended' to say, may have been to order some llamas: I might have been confusing llamas and sheep and misunderstanding the meaning of the word 'goats'.

The Lockean model suggests that mental images are required for my understanding the meaning of words. The images are the meanings. Now, suppose someone tells me, 'Draw a goat climbing a mountainside!' On the model, I need to check with which images the words 'goat' and 'mountain', and so forth, are associated. I find the 'right' images, and then I can start drawing appropriately. Were that model correct, then if told to *imagine* a goat climbing a mountainside, before I could do so I should need to engage the same checking of images and then do the imagining. But that is crazy. I just imagine a goat – and, indeed, I may just draw a goat without a mental image.

The mental image, even when it exists, is not required. Furthermore, it does not help. Whatever image I conjure up (when one is possible), there remains the question of its interpretation. Do I interpret the image, or, indeed, the drawing, as of a goat climbing or as of one sliding down backwards? Neither image nor drawing determines how the image or drawing is to be read. Yet climbing is, of course, radically different from sliding down – as our language can express – and if instructed to climb a hill, I manifest my understanding by climbing, or by refusing, saying that it is, for example, too steep or too distant. I do not manifest my understanding by sliding.

Understanding each other, grasping the meanings of words and sentences – or noises – is a matter of how we use the noises and what we do or are disposed to do. Positing mental images as being or giving the meaning of the noises – or supposing physical drawings – usually is of no help. Indeed, it can hinder, for it runs the risk of our succumbing to the Lockean version of the Humpty Dumpty model whereby we think of meanings as some sort of mental entities held within. To understand the meaning of an arrow inscribed on the rock with the words 'dangerous sands' is typically to turn away from the direction of the arrow's head. To understand what someone is doing when pointing, you need to have a grip on the direction of the arm and how you should look away from the arm itself – something that hounds, apparently, fail to grasp.

The bewitching beetle

The stress on common language is all very well – and fits well when our conversations, our descriptions and instructions, concern public objects and actions: for example, feeding the goat, ordering a drink or describing the seascape in letters to lovers. Humpty Dumpty dangers return, though, when we focus on the words we use for our own sensations. We typically want to say that sensations are private. We may make claims such as the following: only I know what my pain right now is really like. What I mean by 'pain' is the sort of thing going on here in my arm. No one else has access to that. This move of giving meaning to a word by using it to designate what 'only I know' provides a seeming basis for a private language, a language that is essentially private to me. The idea bewitches – and it is an idea that Wittgenstein fights in his argument against the possibility of such a private language. Indeed, Wittgenstein writes of philosophy as being 'the battle against the bewitchment of our intelligence by means of language'.

Let us separate out the discussion into one that concerns the existing words, in a common language, for our private experiences and then one that concerns an attempt to generate a new word.

With existing words, such as 'pain', 'ache' and 'tingle', they manifestly are part of a common language. We were taught to use them. A parent may have said 'that must be painful' when the child grazed her knee. When the child clutches at her cheek, whimpering, she may have been taught the term 'toothache' – and so on. That is, our understanding of such words is tied to our public behaviour, circumstances, and expectations.

One approach to this is to say that the sense of those words – their meaning – is given by such public uses and behaviour. We may still separate that sense from what we use those words to refer to or designate: the throbbing pain, the ache. We may do so just as we may recognize that the sense of the words 'Prime Minister of the UK' differs from the sense of the words 'Leader of the Tory Party', yet they are sometimes used to designate one and the same person. Words such as 'sensation', 'pain', 'ache' and 'tingle' have a common public meaning, in the sense of sense, but the objects that they are deployed to designate are private: the words have private referents. As the referents – the throbs, the aches – allegedly are private entities, they can have no role in those terms' meanings.

Arguably, Wittgenstein is more radical than the above. Picturesquely, he supposes that we each have a box with an item within that we call 'beetle'. No one can look into anyone else's box. I know what a beetle is only by looking at what is within my box. Now, if the word 'beetle' had a use in our common language, what is in the box would be utterly irrelevant to that use. The item could be different from box to box; it could change; it could even not exist – for what is in the box contributes nothing to our grasp of the word 'beetle'. So, too, for us to think of pains and aches as somehow 'things' to which we refer by our language of 'pains' and 'aches' – to which we make a sidelong glance – is a misleading picture. Our language is necessarily grounded in our public behaviour. Further, it is a mistake to think that when I say, 'I am in pain', for example, I am pointing to something about me, and describing it. Rather, I am expressing my pain, giving, so to speak, a sophisticated shriek.

Marching in step

But, we may respond, whatever the case with words in our public language, surely I could invent a word, a noise, for my own private sensation – say, for the sensation that I herewith call a 'thrib'. I point inwardly as it were – and mean by 'thrib' this type of sensation. Yet, does this give the meaning of the word 'thrib' for me?

Wittgenstein answers 'No'. I have gone through a ceremony, but what would constitute my using the term 'thrib' correctly in future? There appears to be no constraint on my use of the term for 'whatever is going to seem right to me is right'. And, says Wittgenstein, 'that only means that here we can't talk about "right".'

The argument – and there is much more to this famous 'private language argument' – has generated reams of discussion and remains highly controversial. What is not controversial is that if we are to use a term meaningfully, there must be sense to the idea of something counting as a misuse – a wrong use. In our public language, we have the possibility of the community correcting my use of a word. If, for example, I suddenly start to apply the word 'yellow' to the blue colour of the sky, others could correct me. My correct use of words means that, with regard to standard items, I march in step with others. With my seemingly private language of 'thrib', my correct use means that I march in step with myself – and that is no 'marching in step' at all.

'Thrib', it seems, as an essentially private term, cannot be used meaningfully by me. It was meant to stand for a private item from whence it gained meaning. Others, of necessity, could not grasp its meaning; but therefore, it seems, I also cannot – for there is no meaning to grasp. To grasp the meanings of words and sentences, we need acquaintance with their use – and the possibility of their misuse.

Humpty Dumpty asked which is to be master. The community of language users is master – and it is that master to whom we defer.

CHAPTER 13

How to know what we are talking about . . .

if we do

When we talk about water, surely we know that we are talking about water. When we speak of Plato, we know that we are speaking of Plato. We manage to talk about the world, yet how do our words latch onto the world? After all, we may be talking about water miles before we reach a tap; and Plato lived over 2,000 years ago, yet we know that we are writing of him and not of Plato the next-door cat. Despite distances in time and space, we succeed in referring to items and, it seems, know to which we refer.

Sense and reference

One standard line of thought is the following. The way in which we use our words is the way in which they have the meanings that they do. Yet we may also speak of what people *mean* in their use of the word 'water' by our pointing to water. That suggests that we should distinguish between 'meaning' understood as what we talk about and 'meaning' as the route that leads us to those things about which we talk. The distinction was touched upon in the previous chapter. Here we are, in fact, focusing solely on those words that we use to refer to worldly items.

Water – the wet stuff in the world – is the *referent* of the word 'water'; it is also known as the 'extension' of the word. The route that leads us to the water is the *sense* of the word, also known as its 'intension'. A traditional way of understanding the sense or intension is in terms of the descriptions that we grasp and that apply to the referent or extension. The distinction between sense and reference was put forward by Gottlob Frege; but, bearing in mind what is to come, let us hereafter use the intension/extension terminology.

Language users encountered water over the centuries through its properties. It is a colourless, odourless liquid that typically quenches thirst. At low temperatures, it freezes; at high temperatures it turns to steam – and so forth. The word 'water' has those descriptions associated with it. What are we talking about when we use the word 'water'? Well, that stuff to which those associated descriptions apply – that stuff which satisfies those descriptions that we associate with the word. The position is linguistic internalism. In summary, the position gives us a definition of 'intension' as follows:

> The intension of a referring word (such as 'water', 'Plato') specifies the properties something must have for the word to refer to or designate that something.

The position then has the substantial claim, namely: a word's intension is what people know or grasp when they use and understand the word; it determines what they are talking about.

Talk of 'knowing, grasping and understanding' suggests that intensions are matters of the speakers' being in certain psychological states – and the existence of those psychological states is assumed not to depend on the existence of certain items in the environment. Your thoughts about water are doubtless grounded in your brain states, but, at this stage in the argument, it seems that your grasp of the sense of the word 'water' does not depend on items outside you. At least on the surface, what you grasp in using the word 'water' is the same whether or not there is any water in your vicinity and even whether or not water exists. Your grasp is in terms of the description, 'colourless, odourless liquid and so forth': whether anything satisfies that description is a separate matter. Consider: we have a grasp of the word 'unicorn'; we associate descriptions with the word – yet there are no unicorns.

Twin Earth

Linguistic internalism has a lot going for it. People in our community must surely understand some descriptions as associated with, for example, the name 'Plato' – and those descriptions would seem to be all that is available whereby a particular philosopher, say, Plato, may be picked out from other philosophers and be the man to whom we refer.

Although linguistic internalism has a lot going for it, it is under attack. One famous attack is courtesy of Hilary Putnam's Twin Earth thought experiment. Putnam does not, of course, believe that another Earth exists; but his scenario is intended to show that linguistic internalism cannot be the right way of understanding how we manage to talk about things. What Putnam's experiment apparently shows to be possible is impossible according to linguistic internalism. (Hereafter we shall focus on natural kind terms such as 'water', 'gold', 'elms', rather than proper names.)

Suppose that there is a planet far away. Apart from a few differences shortly to be specified, physically it is identical to our planet Earth. There can even be doppelgangers of us on Twin Earth. Putnam then specifies the following:

> One of the peculiarities of Twin Earth is that the liquid called 'water' is not H_2O but a different liquid whose

*chemical formula is very long and complicated. I shall
abbreviate this chemical formula simply as XYZ. I shall
suppose that XYZ is indistinguishable from water at normal
temperatures and pressures. In particular, it tastes like
water and it quenches thirst like water. Also, I shall
suppose that the oceans and lakes and seas of Twin Earth
contain XYZ and not water, that it rains XYZ on Twin Earth
and not water, etc.*

Speakers on Twin Earth seem to speak English, just
as we do. In particular, just as we call the stuff in the
oceans and swimming pools and out of the taps 'water',
so do they. But, remember, the stuff in their oceans
and swimming pools and taps has a different underlying
chemical structure.

Putnam asks us to roll back the time to 1750, before
Cavendish's discovery of the chemical composition of
water – and before any Twin Cavendish's discovery
of the XYZ composition of Twin Earth's wet stuff.
Now, consider a speaker, Oscar, on Earth – and a
similar speaker on Twin Earth, let us call him 'Toscar'.
They could both be in exactly the same psychological
states with regard to their grasp of the sense of the
word 'water'. Yet, surely their words 'water' have different extensions, even though they would not know
this if they were magically switched from one Earth
to the other.

For Oscar on Earth, when he referred to water, it was to H_2O; yet Toscar was referring to XYZ. As they were in the same psychological state with regard to grasp of sense, associating the same descriptions to what they called 'water', their psychological states cannot be what intensions are. As Putnam eloquently put it, 'Meanings ain't in the head'. We no more carry meanings, intensions, in us than we need carry the objects to which we refer. Readers may recall the Jonathan Swift satire, *Gulliver's Travels*, where a professor of Lagado argued that as words are names for things, 'it would be more convenient for all Men to carry such Things as were necessary to express the particular business they are to discourse on.'

Challenging Putnam

We may challenge Putnam's reading of his thought experiment by bringing out certain assumptions. Putnam assumes that the extension of 'water' on Earth is H_2O and not XYZ. But it may be better to describe the situation as one in which both Oscar and Toscar are referring to the same stuff, namely the kind: H_2O and XYZ. Even our water in everyday life, as it dribbles from the taps, contains some heavy water and other isotopes – yet they are water. Whether that is a plausible response depends, no doubt, on what is involved in XYZ and how it accounts for the properties of being a colourless odourless liquid and so forth.

It may be all too easy to announce how different XYZ is from H_2O, yet in our everyday dealings, XYZ and H_2O are indistinguishable. Reflect, for example, that XYZ and H_2O must have the same effects with regard to keeping the biology of Oscar and Toscar working. A further assumption that Putnam makes is that the word 'water' on Earth and 'water' on Twin Earth have not changed their extensions. In 1750, with Oscar and Toscar in the same psychological states, we could argue that the extensions of their words did not differ – the extension being *whatever* is a colourless, odourless liquid that quenches thirst and so on. Today, with our knowledge of chemistry, Oscar and Toscar's psychological states, regarding grasp of intensions, would differ – for the intensions would differ, accounting for the fact that today Oscar's 'water' refers only to H_2O and Toscar's only to XYZ.

'Here', 'now' – and 'water'

Putnam offers a different picture from the traditional Fregean theory of how extension is determined. And that different picture would not yield to the criticisms just made. What determines what we talk about, according to Putnam, is in part the physical facts around us – and not solely the descriptions that we associate with a word. After all, Earth is isolated from Twin Earth; so it is odd to think that our Earth term 'water' that refers to H_2O somehow captures as referent the different XYZ stuff on Twin Earth. On Putnam's account, the content of what we assert or say, when we assert or say, depends in part on our surroundings. He speaks of an indexical element involved in determining the extension of natural kind terms, such as 'water'. Indexical words are words such as 'here', 'now' and 'I'. Their extensions depend on context, on who is using them and where. 'Water' is seemingly like an indexical term because what is being spoken about, when it is used, depends on the environment, on whether we are on Earth or on Twin Earth. 'Water', says Putnam, is true of anything that bears the relation 'is-the-same-liquid-as' to typical samples of 'water' *round here*. A typical sample for us – for Oscar and Toscar in 1750 and for them today – would be what comes out of our taps or when it rains. But, of course, that liquid is XYZ on Twin Earth, H_2O on Earth – and so it is the surrounding physical difference that accounts for intensions not being 'in the head'.

The introduction of the indexical element in understanding intensions, though, permits another line of attack on Putnam. What is notable about indexicals is that their intensions do not change, even though they may be used to refer to different locations. The intension of 'here' is 'the place in which the word is spoken'. The intension of 'tomorrow' is 'the day after the day the word is spoken'. So, if Putnam does understand 'water' as being akin to an indexical, we should argue that Oscar and Toscar, be they in 1750 or the 21st century, use 'water' in the same way, with the same intension. That is: 'water' is understood as being whatever is the colourless, odourless liquid that quenches thirst – and so forth – in the speaker's environment, and also anything that resembles that liquid in its chemical composition. Given Oscar's and Toscar's different locations, they would indeed be talking about different things, Oscar of H_2O and Toscar of XYZ. They would also be in the same psychological states, grasping the same intension.

Spreading the mind

There is, as can be imagined, much more to be said for and against Putnam's approach. Controversy still rages, and two intriguing proposals are suggested by Putnam's approach.

The first proposal is the following. Supplementing the contribution that the physical environment allegedly makes to our understanding of how words refer is a social contribution. Putnam speaks of the 'division of linguistic labour'. We all use many words to talk about items in the world, yet we have little idea of how to pick out those items: we lack adequate descriptions of the items. We may speak of beech trees and elm trees, yet be unable to distinguish them. However, although the descriptions we associate with such words would not enable us to pick out the relevant items, we still manage to talk about how beech trees differ from elms. How is that possible? Putnam's answer is that such reference is possible because we are disposed to defer to experts: we, so to speak, pass the intension and reference-determining buck to others – and they may be able to offer adequate descriptions. Mind you, we still must not forget the contribution of the physical environment: after all, the experts in 1750 would have been unable to distinguish between H_2O and XYZ.

A second proposal picks up on a point made earlier. Putnam's Twin Earth example can only work by assuming that Oscar's and Toscar's psychological states, grasping the intension of the term 'water', do not themselves depend on anything outside those psychological states and neural networks. That is known as a 'narrow' understanding of psychological states. It is psychological internalism. But if – *if* – Putnam is right with regard to how the intensions of some words include a contribution from the environment, this has consequences for how psychological states should be understood. Let us see how this works.

If my thoughts are adequately given by the intensions of the words that I use, then the identity of those thoughts should include, in some way, contributions from the surrounding physical world. If that is right, we need to revise Putnam's understanding of Oscar and Toscar in 1750. Their psychological states should now be understood as different, even though 'from within' they would appear exactly the same. Their thoughts are different because those thoughts, just as with the meanings of words, too depend on external factors, such as whether surrounded by H_2O or XYZ. Mysteriously, it seems, the very contents of my thoughts may stretch out and enfold the world around me.

It has be said that philosophers should be content to go to wherever the argument leads, but sometimes where the argument leads may be good evidence that something has gone wrong with the argument.

CHAPTER 14

How to live on slippery slopes . . .
without slipping and sliding

Debates on voluntary euthanasia and drug laws invariably lead to 'slippery slope' arguments. Opponents of change conjure up pictures of society sliding into approval of enforced suicide and people living in a drugged haze. Of course, slippery slopes do exist, and care needs to be taken in their vicinity. Indeed, some communities appear to have slipperier terrains than others, as if slipperiness were a relative matter. So, we need to understand where slippery slopes exist and what can and cannot be done to stop us from sliding.

Voluntary sexual intercourse

Whether we speak of slippery slopes or thin ends of wedges, in matters of ethics and law the worry is that of moving from something that is good, or that at least overall possesses acceptable features, to something that is bad and certainly unacceptable. Of course, opponents of proposed changes, such as those concerning voluntary euthanasia and relaxation in the drug laws, may have other arguments to support their position. This chapter is concerned mainly with slippery slope arguments – and slippery slopes, it is often claimed, would lead to likely outcomes such as the following:

If voluntary euthanasia is permitted, we should slide into accepting involuntary euthanasia. Were cannabis to be legalized, we should end up legalizing hard drugs as well. If research on early embryos is allowed, we shall soon be accepting research on foetuses and even on infants.

Let us try some others, though. If the voluntary study of philosophy is permitted, we shall soon be accepting the enforced study of philosophy. If taxation at 40 percent is acceptable, then taxation at 100 percent will become acceptable. If women are free to go for beauty treatment, then soon they will all be frogmarched and forced into such treatment. Curiously, those three examples do not worry people. No one seriously holds that we shall slide down those implied slopes to such unacceptable consequences – though perhaps the enforced study of philosophy would be desirable. To give an example with more significance in the lives of most people, consider:

If voluntary sexual intercourse is desirable, we shall soon be sliding into accepting rape as desirable.

We are aware that sexual intercourse can take place when people are tired or drunk – where it is not clear that it is entirely voluntary – and we can recognize the pressures that lead to the intercourse being 'well, okay, old friendship' sex; 'well, I guess I had better' sex, and sometimes moving into date rapes, acquaintance rapes or rapes within a marriage. And we know full well that there are brutal rapes. But we do not conclude that, as there is a slippery slope here that starts from voluntary sexual intercourse, we are justified in prohibiting voluntary sexual relations.

Types of slide

How may slippery slides from A to B occur? We need to distinguish between slides that occur as a matter of logic, of what necessarily is so, and slides that may occur because of what the world just happens to be like.

Logical slopes are slopes whereby – as a matter of logic – the 'slide' must take place. In logic, of course, we would not usually call it a 'slide', but rather 'what logically follows'. Consider an exceptionally simple mathematical example. If you order ten crates of champagne, each crate containing six bottles, then you have ordered 60 bottles in total. You have allowed yourself to be committed to, to slide into, the 60 bottles' order. If you accept a loan of £1,000 and you promise to repay by the end of the year, but you do not, then you have allowed yourself to slide into being someone who breaks a promise. In contrast to logical slopes, there are empirical slopes. It may be true that, given how certain human beings are constituted, if they drink one beer, they may slide into accepting a second, and then a third – and so forth. There is no logical inference which takes us from the fact that Wayne drinks one beer to the fact that he will drink another. Wayne's weak nature, though, may be such that he does slide from one to two, and maybe to many more.

With both types of slope, the key objection is that once you are on the slope, you cannot get off it – and that what you slide into is objectionable. We could, though, flip slopes the other way round. If the morally obnoxious involuntary euthanasia is permitted, then presumably we would also easily slide into accepting the morally benign voluntary euthanasia. With empirical slopes, they may give rise to the important objection, namely, that the slide can be stopped only by arbitrary decision. Once abortion is permitted, we can only avoid the slide into permitting very late abortions by arbitrary fiat – such as permitting none after 22 weeks. Let us look more closely at the slopes that worry many people.

Voluntary and involuntary

First, when the slope allegedly *must* take us sliding down from voluntary X-ing to involuntary X-ing, that is but an illusion: there is no such slope. There is a clear distinction between someone voluntarily going to the hairdresser and someone being frogmarched to the hairdresser. A vast amount of our moral and legal judgements recognize that there is a distinction between the voluntary and the involuntary. That is not to say that cases never arise when we are in grey areas – when we may think that an action in a way is voluntary, in a way is not.

Secondly, when debates about the voluntary arise, people sometimes confuse questions of what is really so with questions of how we can tell what is really so. There is a clear distinction between Onslow deliberately murdering someone and Onslow killing someone accidentally: that is a constitutive distinction. What constitutes a deliberate action is different from what constitutes an accidental. Yet there may well be occasions when we cannot *tell* whether Onslow acted deliberately or accidentally. That is a problem about what we can find out about: it is an epistemic matter, a matter concerning knowledge or belief.

Both the above points directly apply to voluntary euthanasia (including assisted dying). There is no logical slope sliding us down from allowing voluntary euthanasia to involuntary euthanasia, though there may be some difficult cases when it is not easy to tell whether an action is a case of the voluntary or the involuntary. The euthanasia slope is an empirical slope. There is the danger that a few people, eager to take advantage of any permitted voluntary euthanasia, will try to persuade elderly relatives that they should opt for euthanasia – and then those acts would not be truly voluntary. The slide would allegedly continue down into people feeling that maybe they had better opt for euthanasia, and further down into the state deciding when people should die. Those difficulties, however, arise in other morally important areas, such as sexual relations. Instead of prohibition, the answer is to have laws that help to prevent empirical slides, combined with moral education so that people see the wrongness of abusing others.

Here is another analogy: we permit people to harm others in self-defence, and the harm may even lead to death. Yes, permitting self-defence can lead to abuse; and yes, sometimes, it is difficult to tell whether the harm was really necessary. None the less, the value of permitting self-defence outweighs such possible dangers. The value of permitting voluntary sexual relations outweighs the risks of slipping into abuses. So, too – unless other reasons can be given – the value of permitting voluntary euthanasia, giving people the opportunity to end their lives as they want, outweighs the risks of abuse. The risks of abuse, not the voluntary euthanasia itself, are what merit attack.

Speed limits, colours and abortion

Slippery slope arguments regarding abortion are not usually concerned with what is voluntary, but with when an embryo or foetus is a person or should be deemed to be a person – or to be a potential person or to have the right to life. Historically, various cut-off limits have been suggested for when a foetus has a right to life, but they usually strike people as arbitrary. If something is arbitrary, does it follow that it lacks justification? Well, in certain areas of life, arbitrary limits are perfectly acceptable. The speed limit of 30 mph is arbitrary. There is, though, a feeling that a limit around that speed is appropriate; but no one seriously suggests that 30 is right whereas 29 would definitely be wrong. In contrast, if the limit for permissible abortions is to be determined by when a foetus becomes a person, then that possesses a 'black or white' feel about it. That, though, is a mistake. Let us consider an analogy.

'ROYGBIV' is an acronym for the spectrum of colours in a rainbow, stretching from red, through orange, yellow, green, blue and indigo to violet. Now look at the part of that spectrum before red shades into orange. If we focus on one thin line of the red colour range, then move our gaze slightly to the adjacent section, towards the orange, we cannot tell any difference in colour: it still looks red. Any two adjacent areas cannot be distinguished in colour by us. Yet we know full well that, as we move our gaze along the spectrum, we shall end up seeing some clear cases of orange, then yellow – and so forth. The moral of the ROYGBIV example is that even though any two adjacent lines of colour are indistinguishable by us, it does not follow that we cannot distinguish *any* of the lines from others with regard to colours. Just because we cannot, with regard to colour, distinguish line A from line B, and cannot distinguish line B from line C, nor line C from line D, nor line D from line E, we may none the less be able to distinguish A from E. A may be a clear case of red and E a clear case of orange, yet the transitional stages are just that – transitions and, further, transitions between which we cannot distinguish.

Applying the above thought to abortion, just because there is no morally perceptible difference between abortion permissibility at 14 days as opposed to 15 days, none between 15 days and 16 days, none between 16 days and 17 days, and so forth, it does not follow that there is no morally relevant difference, and no perceptible one, between abortion at 14 days and abortion at 30 weeks. That there is a big difference, though, does not mean that there exists a non-arbitrary line before which it is right to permit abortions and after which it is wrong.

Anxiety on such matters often arises because people want to find black or white lines in nature and in morality; yet often they do not exist. There is no particular place on the colour spectrum where red suddenly becomes orange; and there is no particular minute when a tadpole is suddenly a frog. There is no particular hour when a baby changes into a child; and there is no particular day when what previously was morally permissible by way of an abortion becomes morally impermissible.

Hiding behind slopes

Some slippery slope considerations are ways of presenting points that are not essentially slippery. When opponents of abortion claim that permitting abortions would slide us into permitting infanticide, they may well be trying vividly to bring home to us that early abortions are morally the same as murder. From conception, abortion is wrong – and not because of the slide. For some, it is wrong because the fertilized ovum really is a person; but usually the anti-abortion arguments are grounded on the claim that the fertilized ovum is a potential person. A quick answer to the 'potential' argument is that it is not usually right to treat a potential X in the same way as we should treat an X. We neither treat acorns as oak trees, even though acorns potentially are trees, nor treat human beings as corpses, even though human beings potentially are corpses. Friends would not see the joke if, our having invited them round for chicken and chips, we dished up chips with fertilized chicken eggs.

To end this chapter, we may ourselves make use of a slippery slide, but arguably with legitimacy. If, as the potentiality argument implies, what is wrong about abortion is the loss of the future person, well, contraception and sexual abstinence also have that consequence. A fertilized ovum is a potential person, and the spermatozoon and ovum *before* they combined must have possessed the potential to become the fertilized ovum. So, if preventing the fertilized ovum from developing is morally wrong, then preventing the ovum from being fertilized is also morally wrong. And so it is that, if people really believe that 'potentiality' is key, then this chapter ends as a Casanova's charter, for sexual abstinence would also be morally wrong. Watch out girls – and watch out boys. . .

CHAPTER 15

How to judge whom to save . . .

with morality on your side

When a red-blooded male is faced with drowning – not his, but the drowning of Jack-the-lad and the delicious and delectable Jill – we may understand that, if he can save only one, he saves Jill. When faced with such choices though, how *ought* he to act? We may argue that 'tis better to save more life than less. So if Jack is 20 and Jill 40, then Jack merits the rescue. Yet, if Jill is your lover and Jack is unknown, would morality demand that outcome?

Ought we to calculate before kissing?

Morality is usually associated with duties derived from principles. The principles are expressed in very general terms, such as always tell the truth; do not break promises; always save human life whenever you can. Expressed as such generalizations, guidance is lacking over what to do with Jack and Jill. Of course, we may revise principles, anticipating certain clashes. We may hold to the principle 'always save the person with most life years ahead'; but why should morality discriminate against the elderly?

There is an answer to such questions, an answer that derives from the ultimate grounding for morality – well, one commonly suggested. The grounding is happiness. Happiness is self-evidently valuable, if anything is – and something is, namely happiness, at least if properly understood. Given the value of human happiness, the moral stance must be that of maximizing happiness; and that maximization involves considering the likely consequences of actions. Morally, you ought to select, in any circumstance, the action most likely to promote the greatest happiness. Such is the approach of utilitarianism, a moral doctrine that is consequentialist: it looks to the future, to consequences, for establishing what it is right to do now. It is hedonistic. It is hedonistic because the relevant feature of those consequences is happiness maximization. The approach is often summed up as the Greatest Happiness Principle, most famously associated with the 19th-century philosophers Jeremy Bentham and John Stuart Mill.

Utilitarianism in principle has an answer to the drowning dilemma. If only you knew the overall consequences for happiness, you would know whom to save. To take an extreme example, if Jack has an extremely gloomy disposition, no one likes him and he does nothing to aid society, then his claim for saving should receive rejection if Jill has a great propensity for happiness, brings happiness to others and is, say, a brilliant surgeon. Were those factors known to be so, the duty would be to swim to Jill. We assume, of course, that you, the saviour, can swim and can save one, but only one.

The calculative aspect of utilitarianism has immediate downsides. One downside is that often the relevant information is unavailable; also, there may be little time to calculate likely outcomes, even if such in theory were possible. Another downside is that if we treated others in calculative ways as means for maximizing happiness, we should paradoxically ruin much that is valuable for happiness. As a certain John Austin, a friend of Mill, stated: for love to flourish – surely an element of happiness – the lover ought not to check the benefits to mankind before kissing his mistress.

After consideration of such downsides, utilitarians stress that, while the maximizing of happiness is the overall moral aim, individuals on a day-to-day basis must rarely be motivated in that calculative way. Overall happiness is best achieved, as it happens, by following some of the dictates of conventional morality, such as not killing, keeping promises and saving life. That, of course, returns us to the initial dilemma, the one where nothing is known about Jack and Jill's prospects. It is a dilemma – and when you have no good moral reason for saving one rather than the other, let what comes naturally take over. In the case first outlined, that probably means, though, that the red-blooded male will have his motivations challenged. After all, Jill does look a far more desirable catch than Jack, at least for our red-blooded male.

One thought too many

Now reflect on the modified 'drowning' example, where Jill is your lover and Jack is unknown. Let us revise the case further: your relationship with Jill is deep and important, despite Jill being somewhat flighty and frivolous; furthermore, you happen to know that this Jack has far more about him, a charity worker, aiding the poor and improving people's lives. Whom should you save? Well, on utilitarian grounds, the calculation may initially point to Jack being saved – but is that right? That may be right neither for those of a utilitarian persuasion nor for others. Were our relationships to be manhandled, even womanhandled, in that way – where no special moral weight is given to intimacies and commitments – much that is of value in human life would be undermined. If we spent our lives seeking to be completely objective, giving no privileged place to our families, lovers and personal projects, then our lives – it is argued – would be empty. Human life would lack substance if morality demanded complete neutrality with regard to our projects, relationships and treatment of others.

Utilitarians have a response. They can reasonably argue that the considerations just launched show that, in working out overall consequential benefits, extra weightings must be given to certain significant relationships, such as those of parent, lover and even devotee of philosophy tutors. Such relationships count for a lot in judging likely overall happiness. Let us assume – a big assumption – that the correct weightings can be assessed, and that the right action is indeed for you to save Jill. Now, what picture does it give of you? Even to think of the situation in those terms – of a calculation – is, as has been said by the non-utilitarian Bernard Williams, 'one thought too many'.

Splash!

Morality would not demand a thought in the circumstances in which your lover Jill – or child or parent – is one of those drowning. (We say no more about philosophy tutors.) Morality would demand just the opposite, namely, an immediate and unthinking action to save Jill. *Splash!* What sort of person would you be if you had to think about it?

The above brings out how morality needs to have

regard for 'real life' people, who live enmeshed lives of attachments, be they those of love, family, employment, or interests, projects and other commitments. Were human beings to lack such attachments, their lives would be empty. Williams expresses the thought thus:

> . . . one reaches the necessity that such things as deep attachments to other persons will express themselves in the world in ways which cannot at the same time embody the impartial view . . .

Consider: what would a human life be like – would it be a *human* life – if it were not a life that viewed the world around it from a particular perspective, with some concerns in closer proximity than others, with certain partialities more important than others? How could you live a life, or at least a full life – at least a human life – if you lacked a particular position in the world, but instead stood detached, outside all particular human affections, interests and attachments?

One tension in our morality exists between our wanting, in the abstract, a detached, unprejudiced perspective and our needing, in reality, an attached life, which focuses concern on special relationships. Now, utilitarianism may try to make sense of attachments as just another weight to enter into the detached calculations; but that undermines the significance to our lives of those attachments. Loyalty, love, laughter – all parts of a flourishing life – cannot be treated in the detached way of fairness, impartiality and equality, also parts of a flourishing life. Morality juggles attached values and detached values, as we see when we contrast two further approaches to morality.

Duty or compassion?

Sometimes morality demands no thought – and that thought reminds us that morality involves having the right feelings as well as doing the right thing. Further, morality involves doing the right thing for the right reasons, when reasons are involved. Let us pop utilitarianism to one side for the moment. Here comes a simple contrast that leads us into two major approaches to morality that contrast with utilitarianism.

Mr Upright, as he struts along, spies a beggar sitting on the pavement; the beggar is clearly in need. Mr Upright has no desire to be involved with such a down-and-out; but he does possess a sense of moral duty – perhaps it derives from his religious belief. He knows that he ought to help the poor, so he drops some bank notes into the beggar's lap and swiftly moves on. He acted from duty.

In contrast, look at the bent figure of the aged Mrs Stooped. She lives on a small pension, but when she sees the beggar, she immediately feels sorry for him. She hands over a few coins – all she can afford – and lingers and chats with him. She has been moved by compassion. True, she is not saintly: she does not do everything that she could, but she is a good soul. She recognized the beggar as a fellow human being: she treated him as such and did her best. She is, we may say, following Judith Jarvis Thomson, a minimally decent Samaritan, and a bit more.

The contrast in motivations is one of the contrasts found between two moral theories. In rough terms, one line of morality, from Immanuel Kant, considered one of the very greatest philosophers, is based on objective universal principles, which can be derived from reason or God – principles accessible to all in theory. A different line of morality, historically most associated with the ancient Greek philosopher Aristotle, stresses the importance of what sort of person you should be.

For the Kantian, to act morally is to follow the abstract principles: to be motivated by a sense of duty, not by biological urges. You may or may not happen to be the sort of person who has feelings for others, a sense of benevolence, or the strength of courage. They are contingencies of your nature – and morality ought not to rely on such contingencies. Just as the truths of mathematics do not rest on how you feel or whether you live in Iran or in Ireland, so your duties do not rest on your feelings. Morality is, so to speak, other-worldly. Mind you, we may immediately object that just as some people may lack feelings of compassion and benevolence, so too some people lack education and sufficient reason to grasp the dictates of morality. *Understanding* morality as well as, for example, understanding abstract mathematics is biologically grounded.

In contrast to the Kantian approach, the Aristotelian focuses on what it is to have a flourishing life. Part of a flourishing life is to have concern for others, to tell the truth, to be fair, to feel compassion – and these are virtues. Yes, there can be useful moral rules to follow, but the motivation should often involve feelings for others – and having the right feelings.

How would you like your children to grow up?

If you are a parent, how would you prefer your children to grow up with regard to their grasp of morality? Would you prefer them to see morality as consisting in some rather abstract and austere duties that must be followed – the Kantian line – or as part of what it is to lead a good and flourishing life – with right feelings, that is, the Aristotelian line? Utilitarianism may be seen to have a foot in both camps. The Greatest Happiness Principle is meant as an objective universal

157

principle, yet its focus on happiness brings in the Aristotelian concerns. This is because utilitarians, such as John Stuart Mill, recognize that happiness is not a matter of twinges of pleasure but is a matter of flourishing: and flourishing involves a social sense, feelings for others and a sense of integrity. Of course, once the happy life, the good life, is seen to consist of many facets, the idea of a happiness calculator is less and less convincing. Morality is a mishmash of considerations, but none the worse for that. What is valuable for children growing up is for them to understand that morality is the mishmash. What is all the more valuable for children growing up is for them to feel within themselves the moral concern for others and for what sort of people they want to be. And that brings us back to whom to save.

Whom should we save? Well, the inevitable answer is 'It depends.' A non-inevitable answer is to challenge the assumption made by many philosophers that you need a theory to find the answer. Rather, theories are constructed from individual cases. And were your grown-up son to encounter Jill his lover and the unknown Jack both drowning, would you be happy to think that he must consult a theory before deciding whom to save? Would not that be one consultation, one theory, one thought, too many?

CHAPTER 16

How not to eat people . . .

without being speciesist

We have no problem in recognizing that other human beings should typically be treated with respect. Yet many morally–minded people find nothing wrong in allowing animals to suffer to provide for the delights of their breakfasts, lunches and dinners, or to advance scientific knowledge. The morally minded, though, would be horrified at using children for experimentation or adult humans for regular dining delights. Are such people guilty of speciesism? And if we are speciesist, are there good reasons why we ought not to be?

From sexism to speciesism

Speciesism bears comparison with racism and sexism, the background principle being that individuals ought not to be treated differently unless the difference in treatment can be well justified. To pay men higher salaries than women if they do the same work over the same period, with the same skills and experience, is to be sexist: the sexual difference is no justification for a salary difference. To offer cervical cancer screening to women, but not to men, is not to be sexist: there is an obvious relevant difference that justifies the disparity on offer. To provide that screening to women for their well-being, but not prostate screening to men for theirs, would be sexist, unless some appropriate justification is available, for example, that cervical cancer is more prevalent or with higher mortality than prostate cancer.

Time, now, to turn to non-human animals; and, to have some in mind, we think of the medium-sized ones: the sheep and cows, the turkeys and chickens – the chimps and monkeys. Of course, in numerous cases, we ought not to treat them in the same way as we treat human beings. To send children, but not sheep, to school, is not to discriminate against the sheep; for that matter, it is not to discriminate against the children. There is good reason for the difference in treatment. But is there any morally good reason for treatment differences with regard to species and our eating pre-dilections? We dine on sheep, but not on children.

What makes you a person?

In killing cows and sheep, turkeys and hens, but not humans for food, are we manifesting an unjustified preference for our species? Are we speciesist? By way of approach, we need to consider what is wrong with killing human beings. We may say, with some glib, that human beings possess a right to life and a right not to be killed; but, before we say something about rights, let us ask: quite what wrong is done in killing human beings? Typically, humans do not want to be killed. Mind you, cows and sheep, turkeys and hens, manifest no obvious desire for death.

Human beings possess a sense of themselves as conscious beings, as subjects of experiences, that continue into the future: they have plans, hopes and fears, and expectations that they will see another day. By killing human beings, we are thwarting those plans, projects and preferences – we are harming them – and it is that, arguably, which makes such killings morally wrong. In contrast, most non-human animals, it seems, lack such a sense of themselves continuing into the future in that self-conscious way; so, by preventing their biological continuance, we are not thwarting them 'personally': we are not harming them.

Each new day for most non-human animals is a day of a new animal. The animals do not sense themselves as continuing entities with plans for the morrow – or that is the claim. If the claim is the correct and only relevant consideration, then it is not because individuals are members of the biological species *Homo sapiens* that we ought not to kill them. It is because they possess the morally relevant feature of a sense of self continuing into the future. Some philosophers label individuals who possess that sense 'persons' and see that as the sole grounding for a right to life. With that special understanding of 'person', we may now raise two questions. Are all human beings persons? And are some non-human animals persons?

With regard to the first question, pretty clearly some human beings lack the personhood characteristics: individuals in persistent vegetative states, individuals suffering extreme Alzheimer's and, at the other end of life's spectrum, human embryos, foetuses and young babies. We should need fresh considerations to show that killing such individuals is wrong, if it is.

With regard to the second question, there may well be evidence to suggest that chimps, gorillas and dolphins possess a sense of continuing self. So, they may be non-human persons – and hence ought no more to be killed than any other person. If the above line of argument is correct, we are not speciesist in killing sheep and cows, and chickens and turkeys, but not killing typical human beings, chimps, gorillas and dolphins to eat. There is a morally relevant difference that accounts for the difference in treatment. The sheep and cows, the chickens and turkeys, have no sense of themselves continuing into the future – and so they are not persons; hence, it is not wrong to kill them.

Well, it is not wrong to kill them if wrongful killing can only be of persons.

Can they suffer?

The above is a somewhat convenient line to justify our practices with regard to which animals to kill, but, even if correct, it fails to justify the suffering and stress that animals undergo in being farmed and led off to abattoirs. Jeremy Bentham, promoter of morality as grounded in seeking the greatest happiness of the greatest number – utilitarianism – argued that in deciding morally what we ought to do, we should take into account all pleasures and pains – be they of humans or cats and dogs or even ants (were there evidence of ants suffering). As Bentham writes:

> It may come one day to be recognized, that the number of legs, the villosity of the skin, or the termination of the os sacrum, are reasons equally insufficient for abandoning a sensitive being to the caprice of a tormentor . . . The question is not, Can they reason? nor, Can they talk? but, Can they suffer? . . . The time will come when humanity will extend its mantle over everything which breathes . . .

Pain, according to Bentham, is an evil whoever or whatever suffers it; and even though most non-human animals are not persons, they are sentient, conscious, and can and do suffer. Hence, our practices, including those that lead to their death, should cause minimal suffering. Farming non-person animals for food is fine, so long as the animals have non-suffering lives and no painful deaths, assuming that we are maximizing overall happiness.

That, of course, is all well and good; but if – *if* – human beings gain considerable pleasure from eating *foie gras* and if the sole way of securing that delicacy is by force-feeding the geese, then, so long as the overall human pleasure outweighs the geese's distress, utilitarians such as Bentham should have nothing to say against such practices. Utilitarians, though, do seek to persuade human consumers to change their dietary preferences away from the over-fattened geese. Perhaps that shows that the utilitarians have concern for the interests of the geese as well as of humans, and that morality is not solely to do with maximizing happiness. Perhaps the moral aim is more to do with minimizing the suffering of individuals. The sufferings of the geese may outweigh the minor sufferings to humans who end up consuming ham and cheese instead of *foie gras*.

Animal rights – or nonsense on stilts?

Concern about our mistreatment of animals leads some to insist that animals have rights; but talk of 'rights' is obscure. My right to my pencil seems very different from my right to life. One thought is that if 'rights' are to be more than a grand way of saying that certain actions are wrong, we need to spot a special grounding for them. In law, because of certain contracts, I have a right to my flat. I own it. Arguments to one side about how maybe all property is theft, many people would cite that ownership, and my and others' recognition of it, as grounding my right. The right derives from various expectations, recognitions, and assumptions by members of the community.

Contrast the position with non-human animals. We cannot make sense of animals being part of a moral and legal community, recognizing the interests of others and entering into contacts. True, we may recall cases centuries ago when animals were brought to public court as defendants. Through the intervention of St Francis, a wolf allegedly made an agreement not to terrorize the citizens of Gubbio, Italy, in return for regular food. Yet, we do not really think that any non-human animal could recognize duties and rights. Without even the possibility of such recognition, we should hesitate to ascribe them any duties and hence any rights.

The above approach to rights threatens inconsistencies. Babies and children lack concepts of duties, contracts and rights; yet they possess rights. They are usually said to possess rights on the basis that they are potential members of the community; but once potentiality enters the story, things can become slippery, as we have seen. Furthermore, when we speak of persons as possessing the right to life – or the right to free speech – we are surely saying more than that they are members of a community that recognizes such rights. Indeed, they may belong to communities that deny the existence of such rights – and that is why we are insisting that they possess them. This is where 'natural rights' are spun onto the scene. Natural rights are rights that exist solely because of our human nature or because of godly commands. Such rights Bentham deemed 'nonsense on stilts'. While we have a grip on the laws of nature, such as Newton's concerning gravity, it is difficult to see how nature itself delivers us moral laws about what we *ought* to do – about rights.

Whichever is the best way to secure a grip on 'rights' – if there is one – we should emphasize that what we morally ought to do extends far beyond matters of not violating rights. In some contexts, rights are thought of as specially important – trump cards to be played when the moral going gets tough – but none the less there are many other morally important demands on us, such as to be kind, compassionate, courageous and loyal. Even if non-person animals lack rights, that does not mean that we lack all moral duty towards them. We have a duty not to be cruel and not to be careless about their interests. That duty is grounded in the fact that they can suffer. They have interests of their own.

Indeed, in some cases, we have special duties of care towards animals – when, for example, we take them in as pets, when, for example, caring for pigs of Guinea.

And yet ...

We may wonder whether speciesism is akin to sexism's partial prejudices. After all, sexism's wrongness occurs when men and women fail to treat each other with equality concerning respect for how they may flourish; and men and women can engage in dialogue about their different flourishing ways. Inevitably, though, there is no dialogue between humans and sheep, and dolphins and goats. Human beings have to decide how to treat the other species for their sake; the other species are in no position to decide how to treat humans. There is an asymmetry: it would be patronizing and sexist were women to decide how men should be treated – or vice versa.

Further, with regard to moral matters, we may question whether morality must always be impartial – an issue raised in Chapter 15. Some partialities are at the heart of many of our moral concerns. We form attachments. Lovers give preferences to their beloved. Parents are specially concerned for their own children. To feel a genuine moral dilemma over whether to feed the hungry stray dog or your hungry child when food is scarce – well, that would seem to be the impartiality of anti-speciesism taken too far. We should, though, have to say much more to justify when it is right to be partial.

Reason and concern for consistency may encourage us to correct for our spontaneous – speciesist – attachments. People are horrified at the thought of experimentation on mentally retarded human babies, yet accept such experimentation on non-human animals, but such experiments on adult chimps could cause greater direct sufferings than if on the babies. That reflection may, in due course, lead people to challenge all the more the use of non-person animals for experimentation. Even though non-person animals lack any concept of 'what is in their own interests', it is surely right that morally we should have some regard for their interests.

CHAPTER 17

How not to be harmed by your death . . .

BUT I bring you sad tidings

Your death is not good news – well, not for you. Others
may disagree. Of course, you are no longer around to hear
the news, well, not around on this mortal coil. Here, let us
assume that death is annihilation – The End. Is the end to
be feared? After all, once you no longer exist, you are
unaware of your loss of life. And being non-existent there
is no sense in seeking to assess its disvalue to you – for
there is no 'you'. Now, is that good reasoning?

'When death is there, we are not. When we are there,
death is not.' Thus spake Epicurus, of fourth-century
BC Greece, who argued that we should neither look
forward to death nor fear it. Let us check out the
argument, and orient it to a particular individual. Let
him be Benedict.

The underlying assumption is that all times after Benedict has died are times when he does not exist as a subject of possible experiences. That is the Annihilation Assumption – which we are simply accepting. The second assumption, the Existence Assumption, is that an event can be good or bad for Benedict only if he exists at the time of the event as a subject of possible experiences. The conclusion validly drawn is that no event, once Benedict is dead, can be good or bad for him. If we add that it is irrational to fear an event unless it is bad for you – arguably true – then Benedict ought not to fear being dead.

One challenge to the argument is that it speaks of events and states *after* death not harming Benedict, but that does not show that dying and the event of death are not harmful and to be feared. That is the Challenge of the Loss. A further challenge is to question the Existence Assumption. We meet the Challenge of the Loss first of all.

Death is bad because . . .

Death is bad for Benedict because he has lost any future living. Now, obviously, many people have had enough of life and do not want to continue; but our Benedict was a happy man with much happiness ahead, if only he could live longer. He was aware of the impending loss – and that distressed him and was bad for him. Putting aside how his death may be bad for others, has it been bad for Benedict? What is the loss that he feared? It could be argued that the extra years of happiness that he missed need to be compared with those years of his when deceased. Yet what value can we give to his having, say, 40 unexpected extra years of non-existence? We have no idea. Hence, we have nothing with which to compare the extra 40 living years that he would otherwise have undergone – or have we?

We have. We should compare Benedict's actual life – until, say, his 'early' death aged 40 – with his possible life that could have gone on realistically until age 80. That is how we may assess what he has lost. Were he able to judge, would he have preferred his actual 40-year life, or the possible 80-year one? Mind you, Lucretius, who offered arguments in support of the Epicurean stance that there is nothing to fear in death, pointed out that life could be infinite. If so, then Benedict's early death at age 40 meant that he lost an infinite period of time ahead; but that duration is neither more nor less than what people lose when they die at 100 or, indeed, aged 1,000. That is, though, a special puzzle about infinity and how it applies to life and the world.

Samantha, Bondi Beach and Obsession

As a matter of fact, we do feel that the death of, say, a young person is a greater misfortune than the death of a much older person. Consider an example. Samantha is a 20-year-old woman with a lot going for her. She takes a swim off Bondi Beach wearing just her Obsession perfume. In the water, she meets Sheila – aged six. Sheila is a shark with an obsession for Obsession. That is the end of Samantha – though not of Sheila. The loss of life to Samantha is a great misfortune, not just because of the (say) 60 more years she could reasonably have expected to live, but because all that was required for her to have that long life was for Sheila to have been swimming in a different direction. The possibility of Samantha living to a ripe old age is very close to how things actually could have been. Samantha actually living on merely required the shark to have had other plans that day.

Contrast Samantha's case with your ancient author's. I step into the water, having donned my Obsession perfume – and meet a Sheila (clearly a desperate Sheila, if wanting to dine off me). Given my age and dotage – perhaps I am 99 – even if Sheila had resisted temptation to dine on me, there would have to be radical changes in the laws of nature for Peter Cave to be living on for another 60 years. We typically feel that the deaths of the young are greater misfortunes than those of the elderly because we have the background

172

of reasonable expectations, given the existing laws of nature concerning human aging. Yet, with my death and Samantha's, we could say that the deaths deprived each of us of virtually the same durations, say, a million years of life, were the laws of nature so very different. In such circumstances, the difference of 79 years (Samantha dying aged 20; my death at age 99) proportionately is minuscule. To reiterate, though, what we treat as misfortune is against a backdrop of reasonable expectations, given the world much as it is – not given a radically different world where human life-spans are typically millions of years.

In assessing how much death is a misfortune, we also need a clear sense of what constitutes the individual who may undergo the misfortunes. We understand how Samantha has lost a lot of life as a result of Sheila. It is a misfortune for Samantha. Would it be, though, a misfortune for you had the foetus from whence you developed failed to develop? Is it a misfortune for people, who otherwise would have been, that contraceptive use prevented their existence? Recall some similar talk in Chapter 14, *How to live on slippery slopes.*

What you don't know – *can* harm you

Lucretius's argument made the assumption, called the Existence Assumption, that for something to be a harm for you, you need to exist as a possible subject of experiences. The assumption deserves challenge. The backing to the assumption is often the simple thought that you cannot be harmed or undergo a misfortune if you do not experience it as such or if, at least, your quality or quantity of life is not reduced. Clearly a would-be mother, with a drug-crazed and HIV-infected lifestyle, could damage her child-to-be; but for that to be so, the child does need to be – and needs to be harmed because of the mother's lifestyle. Some physical or mental damage must surely occur for there to be a harm – or so it is thought. Yet is that true?

Classic examples that suggest that it is far from true rest on the belief that what matters to you personally goes beyond the boundaries of your skin and what you know or think. What matters to you includes your interests. When your interests are harmed, you are harmed – and it can be rational to fear such harms.

Suppose you value the love of your children and the loyalty of your colleagues at work, yet, behind your back, they talk you down and despise you. They put on an excellent front, so you never know how they really feel about you. They put on the show because, as your children, they require financial support; and, as colleagues, you have power over their employment prospects. In such a world, you have no knowledge of their genuine feelings, yet are you not being harmed, being damaged, by what is happening?

A reply often given is that you are being harmed because you are likely to find out; you are bound to sense that they are not being honest in their dealings. Let us suppose, though – as is surely possible – that you never find out, and that your children's and colleagues' behaviour strikes you as perfectly authentic. You are still being harmed, even though from your perspective all seems well. Here is a consideration to support that view.

Suppose you are in the world in which you never will find out about the disloyalty and the lack of love. We may still consider the hypothetical possibility – counter to fact – of 'were you to find out'. Were you to find out – what then? You would feel distressed. You may say that you wished you had not known. But the distress, the wish not to have known, suggests that what you have found out about was a harm. Why else would it matter that you have found out? The conclusion is that, just because you do not experience a harm, you may still be harmed by it. There are non-experiential harms. So, if nothing can harm you when you are dead, it cannot simply be because you cannot experience the harm.

Harmed, when the subject is no more

The reason harms cannot affect you when you are dead is, it has been proposed, not because you cannot experience them, but because you do not exist at all. If you do not exist after death, then how can you be harmed by any events after your death? The reply is that, again, what is being forgotten is the fact that your interests extend beyond your physical and mental awareness.

Suppose owl-loving Olsen devoted his life to a major work on the migration of owls. He leaves the only copy in London, to be printed and published, and sails to a faraway shore to rest, eager to be free from the anticipated publicity. Bearing in mind the non-experiential harms described above, if the manuscript is burnt and all his labours are wasted, that is a harm to him – even if he learns nothing about the loss. Now, suppose that just before the fire in London that destroys his life's work, Olsen dies on his faraway shore. Why should that suddenly ensure that the fire in London, destroying his labours, is no longer a harm for him?

It should not – and that it should not is something that we seem to recognize in our everyday practices. After all, atheists, when an atheist colleague dies, still respect his last wishes, still manifest a dignified presence before his corpse – and would consider it wrong, bad manners, to talk ill of him for the sheer fun of it.

Yet, they, of course, have no worries about afterlives or about their colleague gazing down on them.

The assumption that is being challenged by these examples is the assumption that an event can only harm someone if that person physically or mentally exists at the time of the event. We have seen how that assumption is mistaken with regard to events before our conception; it is also mistaken with regard to events after our death.

The mirror: pre-birth and post-death

'Look back at the eternity that passed before we were born,' instructs Lucretius, 'and mark how utterly it counts to us as nothing.' Lucretius sees this as a mirror that Nature holds up to us, in which we may peer into the time when we are dead. 'Is there anything terrifying in the sight – anything depressing – anything that is not more restful than the soundest sleep?' he asks. This is another stab by Lucretius to stop us worrying about death. Just as we do not typically regret all those years we failed to exist before we were born, so we ought not to be depressed by all those years we shall fail to exist in the future as a result of our death.

Lucretius's argument ignores the asymmetry between our life continuing further into the future and our having been conceived earlier. I can easily imagine

177

living for longer than in fact I shall, having some decades, even many more decades, and it still being me. But what sense can I make of its still being me, had I been born, say, 50 years earlier? To make the problem vivid, what sense can you make of having been born five centuries earlier and yet it still being you? The upbringing, the surroundings of that individual – no utilities; none of the music that actually nurtured you; no schooling; no emails, tweets and Facebook – would be so radically different that that individual could not be you.

For death to deprive me of anything, there needs to be a 'me' – the self – existing at some time. Mind you, as was demonstrated in the first two chapters, the self remains as enigmatic as does the state of being no more.

CHAPTER 18

How to be God . . .

if God be possible

'It's not easy being God. After all, I am that most perfect of beings, and so, I must be possessive of maximum reality. I am omnipotent: I am able to do anything doable. Everything that exists depends on me, at least to the extent that I permit its existence. I am omniscient, for no truth can escape my intellect. Being morally perfect, I am all good in all possible ways. With all those distinctive attributes, I mystify most human beings – yet those attributes should surely manifest themselves for all to see. How could people fail to notice me? I am not exactly insignificant. I am no underachiever.'

Things that happen to be

Many people do fail to notice God. So, by way of aiding God, let us see what there is about God – and the Universe – that could reasonably lead us to notice him. Purely out of deference to tradition, we use the masculine pronouns 'he' and 'him'. As God is omnipotent, it may be argued that he does not merely happen to exist, but necessarily exists. If he just happens to exist, then it would seem that his existence depends on something else – or on nothing at all – whereas if a being is all-powerful, its existence should depend solely on itself, on its nature. Now, all the items around us – in the physical and psychological worlds with which we are acquainted – are not necessary beings, but are contingent beings. They just happen to exist. Their existence typically depends on the existence of other things.

Here are some contingencies. Your existence depends on the existence of your parents, and your parents' existence on their parents, etc. They – you – would not have existed had the Earth been different, and the Earth might have been radically different, even non-existent. Its atmosphere might have been shattered by cosmic explosions. You are reading these words; but that is only a contingent truth. You might not have been reading – you might have been having a fun time instead – and this book might not have existed.

Contingencies differ from necessities. It is a necessary truth that the number between 18 and 20 is an odd number and also a prime number. Necessarily, round squares do not exist. Now, although some truths are necessary truths, we do not encounter any necessarily existing entities in our everyday experience of the world around us. The nearest that we may get is the necessary existence – some would say – of some abstract entities. Maybe numbers necessarily exist, but numbers cannot do things: they cannot cause effects in the way of hurricanes, fires and people. God, of course, is not meant to be an abstract entity.

To be God is to be something that is a completely different sort of entity, with regard to existence, from everything we encounter in everyday experience. Yet some people claim to work out that such a completely different sort of entity must exist. One argument – the argument from contingency – takes as its starting point the contingency of the surrounding items. Another radically different argument – the ontological argument – depends not on the existence of surrounding items, but simply on our concept of God and what we can reason about that concept. We set off first with contingency.

The argument from contingency relies on a principle that has been called, by the great 17th-century German philosopher and mathematician Gottfried Wilhelm Leibniz, the 'apex of rationality'. The apex is the Principle of Sufficient Reason: there must be a sufficient reason for everything. My existence can be explained by reference to the existence of my parents and certain of their actions; and their existence has a similar explanation. But what is the explanation for the existence of that whole sequence of human beings? Well, maybe we can find further explanations in terms of the existence of cells, variations and natural selection – but all those also are but contingencies. The only way in which there can be a full explanation of *all* the contingencies – of this Universe of contingency – is by reference to a being that does not merely happen to exist, but to a being that *must* exist. The being that must exist is God. We may immediately point out that the argument, as it stands, does not justify the existence of the just one God rather than many necessarily existing gods; and, of course, there is no reason to see the proven God as possessing the characteristics often ascribed, such as loving.

The argument can accept that the Universe, the sequences of contingent items, may go back infinitely, endlessly, into the past. If the sequences do, there remains the principle's demand for a reason why such sequences exist. To suggest yet more contingent items to explain those sequences raises the same demand again – and again. The demand can only be quietened – the intellectual quest quelled – if we realize that there must be a necessary being that underlies, that grounds, the contingent beings. There are, though, substantial challenges to the argument. Why assume that, because the individual items in the Universe are contingent, the whole Universe is also contingent? What is true of parts may not be true of the whole. Parts of an aircraft cannot individually fly; but the aircraft as a whole can fly. Further, accepting that the Universe is contingent, why assume that there must be a sufficient explanation for everything? Perhaps it is just a brute fact – without explanation – that the Universe exists.

We may also cast doubt on the explanatory power in saying that God, a necessary being, must 'ground' the Universe. If his existence and characteristics are all necessary, then we may wonder how any entities that are contingent can arise: must they not necessarily flow as necessities? We may also question what it means for an existent being to exist necessarily. Such a being seems as great a mystery as simply living with the mystery (if it is one) of the Universe of contingent items happening to exist. But. . .

The purr-fect pussycat

We turn to the ontological argument, for it seeks to show that reason alone proves the existence of a necessary being, however mysterious such a being may be. The argument from contingency rests on the existence of contingent items; it is *a posteriori* – that is, it makes use of our experience of the world around us. The ontological argument – 'ontological' because it seeks to show what must exist – does not rest at all on certain items existing. Instead, it relies on what is involved in the concept of God. It is *a priori*: we are reasoning without needing to have reference to what exists in the world. Another example of *a priori* reasoning is mathematical. We do not need to consult the world around us to reason out that the number seven is a prime number or discover the necessary properties of triangles.

We may investigate our concepts, reasoning *a priori*, without being committed to the existence of any items to which the concepts apply. We can describe unicorns and mermaids, even though such items lack existence. Yet, once we investigate the concept of God, reason shows that he must exist: well, that is so, according to the ontological argument. Here is one version, derived from Descartes' *Meditations*:

> God has all the perfections.
> Existence is a perfection.
> Therefore, God has existence.

The first premise is true by definition. That is what we mean by 'God'; well, let us assume that we do. The second premise, it is said, is also true: after all, not to exist would be a defect. The conclusion follows and so, as the premises are true, we must accept that the conclusion is true. Yet we may rightly feel that the argument is a cheat. Surely, just 'by definition' we cannot prove the existence of God – or of anything.

We may have the regular understanding of what unicorns are. We could then define a new concept, 'perfect-unicorn', insisting that by definition 'perfect-unicorns' are perfect; and then we could argue that, as existence is a perfection, perfect-unicorns possess existence. Yet, once we have done all that, we may surely still question whether there are such beasts.

Pussycats exist. We wonder, though, whether there could be a perfect pussycat: that is, one with ideal whiskers, the finest coat and finest meows possible – and one which *must* exist. So, we attend to the concept of the purr-fect pussycat. By Descartes' argument, it looks as if we can insist that such a creature must have existence. That is surely crazy. Whatever we say about the concept of X – even that X includes existence – there is always a leap with regard to whether there is anything that is X. 'Exists', if truly said of an item, is not another feature of the item to look out for; rather, it flags the fact that we have looked and found.

Describe the woman of your dreams to a dating agency – and then add 'and exists'. You have not given the agency another characteristic for the woman to manifest. On reflection, though, things are not quite as straightforward as that suggests. Were there not the assumption that people seeking dates want existent people, dating agencies could deliver fictional characters as possible dates by supplying appropriate novels. The individuals could be lovely and curvaceous and intelligent and kind, but mere characters, existing only in the novels – not quite what lusting males may be requiring.

That being than which nothing greater can be conceived

The original ontological argument, from whence Descartes' argument derives, was presented by St Anselm of Canterbury in the 11th century. Anselm's argument brings out that maximum perfection, understood as the greatest possible reality with no defects, is a special case – and not at all akin to perfect unicorns and purr-fect pussycats.

Anselm describes God as that being than which nothing greater can be conceived. Now, suppose that such a being fails to exist. Then we should be able to conceive a being greater still – namely such a being that does exist and, indeed, necessarily exists. But that being would then be greater than the greatest conceivable being – and that is a contradiction. Contradictions, though, are not possible ways of how things can be. So, having reached a contradiction on the assumption that God – that being than which nothing greater can be conceived – does not exist, Anselm concludes God must exist.

We may, though, object. Possibly Anselm's argument confuses God with the idea of God. It would be as if someone confused the concept or idea of water with water. Water is wet; but the concept of water is neither wet nor dry. Consider this part of Anselm's argument:

> If we suppose that the greatest conceivable being fails to exist, then, were he to exist, he would be greater than *the greatest conceivable being* – but that is a contradiction.

The argument presents the concept of the greatest conceivable being as if that concept could be a contender for the greatest conceivable being (as represented in italics above). But, were there to exist the greatest conceivable being, then that being would be just what the concept is a concept of. Were mermaids to exist, then arguably they would be the items to which our concept of mermaid after all does apply. Our concept of mermaid is not a contender for being a mermaid.

Perhaps Anselm is not guilty of the above confusion. Perhaps he is merely asking us to reflect on what we grasp when we think about the greatest conceivable being. We ought to grasp that existence must belong to such a being – just as we grasp that seven must be a prime number. Yet we can now see another possible defect in the argument. Why assume that we can make sense of the concept of the 'greatest conceivable being'?

After all, we cannot make sense of the concept of the greatest number. Mention whatever number you want: we can always add another to make a larger number still.

And paradoxically so...

Paradoxically, if to be God is to be the greatest conceivable being, then arguably no one can be God. Of course, maybe there are better ways of understanding what it is to be God – and better arguments to show that he exists. Whatever the ways, paradoxes remain about his nature – and, some would say, it remains paradoxical that so many people can believe in something so paradoxical. But quite what it is that they believe, and why else they may believe, are uncovered in the next chapter.

CHAPTER 19

How to sympathize with the devil

. . . and view religion afresh

'Praise be to God,' proclaims the woman. She has been rummaging through the earthquake's devastation and found her child alive and well. Of course, the woman is not blind to the suffering of mothers whose children perished in the quake, yet for non-believers she seems blind to an absurdity. If God is to be praised for the saved child, ought he not to be blamed for the death of the others? That is the puzzle of evil. But, after viewing that puzzle, we may succeed in casting some light on the nature of religious belief.

The puzzle of evil

Belief in a loving deity that is all powerful and all good sits uneasily with the immense evils in this world so earthly. Taking 'evil' to cover the wide range of sufferings and distresses, pains and anguishes, that human beings and other animals experience, the puzzle may be expressed as follows:

Either God cannot abolish evil or he will not.
If he cannot, then he is not all powerful.
If he will not, then he is not all good.
So, either God is not all powerful or he is not
    all good.

We may add that if God is all powerful and all good, then the argument, if sound, shows that he cannot possibly exist.

Evils appear in two forms. There are moral evils, which result from our choices when we deliberately cause harm to others. And there are natural evils, which occur outside of human control – for example, when hurricanes devastate all in their paths. Religious believers, of course, attempt to reconcile God, as all good and all powerful – and, indeed, all loving – with both types of evil. Some have argued that just as, for people to be tall, some people must be short, so, for goodness to be present there must be badness, wickedness, evil; and, for there to be pleasures, there must be sufferings. Others have argued that for mankind to grasp what is good and bad, examples of good and bad need to exist. There are complexities and challenges to those claims, but, even if we accept the claims, they in no way justify the vast quantity of evil that exists.

Of course, sufferings – pains, hardships – are sometimes good. They may be the sole, the necessary, means to some beneficial outcomes. The pain at the dentist is worth suffering for the ultimate escape from toothache. The satisfactions of achievements require the stresses of revisions, examinations or the exhaustions of training. It is, though, difficult to believe that a benevolent God almighty could not have created a universe that lacked the seemingly gratuitous tragedies that befall people when, for example, they see loved ones ageing and dying – and when they age and die themselves. And even if this life is meant as a trial to test which humans merit an afterlife of heaven – a curious idea – it is difficult to grasp its value to the millions of non-human animals who suffer, with Nature, 'red in tooth and claw', as expressed by Tennyson.

So much for automata

A mainstream attempted resolution of this puzzle directs attention to human free will. Human beings, possessive of free will, are intrinsically more valuable, it is claimed, than automata. Possessing free will, human beings frequently need to choose between doing good and doing bad. We may choose to commit evils, by harming others, by being mean or cruel, cowardly or unjust. The value of a universe containing some creatures with free will, apparently outweighs those evils, evils that God presumably foresaw.

There are deep puzzles about what constitutes free will – as we have seen – even without the theological supplement. Let us, though, assume that sense can be made of free will, understood as people being able to act otherwise than they in fact do; and let us challenge the free will defence, which accepts that God creates individuals with free will. Now, assuming that God's omnipotence includes his omniscience, it follows that he must have known what those created individuals would freely choose to do. That in itself does not undermine their free actions: just because someone knows what we shall do, it does not follow that we must do it. That thought is in line with the lesson about necessity towards the end of Chapter 1, *How to know that you exist*.

In creating this world, which gives rise to the human beings who do exist, God would have known that many evils and bad deeds would be done. It would, though, have been possible for the world to have given rise to individuals who freely choose to act morally, to help others, to be honest; and God would have known which world would have generated individuals possessed of such benign characteristics. Hence, the puzzle is: why did God choose to create this world with the 'fallen' individuals rather than another world in which its individuals acted without wickedness, or, at least, without so much wickedness?

It is no good answer to say that such created individuals could not then have been free agents. It is no good answer because the free will defence itself accepts that God's creation of individuals is compatible with there being free agents; further, believers typically accept that God possesses foreknowledge of everything that will happen.

The free will defence also fails to account for natural evils resulting from earthquakes and the like, unless people suffer those evils because of their way of life or their fathers' sins. Even today, some clerics blame humanity's greed for recent floods. As for the thought that people today are being punished for the sins of their fathers – well, that is morally horrendous. What can be just about people suffering now because of the actions of great great grandfathers?

In the face of evidence

John Stuart Mill, the Victorian utilitarian and reformer, pointed out that if we looked around the Universe without a prior conception of God as good and loving, we should find considerable evidence to blacken God's name and not much evidence to praise it. We add that we may be tempted to have sympathy for the devil, for, if the world is evidence of a designer, arguably it points more to a malevolent power than a benevolent – or, at least, to such powers in conflict. God does not deserve to get all the press coverage.

It looks as if for many religious believers, nothing can undermine their belief in God. Once upon a time, certain events were considered evidence for God's (or gods') existence. If the events were desired, they showed God to be good and pleased; if undesired, they showed God to be good and displeased. Sometimes praying for rain – to the right god – would bring forth rain; sacrifices for victory in battle would bring victory. Prayers and sacrifices, though, are unreliable ways to desired ends. Further, there is a conundrum when both sides in a battle pray to God for success. Since believers typically refuse to accept any evidence as evidence against the existence of God, we may question whether religious belief should be understood as *belief*. If nothing can possibly count against a belief that some being exists, be it natural or supernatural, then we may wonder whether the belief has content: recall Popper on this in Chapter 11. Consider the following often told by the author, concerning Abe's 'belief' that Zoe secretly loves him. Abe reflects thus:

In seeking loving demonstration, I invite her to the opera, ask her round for a drink and send her earrings. My offers are spurned. I conclude that opera is not her cup of tea, that she is a non-drinker, and that she doesn't wear earrings. When, the following week, I see her at the opera, having a drink, and with sparkling earrings jangling – well, I conclude she plays hard to get.

The tale continues, building up more and more ways in which Zoe resists Abe's advances. She changes her telephone number, threatens court orders, calls the police. If Abe still protests that she loves him really, it is time to recognize that he no longer has a belief at all. Rather, he suffers a desperate obsession or is possessed of a mental state requiring medication.

Now, religious belief need not be an obsession in Abe's way; but given how religious believers respond to the world, religious belief should not be treated as regular belief. Indeed, this comes out when we reflect that many believers speak of *faith*. Kierkegaard, the 19th-century Danish philosopher, suggested of a 'leap of faith'. Some speak of putting their trust in God. Of course, if you place your trust in someone, you will speak of believing that that someone exists; but maybe such talk need not be taken at face value.

'My dear, it's the Taj Mahal!'

A tale has been told of a woman in a dress shop trying on a new hat. She looks at herself, unsure what to think. Does it suit her? There is something appealing, yet also something not quite right. Her companion exclaims, 'My dear, it's the Taj Mahal.' Of course, the hat is not literally the Taj Mahal; yet we ought not to reject the exclamation. It brings forth a new way of looking at the hat, drawing a previously unnoticed connection. The indecision vanishes. The hat is all too much for the purpose at hand – or head.

When considering religion, perhaps it is better to focus not on God but on the believers. Perhaps religions are best understood as offering ways of looking at the world, as, somewhat trivially, the exclamation 'Taj Mahal' cast a fresh light on the hat. We should remember that religion involves far more than the proposition 'God exists'. Religions, and the 'beliefs' within, should be understood, at heart, as a collection of attitudes, intentions and encouragements to certain types of behaviour. The assertion 'God exists' may then be seen as part of the web – or a summary of the web – that expresses such attitudes. The web manifests a commitment to a way of life – be it to help the poor and sick or to murder infidels and wipe out the Jews.

Certain ugly beliefs apart, mainstream religious belief often emphasizes a reverence towards life: life is a 'gift'. Some religions inspire through music and words, manifesting awe at the natural world and respect for others. Religions may encourage an attitude towards the self. One may stress humans as base and *un*worthy; others may see humans as reflecting the divine.

Really, really. . .

For some Christians, stories of Jesus's life, of his days in the wilderness, of the parables and the Last Supper, lead to living agapeistically – that is, in brotherly love. Viewed in that way, religious belief is seen by some – for example, by Marx and Freud – as but a projection of the hopes and fears of man. But whether a projection or not, religious belief encourages us to see life in a certain light. Viewing the world through the light of, say, Christian scriptures, is different from viewing it solely in the light of evolutionary theory. In summary, religious assertions, it may be suggested, are expressions of moral intentions. Certain religions may be understood as humanistic in so far as there is concern for the flourishing of others and oneself, but a humanism wrapped up in certain traditions and assertions about God.

Most religious believers, of course, take their godly belief to be that there literally exists a supernatural being. On the proposal here, that claim of a supernatural existent should be treated as of the fictional; but the fictional can none the less be valuable. Through reading poetry, attending performances of Shakespeare, delving into operas by Monteverdi or Britten, we learn about people and their emotions. We may come away viewing the world afresh, perhaps more able to deal with difficulties in life. A key worry remains: some religious beliefs lead people into lives much worse, lives blinkered, intolerant and closed.

The proposal that religious belief is akin to fiction that uplifts, lacking any genuine beliefs about an existent supernatural being and life hereafter, does not go down well with most believers. They insist that their words should be taken literally: God really does exist. Our response is thus: that is but a way of saying that, for example, brotherly love is to be encouraged. The response, though, is likely to be met by, 'But God *really* does exist.' We, once again, may take those words to mean that the speakers really do have the commitment mentioned to brotherly love. This is where the 'really's multiply. 'But, really, really, really God exists.' 'Yes,' we reply, 'really, really, really you are committed to loving your fellow man. . .'

Belief in God, we suggest here, is at heart an attitude towards how best to live and flourish. For those who insist that their belief in God is a genuine existential belief, with content, all we can do is to quote Charles Dunbar Broad, a 20th-century Cambridge philosopher, 'Wait and see – or, alternatively, wait and don't see.'

CHAPTER 20

How to be a monkey endlessly typing . . .

yet never Shakespearean

Were monkeys forever to tinker on typewriters, they would eventually – it is casually said – type the complete Shakespearean oeuvre. Not our monkeys! They may type forever, yet still miss the bard's wordy and worldly ways. Infinity allows for that possibility, for, to take another example, an infinite number of numbers may not at all be all the numbers there are. Indeed, once infinity is on the agenda, we may find our eyes opened to it everywhere and even every 'when', with some bewildering puzzles for philosophers.

Doing the monkeys first

Physicists – such as Paul Davies, mathematician and physicist of some fame – are prone to insist that, were the Universe to have an infinite lifetime, 'any physical process, however slow or improbable, would *have* to happen sometime'. And that includes the aforementioned monkey business. If such insistence is right, and were the world temporally infinite, interesting conclusions flow: all lottery entrants would eventually enjoy top prize winnings; there would never have been a global banking crisis – as well as having been one – and pigs would fly. Bearing the latter in mind, and how your English author would mysteriously be a Dutchman too, we may meet the scientists' insistence with some caution, nay scepticism.

Scientists may be operating with technical terminology when using the word 'infinity', but that should not inhibit us from making such simple and true points as the above, using words in their ordinary meaning. 'Infinite' applies when there is no end. Just because a sequence of different events goes on and on – endlessly, infinitely – it does not follow that all possible events must sometime occur. Events could be endlessly repetitive. It is logically possible that – there is no contradiction in the thought that – Tinkerbelle, the horse, will win the 3.30 race tomorrow. But once tomorrow has come and Tinkerbelle has limped in last, nothing about the Universe, even if endless, could make it true that her possible winning had also then been actualized. In radioactive material, which atom decays when is apparently random; so, although it is logically possible that this atom did not decay at time t, if it does decay at t, the logical possibility of its non-decay at t is ruled out for good.

Moving on from monkeys – moving?

Courtesy of the ancient Greek philosophical wizard of paradoxes, Zeno of Elea, a story is told of Achilles and a tortoise. They were in a race, yet Achilles failed to win, despite being the faster runner by far. Achilles failed, not because he fell asleep or headed in the wrong direction, but because the tortoise was given a head – well, many heads' – start. Allowing the tortoise to start some way ahead, even just a small way ahead however small, generates the problem.

Imagine the scene. Before Achilles can win the race, he must overtake the tortoise; and before he can do that, he must get to the tortoise's starting position. The firing gun is – er – fired. So, Achilles heads for the tortoise, yet by the time he reaches the tortoise's starting position, the tortoise has moved forward a further distance. And by the time Achilles reaches this next position of the tortoise, it has moved a little further still. Those distances whereby the tortoise is ahead diminish – after all, the tortoise runs more slowly than Achilles – but none the less those distances exist; and there is always a fresh distance for Achilles to travel. Although those distances decrease in size, there is an infinite number of them.

More easily to picture, start to walk to the wall opposite – but reflect. You need to reach the point halfway between you and the wall; and then the point halfway further on, then halfway further on still – and so on, without end. It looks as if you cannot reach the wall; yet, of course you can. Today, philosophers recognize that something has gone wrong with the reasoning. Zeno, with his paradoxes of motion – and with some conceit – thought his reasoning impeccable. For Zeno, something must have gone wrong with our common-sense view of the world. Something has gone radically wrong because such paradoxes, when properly thought through in the spirit of Zeno, appear in the end to show all motion is illusory.

There are also puzzles which focus on trying to prove that we cannot even get started. Before I can reach the wall, I need to get halfway, but before I can do that, I need to get half of that first halfway, namely a quarter-way; and so on. Or not casually 'and so on' because there is no smallest distance I may start to traverse. Mention any distance – and half of that distance can be conceived. Hence, I cannot get started. Related puzzles arise even for those spatially stationary. For you to exist over the coming minute, you must exist for one half-minute, then an additional quarter minute, then a further eighth of a minute, and so on. Those time periods diminish, yet there is no end to the series of them.

Making infinite moves – without loss of breath

The paradoxes apply whenever there are extensions, be they in space or time. Any extension, it seems, can be divided again and again without end. All extensions, be they spatial lengths or durations of time, generate the puzzle; all extensions are infinitely divisible. Yet we do, of course, move around the world. We do persist through time. So, it looks as if we are managing to do an infinite number of things whenever we do anything or even just persist – and we do these infinite tasks often without becoming tired or breathless.

Sticking, so to speak, with movement: two assumptions lead to Zeno's paradoxical conclusion that all movement is illusory. First, movements involve infinitely many smaller movements. Secondly, nothing can perform infinitely many anything. Performing an infinite number of tasks, that is, an endless number of tasks, would be to perform a 'super-task', which should surely be beyond anyone's ability, even God's. Yet many mathematicians – like our scientists predicting monkeys' eventual authorial success – accept, quite casually, that an endless series can have an end, and hence that we can perform an infinite number of tasks. Yet are things as easy as that?

Consider the series that may represent the repeated accumulated half-ways to the wall opposite, as we draw nearer to that wall:

$\frac{1}{2}, \frac{3}{4}, \frac{7}{8}, \frac{15}{16}$, and so on. . .

The series has terms that draw closer and closer to the number one – to the wall. The series converges to one; and mathematicians may define the 'sum' of a convergent arithmetical infinite series – a half, a quarter, an eighth and so on – as the limit to which the sequence of partial sums converges. Such defining, though, fails to explain how the point can be reached by following an *endless* series. To converge is not to reach. To make this vivid, let me introduce a flea, a flea which for some reason is keen to hop along in one direction. Suppose the series above is written out – the fractions inscribed. Perhaps they are all one inch apart, going on and on, out into the Universe. They will go on and on without end. No one could rightly argue that the flea, however speedily she fled, would end up hopping on an inscription of the number one. She cannot achieve that feat for the simple reason that that number does not occur in the endless series inscribed. The fractions draw closer and closer to that number; but they never reach it. She is defeated.

Some rain and some chess

The paradoxes arise, at least in part, because we are being rather casual in applying the concepts and theorems of abstract mathematics to the world around us. Naturally, in various ways mathematical models can be properly applied to what we do: to Achilles chasing the tortoise;

to my reaching the wall. After all, computer simulations can model weather changes and be applied to the weather. We should, though, conclude neither that everything about the simulation applies to the weather nor that everything about the weather applies to the simulation. The models may involve colours and graphs, but the weather is not similarly coloured. The simulation and the computer, when modelling rainfall, usually remain dry.

We need to turn once again to Ludwig Wittgenstein, the tormented philosophical genius of the 20th century. He reflects on a knight's move in a game of chess: two squares in one direction followed by one square at a right angle. That is a single move for a knight. Despite the description given, in chess there are no partial moves for a knight. Although the knight moves over different squares, the rules do not permit a part move. In contrast, you may eat a bread roll or half a bread roll. Now, it is a misunderstanding of chess to think that, as there are *moves* in chess, there must be partial moves.

The piece of wood that is shaped into the knight – yes, that could be moved just one square; but the knight in the game cannot make a one-square move. What is possible with pieces of wood is not thereby possible with the pieces in a game of chess. So, too, what is and is not possible with regard to abstract mathematical series does not carry over to what is and is not possible in the world of wood, of individuals running, resting and counting. We need to remember that an infinite collection should not be thought of as just a very big finite collection. Doing something an infinite number of times and completing that task – performing a super-task – does not have the problem of being very tiring and a danger. Doing something an infinite number of times simply is impossible. Let us use an example derived from Wittgenstein.

First, imagine some individuals, exhausted by a marathon event, perhaps one of counting in unison the numbers down from one million. Here they are, in front of us, gasping out the last few numbers: 3, 2, 1. That has doubtless been exhausting for them, but such a vast task makes sense – and it makes sense finishing it. Secondly, imagine a similar set of circumstances. The individuals before you are indeed wearily counting down to the last numbers: 3, 2, 1. The difference is that they have been counting down *all* the positive whole numbers. Any number you think they may have started from could not be the starting number, for there would always be one greater. Reaching the end of counting an infinite number, it seems, does not make sense.

The cable guy

Here is another example (devised by Alan Hájek) of the troubles we encounter when misapplying the infi-nite – infinite divisibility – to the empirical world. The cable guy – utility man – will definitely arrive today any time after 8.00 am up to and including 4.00 pm, the times being equally likely. To be so certain may strike us as implausible; but we are certain, and it is true. He will arrive. So, it is equally probable that he turns up from 8.00 am up to and including midday as from midday up to and including 4.00 pm. The tale excludes a precise 8.00 am arrival. If the guy arrives exactly at noon, that belongs to the morning; if he arrives exactly at 4.00 pm, that belongs to the afternoon. There is parity in the durations. Were we to take bets, the night before, on when he will arrive, it would be rational to bet that a morning arrival is as likely as an afternoon arrival. The problem is the following. However short a time after 8.00 am it is, we should then think his arrival more likely (very slightly initially) in the afternoon than the morning. After all, some of the morning has gone. There is no 'first moment' after 8.00 am, so we know that whenever he appears, even seconds after 8.00 am, there are times between 8.00 am and his arrival when it would have been rational to have bet on the afternoon appearance as more likely. So, paradoxically, it must surely be irrational to bet on morning and afternoon being equally likely – given that in principle there is a time when we are *bound* to think the afternoon more likely.

How do we handle the puzzle? Well, what it is rational to bet on at one time may, of course, differ from what it is rational to bet on at another. There are likely to be times after 8.00 am when it would be rational to change our bets in favour of the afternoon. The puzzle, though, leads us into thinking that we are bound to change our view that both morning and afternoon are equally likely; so why hold to that 'equally likely' view in the first place? We need to recall Wittgenstein and the chess example. Perhaps the Cable Guy problem is solved by resisting the casual abstract division of time when actions are involved. Bets and thinking take time. The cable guy could appear so soon after 8.00 am that there would be no time for us to revise our initial betting or thinking. There is nothing irrational in betting on morning and afternoon being equally likely.

Georg Cantor mysteriously wrote:

> *The fear of infinity is a form of myopia that destroys the possibility of seeing the actual infinite, even though it, in its highest form, has created and sustains us, and, in its secondary transfinite forms, occurs all around us.*

We should remember, though, that bets and runs, fleas a-hopping, and monkeys a-typing, once taking place in the real empirical world, make sense. Translate them into the realm of abstract mathematics and things may well get changed; impose them, with the changes, back onto the empirical world – and no wonder we are baffled.

CHAPTER 21

How to be seduced by logic . . .

and how not to be tricked

Casanova's methods of seduction almost certainly did not depend on logic. Yet as with human beings when motivated by love or lust, Mistress Logic may have some wily ways. Of course, being an upright woman at heart, Mistress Logic will show us how those wily ways work, and where they go wrong, if we want to be fair, just and consistent. None the less, where love is concerned, we may prefer to draw a veil over logic, and succumb instead to the wiles – depending, of course, on whose ways they are.

A silver-tongued seducer

Sylvester, keen on logic, spies a lovely young woman Emilie and yearns for her company and more. Urged on by Mistress Logic, he approaches the desirable creature and soon they are chatting easily. After a while, Sylvester confesses his interest in logic. Emilie, instead of fleeing, is fascinated and asks for some lessons. Little does she know how she will become ensnared. Sylvester says that naturally he would love to display his logical acumen. With that in mind, he asks Emilie to consider the following question:

> Q1: Will you give the same answer to this question as to my next question?

Emilie is a little bewildered, thinking 'How odd', and reasonably responds, 'But how do I know? I know not what your second question is.' Sylvester has no problem with such caution. 'Look,' he says, 'the question that I have given you requires a yes-or-no answer; but so long as you agree to give that type of answer, one way or the other, I'll tell you what the second question is. First you need tell me whether you will answer yes or answer no to my first question. I can't be fairer than that.' Sylvester adds that, if she is happy with the conditions, he will take her out for a fine dinner beforehand.

Emilie readily agrees, the chit chat moves on; but later, over that dinner, Sylvester returns to his question. And so Emilie, having acknowledged that she must answer yes or no to the first question, waits to hear the second question. Sylvester is now a little sheepish, but – with naughty Mistress Logic's urgings – he spills forth the second question:

> Q2: Will you sleep with me?

Emilie is shocked. She is not that kind of woman, well, not after only one dinner. 'No!' she says spontaneously. 'Hold on,' replies Sylvester. 'You need to tell me the answer to the first question, Q1.'

'Well, it's "No",' shouts Emilie, looking all indignant.

'Ah,' replies Sylvester, 'how splendid. As you've said "No", that means you will not be answering Q2 in the same way; so you are saying that, yes, you will sleep with me. How wonderful – and wise, if I may be so bold.'

'I'm confused. I must mean "Yes" to the first question,' insists Emilie heatedly.

'How wonderful,' beams Sylvester. 'So that means you're saying yes to my sleeping proposal. What a wise choice – and to reiterate it so forcefully.'

Emilie's heart sinks.

What was Emilie's mistake?

Emilie has been trapped. Whichever way she answers Q1, she is succumbing to Sylvester's slippery seduction. If she agrees that she will answer in the same way – 'Yes' to the first question – then she will have to say 'Yes' to the sleeping question. If she goes for 'No' to the first, then she cannot answer 'No' to the second, but must again answer 'Yes'. Acquiescing to the yes-or-no demand leads to a 'Yes', come what may, to the seduction. 'Yes' to a 'Yes' generates a 'Yes'. 'No' to a 'No' also generates a 'Yes'.

What a fine mess Emilie has got herself into! Mistress Logic, though, takes pity on her and explains how she has been ensnared. The questions have been unfair – for let us assume that Emilie has, indeed, no intention of sleeping with Sylvester: she wants her answer to the second question to be 'No'. Obviously the first question must not be answered with a 'Yes' or a 'No'; but what is it about the situation that makes that so? Mistress Logic reminds us all of a typical example where it is unwise to accede to a yes-or-no request. In a court of law the defendant, an innocent husband, is asked, 'Have you stopped beating your wife – yes or no?' If he answers as requested, he is bound to condemn himself. If he answers 'Yes', then he confesses to having been bad, but he is at least improved. If he answers 'No', then he confesses to having been bad and to have made no improvement at all. If he refuses to answer, spectators may consider him shifty.

The husband should obviously decline the yes-or-no demand; we often should decline such demands. True, refusing to answer yes or no may make us appear evasive, but in reality the refusal may be the proper response, ideally combined with an explanation of why. The refusal to consent to the yes-or-no by the husband is justified because the question falsely presupposes that the husband used to beat his wife. The question contains two elements: a claim of what used to happen and then a question. An innocent husband obviously wants to challenge the presupposition, saying that, no, he did not beat his wife, and then also saying that, no, he does not beat his wife now. Only if the presupposition is true, namely that he did beat his wife, is it legitimate to ask that the question be answered yes or no.

Returning to Sylvester's question, Mistress Logic reminds us that a yes-or-no answer cannot be given by Emilie to the first question, Q1, assuming that Q2 is to be replied to negatively. One way of seeing why that is so is to draw attention to the existence of two elements lurking within Q1. Here are the two elements, E1 and E2:

E1: What is your answer to this question?
E2: Is your answer to E1 the same as the answer to Q2?

Of course, E1 is baffling and to answer yes or no would be arbitrary. E1 is as vacuous as the command 'Obey this command' with nothing else said. Still, if Emilie played along and gave a yes-or-no answer to E1, E2 could then be answered, but it would be answered differently. Suppose Emilie answered E1 as 'Yes'. Her answer to E2 would be 'No'. Suppose Emilie answered E1 as 'No'. Her answer to E2 would be 'Yes'. Seeing Sylvester's Q1 as containing those two elements brings out how there cannot be fairly demanded of Emilie a yes-or-no answer to the Q1 question.

More seduction – being hit upon

Emilie fled, but a few hours later, we find Sylvester back in the bar, engaged in excited conversation with another desirable woman, Lolo. Sylvester can hardly believe his luck. Lolo is checking that he really is happy with the following conditions. 'You may have a passionate week's holiday with me in Nice. The sole payment is £50. Everything otherwise is free. There are no strings: return first-class tickets, five-star hotel, and me, filled with passion, at your beck and call. Here is one further condition. I shall shortly be saying something important for you to assess. Let us call what I shall say "the key". If what I say next (as the key) is true, then I keep the £50 and you have the holiday at no further cost as explained; if what I say next (as the key) is false, then you must accept the £50 back, but still have the holiday and me free.'

Lolo's announcement above is taken to be true; so let us stand aside for the moment and reflect on the position for Sylvester. How can he lose? There are no snags concerning the holiday and passion. Sylvester would love

214

a trip to Nice for just £50 in any case – and with such a desirable woman thrown in with the seduction, well, what could be better? Either way, with regard to whether the key is true or not, he is bound to have the splendid trip and the passion. At worst, it costs him a mere £50. Rational man that Sylvester is, he eagerly accepts. Lolo takes Sylvester's £50, with a coy smile; and then says – and this is the key to be assessed for its truth:

'Either I shall return the £50 or you will pay me £1 million.'

Now, is that true or false; and, whichever it is, what are the consequences?

Beware of Mistress Logic

With an either/or proposition, the proposition is true so long as at least one of the elements is true. Either I shall go to Cambridge today or to Oxford tomorrow. So long as one of the elements is true, the whole either/or proposition is true. Logicians are also happy with both elements being true and the either/or remaining true. So the either/or proposition just given is true, if I both go to Cambridge today and to Oxford tomorrow. Now, let us return to the key proposition given by Lolo, bearing in mind that for an either/or proposition to be false, both elements need to be false.

First, suppose that what Lolo says, the key, is false. For it to be false, just considering the key set, she must not return the £50; but the deal's conditions are that she does return the £50 if it is false. Hence, there is a contradiction, whether or not you pay the £1 million. So, what she says cannot be false. Therefore, what she says must be true. Secondly then, let us consider it true. As a truth, that must be because either Lolo returns the £50 or Sylvester pays her the £1 million. It cannot, though, be because she returns the £50; the deal's conditions state that she keeps the £50 if the key is true. Hence it can only be true because Sylvester pays her the £1 million. That must – magically and logically – be the case. The so-called magic arises, though, because a contradiction has been set in the conditions to ensure that we rule out the possibility of the key being false. What we should usually expect – that the key would be either true or false – turns out mistaken.

Sylvester is, of course, upset at being trapped. Indeed, he has ended up thinking that maybe Lolo is but Mistress Logic in disguise, making amends for his having earlier tricked a member of the sisterhood, namely Emilie.

Lolo's trap may be likened to a more blatant one by Mistress Logic. She says to you, 'I am not going to give you £100; and what I say next is true.' She then says, 'Either I am going to give you £100, or you must give me £1 million.' Well, if that either/or claim is true then, if what was first claimed is also true, the either/or claim can only be true because you must donate £1 million. Of course, we can easily respond to this by pointing out that, presumably, Mistress Logic is not speaking the truth when saying that her next utterance would be true. It is false; but with our more complicated Lolo offer, the conditions seek to rule out the false option because it leads to a contradiction. And once we have contradictions involved in conditions, we may find ourselves trapped into all manner of things.

The Barber

To end on a classic contradiction that sometimes sends minds reeling, let us relay the tale of the Barber of Alcala, courtesy of Bertrand Russell. The barber shaves all and only those who do not shave themselves. So, does the Barber shave himself? If he is someone who shaves himself, then he does not shave himself. If he is someone who does not shave himself, then he does shave himself. What does he do?

With the seduction puzzles above, we should now be wary of thinking that it must be either true or false that he shaves himself. A little reflection can lead us to see that there is a presupposition that such a barber can exist. But there cannot be such a barber. The situation described is contradictory. Had our barber of Alcala been shaving all and only those in the next village, say, Balcala, then there would be no problem. The problem arises here because he himself is included as seemingly an individual who does or does not get shaved. Self-reference is involved and this leads to the contradiction – as we saw with some propositions above spinning back on themselves.

When we engage with Mistress Logic, we need to be careful of presuppositions, contradictions – and simple mistakes. Learning how to handle and tame Mistress Logic, though, has its own charm; arguably, however, many will find the seductions of the next chapter to possess greater charm.

CHAPTER 22

How to be an object of desire . . .
yet far more than an object

Being in love is a complex state, but there are complexities enough if we focus solely on the sexual desire within that love, for what is it that we desire when sexually desiring? The desire may appear as an appetite, a lust – a state far more intense than, but akin to, the appetite some possess for chocolate, coffee or even football. Of course, 'Come up for coffee?' is a well-known invitation, often motivated by sexual desire. So, quite what is the object of that desire? For sure, it is not coffee.

Wine, water and a bedroom window

Imagine – though the imagined herewith is reality-based – a girl half asleep, yet aroused, waiting for her boyfriend to slip into her bed to make love. The boyfriend, though, snoozes downstairs while a burglar slides in through the open bedroom window. The burglar sees the half-sleeping figure naked in the moonlight and takes his opportunity. The girl yields, thinking she is yielding to her boyfriend: well, she is sleepy. So, yes, the girl had sex; yes, her desire for sex has been quelled – but her sexual desire was for her boyfriend. That desire was not satisfied; it was interrupted, abandoned or misdirected. The object of sexual desire – an obscure object, as we shall see – involves a particular individual. The desire is directed towards *that* individual. The desire gives rise to talk of possessing the other, taking the other, wanting the other – or being possessed, taken, wanted. Now, we may possess some property or want some wine, yet such instances may appear radically different from what lovers want from each other or have when possessing each other.

You have been running. Oh, how you want some water. There are five glasses of water in front of you. Does it matter which you take? Not at all – you just want some water. You are a wine connoisseur, so you dismiss the shoddy wine in the plastic two-litre bottle; but once you have chosen a fine wine to suit your taste, say the Merlot, it matters not at all whether you have this glass or that. We assume the glasses are the same size and un-sipped by others. Readers, please switch, as appropriate, the examples that follow, if it is easier to identify with a woman wanting a man or with a homosexual relationship.

Sometimes a man may just want a woman. Imagine a sailor landed ashore after weeks at sea, and roaming

Amsterdam's red light district. He wants a woman, maybe a woman of a certain type. He is in need of sexual release – and sexual release through womanly dealings. There is, though, no particular woman whom he desires – yet. His state so far is akin to your wanting a glass of water or, if more discerning, the better wine.

Once a woman is in his gaze – say, Tanya – he may then find his sexual desire well focused. The desire is for that particular woman. His desire possesses a directedness towards Tanya; and that desire can be satisfied only through sexual relations with her. In our bedroom tale, the intruder could not satisfy the girl's sexual desire for her boyfriend. A desire for water, though, may be satisfied whichever glass of water is taken. It does not matter which one in particular; a substitute would be equally good. And, arguably, even with the particular glass of water in hand, the desire is still just for water – any will do.

Being a sex object

We may want a drink of water, a fine wine, or to eat some chocolate. We may want just some woman or other; but we cannot sexually desire just some woman or other. Sexual desire requires a particular in its directedness. Once sexual desire exists for, say, Tanya, that desire would not be satisfied by means of Tanya's twin. Tanya is essential to that desire – she is irreplaceable.

Sexual desire has an irreplaceable object, but that may not count for much. If our sailor has no luck with Tanya, another sexual desire may quickly grow for the next woman he spies, namely Vanya. Where sexual desire is intermingled with love, though, such a casual 'move along the line' feels and is inappropriate. Erotic love typically requires more substance than would be implied by an easy switch from Tanya to Vanya. Many are sceptical of Bertrand Russell's appreciation of love, for instance, given that he said that his love for his then wife vanished during a bicycle ride, just like that.

Thinking more generally, there is an important distinction between what is replaceable and what is irreplaceable. The distinction rests on whether we are concerned for a certain type of item – and any instance of it will do – or whether we are concerned for the particular item, *this* one, with other items possessing the same qualities still not doing at all. Sometimes the distinction is thought to coincide with the distinction between physical objects and persons. If we want a glass of water, any will do; but if we are in love with Belle, no one else will do. The coincidence, though, does not work. True, the beer and the phone, the glass of water and the chocolate are readily replaceable, but then typically so are train drivers and bar staff. True, there is a special relationship with a child or a lover that means a substitute, however similar, would not do – but then such irreplaceability applies to this particular painting by Poussin, those letters from the former loves, these earrings that were a special gift.

In desiring Belle, what do you desire?

Hal sexually desires Belle. Quite what does he desire? Note, Hal does not merely want his desire quelled for that may happen through sudden fears or accident, not through satisfying the desire. Further, Hal may not even want his desire properly satisfied at all or ever: he may delight in the desire, in the deferral of satisfaction. Still, what would properly satisfy his desire?

We are not safe in suggesting that sexual desire is identical with wanting sex – with achieving sexual intercourse or orgasm as the desired end. A 'working girl' may want sex with a client, yet she neither aims at orgasm nor sexually desires the client. An actress (probably mistakenly) believes that the film part demands sex with the lead actor, yet it follows not at all that she sexually desires him. Hal, even though sexually desiring Belle, may not be wanting sex with Belle: perhaps he fears the age gap is too great; perhaps there are health dangers. Those observations, though, should remind us that, in some cases, we can have conflicting psychological states. Maybe Hal possesses the desire to have intercourse with Belle, but also fears satisfying that desire.

The Marquis de Sade wrote that erotic love comes down to sexual desire. In *Juliette*, he speaks of himself having fallen in love with a beautiful woman, yet another man just sexually desires her: 'both he and I want to lie with her – he, 'tis her body he desires: and I, by a fallacious and perilous metaphysic . . . persuade myself that it's only her heart I want . . . Were man to reflect more carefully upon his true interests in pleasure-taking, he would confine himself to the simple enjoyment of bodies.' One way of understanding de Sade's approach is that, in sexually desiring Belle, Hal is yearning for some pleasurable sensations of the flesh. That, though, surely is not the heart of what Hal desires. Were that the heart, then he should be content to secure those sensations, and maybe more success-fully so, through other activities. Pleasurable sensations of the flesh could be caused in Belle's absence, yet Hal's experiences be the same, as if she were present and the cause.

Here is another understanding: Hal's yearning is for skin-to-skin, flesh-to-flesh, bodily contact *with Belle*, leading to pleasure. Now, such desire for bodily con-tact obviously frequently features, yet is it the key to sexual desire? A wrestler desires bodily contact with his opponent, and the pleasure of pinning him down; but that need manifest no sexual desire.

The above considerations suggest that Immanuel Kant's curious understanding of sexual love is way off the mark, when he writes:

Sexual love makes of the loved person an object of appetite; as soon as that appetite has been stilled, the person is cast aside as one casts away a lemon which has been sucked dry . . .

Perilous metaphysic of the flesh

Many lovers have, at times, experienced partners mechanically going through the rituals of sex. They have done so themselves. Such mechanical responses are not usually wanted when sexually desiring someone. While men sometimes do drug women in order to have sexual intercourse with them, that is a very impoverished way of having sexual desires satisfied – and is of course morally repugnant. Indeed, we may question whether sexual desires for the individuals in question are satisfied by such manoeuvres. A word that may now come to mind is 'reciprocation'.

A lover – a human being; a person – is not just a biological blob of flesh to be penetrated or impaled. A person is a conscious being: the flesh is informed with consciousness. Jean-Paul Sartre, the twentieth-century French existentialist philosopher and novelist, draws on this in the following, though it is troubled by his own perilous metaphysic and presentation:

225

> *I make myself flesh so as to fascinate the Other by my
> nakedness and to provoke in her the desire for my flesh
> – exactly because this desire will be nothing else in the
> Other but an incarnation similar to mine. Thus desire is an
> invitation to desire. It is my flesh alone which knows how
> to find the road to the Other's flesh, and I lay my flesh next
> to her flesh so as to awaken her to the meaning of flesh
> . . . Each consciousness by incarnating itself has realized
> the incarnation of the other; each one's disturbance has
> caused disturbance to be born in the Other and is thereby
> so much enriched.*

Hal's sexual desire involves a desire that Belle be aroused by her recognition of Hal's desire that she be aroused. We may picture arousals being enhanced by such mutual perceptions of the arousals. Reflect on how mutual glances can spiral into recognitions of mutual desires. Sartre's words, though, also provide a picture of paradox and conflict. Hal wants Belle to be a separate conscious being, desiring their flesh to be pressed, yet Hal is also wanting to unite with Belle as flesh, as embodied, as an object within his world, which undermines holding Belle as a subject with her own perspective. Sexual desire, in seeking to capture the other, generates the impossibility of turning another consciousness into 'but an object', yet also needing it to be a consciousness desiring the other.

Quite what Sartre is arguing is obscure, but arguably true to life for the object of sexual desire *is* obscure. Desire essentially involves both voluntary actions and many involuntary changes in the body, and both feeling oneself and the other as flesh, as biological chunks, yet also as conscious beings with distinct perspectives on the entwined happenings.

In defence of sex objects

Leather boots do not reciprocate; hence, although Hal can do many things with Belle's high-heeled leather boots, he cannot sexually desire those boots, however much those boots may heighten sexual satisfactions, however much they may be valuable sex objects. Hal can, of course, sexually desire the wearer of the boots, namely, Belle.

Even when aware of how sexual desire is directed at a conscious person and not just a body, some see sexual relations as involving the woman merely as sex object and replaceable. Indeed, as seen, Kant viewed all sexual desire without love as mere appetite, normally the man no doubt using the other as an object to be cast asunder, as 'when a lemon has been sucked dry'. Sexual desire, though, as shown above, is very different from an appetite for chocolate, cake or even lemon sucking.

The 'sex object' complaint has different sources: the 'object' may have her interests ignored or may not be freely giving herself. She may be being used merely as a means to man's sexual satisfaction. Sexual desire, though, does not require such features – and there is no reason to think they are normally present – but sexual desire does focus on our biology, our urges of the flesh, yet as conscious biological beings seeking to arouse and unite with others.

In view of the object/consciousness tension, it is unsurprising that sexual desire can be intermingled with plays of dominance and submission: plays at being sex objects. Playing the role of sex object is, though, very different from being a sex object. The importance of role play – reflect on the fictional accounts of lovers as meant for each other and finding their 'other half' – only adds to the obscurity of quite what constitutes the object of sexual desire; but whatever the obscurity, how many would want to be without such desire?

CHAPTER 23

How not to be nasty, brutish and short . . .

or how to love the law

We find ourselves surrounded by laws, cops and courts
– with threats of fines and jail. Yet we never consented to
living under such forces of law, or in a state where the
spliff needs concealment and taxation pays for much that
lacks our approval. True, in many countries, we are
occasionally allowed a vote, but we know full well that our
votes may be in the minority. The whole apparatus of state
control is not going to be dismantled; and the apparatus
restricts our choices in life. So why ought we obey the law
– if we ought?

Nasty, brutish and short

Were we not to live under a government, with authority
and the means to enforce that authority, we should
surely suffer more than we do now, if, in reality, we
suffer much at all. So, a quick answer to our question

is that we secure benefits from the state and, in return, we should obey its laws, accepting some restrictions.

Below, we shall see how robust, or not, is the quick answer just given; but first let us do what many political philosophers have done, from the ancient Greek Plato, to whom the whole of subsequent philosophy is but a footnote (well, so it has been said, without too much exaggeration). What the philosophers have done is to tell of a life prior to government, state and human-constructed law. Some have spoken as if of historic fact; others, more wisely, have offered tales as reconstructions of pre-governed life, as thought experiments to justify our lawful obedience.

The *state of nature* is that state prior to government; it is the position human beings would be in if left to their own devices, unconstrained by laws and authority. Now, how bad would that state – historical or hypothetical – have been? It depends, of course, on the resources available and what we take human beings to be like, if without law. That, without doubt, is difficult to assess; but the difficulty has not prevented assessments. Some provide glowing reports: at least the natural state gave freedom, with people living with some degree of cooperation. In contrast, we encounter the views of Thomas Hobbes, one of the major political thinkers of the 17th century.

Hobbes had a low opinion of human nature. In *Leviathan*, he noted how, even within society, people lock their doors or arm themselves when travelling. Were he alive today, he would point to mobile phone theft, the desire of many Americans to carry guns and the ruthless capitalist spirit in business. Hobbes saw human beings as competitors, and thought that, for some individuals, pre-eminence over others was a prime aim.

People were motivated, claimed Hobbes with some caveats, solely by perceived self-interest. Indeed a bishop, Bishop Butler, suggested that Hobbes must have looked into his own motivations and wrongly universalized from his one mean instance. By way of further response, we may face 'chicken and egg' questions: did our society create distrust of others or vice versa? Hobbes' state of nature was a state of war: our lives would have been 'solitary, poor, nasty, brutish and short'. There is a wonderful reply: it could have been worse, Thomas. Lives could have been solitary, poor, nasty, brutish – and long.

Effecting escape

If Hobbes is right then it is understandable why humans would want to escape and live under a rule of benign law, yet it is inexplicable how they achieve the escape. Yes, it would be rational to cooperate and agree to an independent authority of some kind; but why would individuals, so distrustful of each other, risk trusting each other – and risk giving powers to a sovereign body? To Hobbes' seemingly impossible position, John Locke responded. Locke understood the state of nature as composed of people who would tend towards some cooperation. Magically, too, many would have a grasp of the divine moral law, the law that apparently teaches mankind that:

> . . . being all equal and independent, no one ought to harm another in his life, health, liberty or possessions. Every one . . . when his own preservation comes not in competition, ought he, as much as he can, to preserve the rest of mankind, and may not, unless it be to do justice on an offender, take away, or impair the life, or what tends to the preservation of the life, the liberty, health, limb, or goods of another.

Locke's state of nature possesses a more contented air than Hobbes', but escape is still desirable: individuals come into conflict and an independent authority would be valuable, making detached judgements and working for the overall good. So it is that from Locke we receive the idea of an explicit social contract, which leads to governments being elected – and which became a source for the United States' Declaration of Independence. In the terms of John Milton, the poet and political activist writing before Locke, the people should be seen as *entrusting* their powers and liberty in the government.

Perishing at sea

The social contract is problematical. What relevance can a social contract, even if (implausibly) historically actual, have to our obligations to the state today? Locke's response is to maintain that today we do consent to the contract. Our behaviour manifests the consent; the consent is tacit. Tacit consent to the state and government, as understood by Locke, seems remarkably easily given. Merely walking the king's (or queen's) highway manifests some sort of consent. A notable withering response came from David Hume:

> *Can we seriously say that a poor peasant or artisan has a free choice to leave his country, when he knows no foreign language or manners, and lives, from day to day, by the small wages which he acquires? We may as well assert that a man, by remaining in a vessel, freely consents to the dominion of the master; though he was carried on board while asleep, and must leap into the ocean and perish, the moment he leaves her.*

Whether people consent to an authority depends on the alternatives available. People are free to leave this country, but only if they can afford passports, travel tickets – and, of course, can find an acceptable country to take them. They may lose contact with family, have language problems and difficulties in finding work. Options available, in practice, may well be little better than perishing in the ocean. Perhaps trying to establish

233

actual voluntary consent, even if tacit, is a mistaken path to follow. A different path is that of the hypothetical. Obviously, we were not involved in any original contract; obviously our living under this state does not thereby establish consent. But, had we been around, deciding on the structure of the state and laws, to what should we have consented?

Behind the veil

A quick quip, before we go further with 'hypothetical consent', is that hypothetical consent is not even worth the paper it is *not* written on. Yet the quip deserves challenge. True, hypothetical consent is not actual consent; but, understood properly, it may, in certain circumstances, be as relevant as explicit consent. You are in a car crash and, being conscious, you explicitly consent to being dragged from the wreckage and given medical treatment. Now, another example: clearly prone to accidents, you are in another car crash and knocked unconscious; you are dragged from the wreckage and given medical treatment. The dragging and treatment could well be justified by the hypothetical truth: had you been conscious, that is what would have received your consent.

With regard to how the state should be organized, to what should we have consented? Well, there is no one answer without more conditions set. After all, our answers may be coloured by our current positions and expectations in society. If poor, we may think that a state should be primarily a welfare state, providing benefits as high priority. If rich and in business, we may emphasize low taxation. If of certain religious persuasions, we may want a theocratic state, following the (alleged) will of God. If we are parents, provision for children may be highly valued. And so forth.

To overcome such partialities, American philosopher John Rawls promoted the 'veil of ignorance'. We need to judge of our consent as if we existed behind a veil, unaware of our race, sex and religion, unaware of our abilities, of whether we are abled or disabled, and so forth. In such a hypothetical original position, we should all, in a sense, be equal. Even though we are still individuals, making our choices, the choices would not be distorted by our own peculiar self-interest in opposition to the interests of others. The veil is a device, it seems, to lead us into an impartial and rational approach to what would count as a just society. Not knowing our own positions in society, we should think it rational to propose some welfare provision, for example. Aware of external dangers, we would see the value of the state being defended. Given the possibility that we could be in a minority group, we should back certain freedoms and rights for individuals. In as far as our current society has such rights and freedoms, our obedience is justified by this hypothetical consent.

The thought experiment involved here is far from plain sailing. If we are made so abstract, through ignorance of our position, we may fail to secure a grip on what could motivate us. Further, we have assumed that we should have concern for welfare, liberty, fairness; but how should we prioritize such prizes – and what justifies our prizing them? Somehow the veil needs to leave us with sufficient moral sense for us to make sense of the exercise. If, behind the veil, we are neither male nor female, then, on the one hand, we may miss out on virtues that ground some important concerns to do with children, caring and marriage; on the other hand, we may not be obsessed with inheritances.

Benefits, obligations and disobedience

If we give up on consent as providing a justification for our obligation to the state and its laws, we may be cast back to the original suggestion, namely, that the laws are to our net benefit. We are better off with law than without; we are better off paying taxes – for they provide many services that benefit us, even though they also pay for services irrelevant to us or which annoy us. Our obligation to the law rests on the benefits received. There is, though, an immediate objection. The justification does not apply to everyone. A significant number of people do badly, often through no fault of their own. Consider those you find sleeping rough or those who are exploited by unscrupulous employers. Why should they feel obligated and obey the law? At the other end of the scale, some of the well-off claim that they contribute more than they receive. In fact, though, it may be that they make their money because of society's stability, because of the law allowing large inheritances – and because of sheer good fortune.

Let us assume that we do benefit from the state's existence and its laws. That alone does not mean that we are under any obligation to the benefactor. If an unknown person buys you a drink, but you did not ask for the drink, you are under no obligation to return the favour. We benefit from street lighting; but if we made no request for it, then we are under no obligation to pay for it (through taxes). Well, that is the argument; but perhaps it places too much stress on 'obligation'. Perhaps we should simply acknowledge that people receive benefits in various ways; so it is right to contribute to the provision of those benefits, even if only some apply to us and none is requested.

Even if we have reasons for obeying the state, there are still some cases when we morally ought to disobey. Civil disobedience is sometimes right. Just think of the many atrocities committed by governments, often in the name of their people. It is, of course, difficult to oppose a powerful state, but when it is engaged in appalling behaviour, opposition is rightly required – yet easy to say. One way of viewing the relationship between the people and the state, as said, is that the people entrust their powers and liberties to the authorities. If that trust is broken, then the people are within their rights to rebel. We end by returning to John Milton and his fine political sense:

> It being thus manifest that the power of kings and magistrates is nothing else but what is only derivative, transferred, and committed to them in trust from the people to the common good of them all, in whom the power yet remains fundamentally and cannot be taken from them without a violation of their natural birthright.

Thus it is, in line with Milton and Locke, that we are within our rights to oppose those governments that threaten our liberty and fail to provide adequate protection of our welfare. Governments are corrupt that dishonour the trust we, as rational agents, place in them.

CHAPTER 24

How to tolerate the intolerable . . .
well, or be as tolerant as possible

Consider some slogans: men are inferior to women; homosexual practices are wicked; abortionists are all murderers; Factor X will prevent ageing. If we love liberty, surely we should tolerate such views, however strongly propounded. There are, though, limits to toleration, notably when direct incitements to harm occur; but how can we justify tolerating any expressions if they are blatantly false, nasty, or seek to persuade people to be intolerant?

The Liberty Principle

Tolerating something already suggests some disapproval. We do not tolerate things that we welcome. Toleration certainly neither implies respect for the views being tolerated nor respect for the individuals who propound the views. There are some dreadful views expressed – for example, that people who leave Islam should be killed – views that certainly deserve no respect. And, as said, the individuals who promulgate such views forfeit any respect, any respect in the sense of approval. We may, though, respect such individuals simply in the sense of acknowledging them as human beings with views to put forward – and views which may be tolerated.

It is, indeed, when people express views deeply opposed to our own – ones about which we cannot be indifferent – that toleration may be required. Paradoxically, toleration may be most demanded when we confront the intolerable. Were the opposing views less than intolerable, we probably would not care much about their being aired, depending upon how adverse the likely consequences. We may simply celebrate the diversity in opinion. In his highly influential book *On Liberty*, John Stuart Mill, our favourite utilitarian, presented the Liberty Principle, known also as the Harm Principle, which offers grounds for toleration – and notes the places where toleration should cease. The 'simple principle', as Mill termed it, is as follows:

> . . . the sole end for which mankind are warranted, individually or collectively, in interfering with the liberty of action of any of their number, is self-protection. That the only purpose for which power can be rightfully exercised over any member of a civilized community, against his will, is to prevent harm to others. His own good, either physical or moral, is not a sufficient warrant.

The principle applies only to sane adults, in a sufficiently developed and informed society. Mill's utilitarianism, as seen in Chapter 15, *How to judge whom to save*, is the theory that we morally ought to maximize individuals' flourishing. The theory underlies his Liberty Principle. Being compelled to live in a certain way – be it by the state or by custom's tyranny – is to be but an automaton, not a person. It is that thought, about what it is to be a person with a flourishing life, which rebuts the common objection to the principle, the objection being that people may be happier if told what to do.

Experiments in living

Mill speaks of 'experiments in living'. Individuals should be free to seek to fulfil themselves and, to do so, they need to possess freedom of expression, the expression being not merely of speech but also of style of life. Observers will then see how well the experiments of others develop. Society overall benefits for, as Mill writes:

> . . . a State which dwarfs its men, in order that they may be more docile instruments in its hands even for beneficial purposes – will find that with small men no great thing can really be accomplished.

Might sufficient experiments in living lead us, one day, to discover an ideal way of life? That is unlikely: Mill recognizes significant differences in human nature;

further, he sees the value of diversity in a society. There is no reason to believe in a 'one fit' lifestyle. Mill's advocacy of different experiments in living implies, of course, neither that all experiments will be successful nor that he approves of all. What Mill approves of is that society should tolerate diversity in living – and, in many instances, welcome it.

The Liberty Principle, it is worth noting, does not allow us to ignore duties that we have voluntarily accepted. People, argued Mill, should not have children unless they are able to support and educate them. By all means, we should tolerate individuals who live in alcoholic or cannabis hazes; but not, if by doing so, they end up harming others, such as their children.

Free speech: individuals and media

Freedom of speech is a manifestation of freedom of thought. It deserves special protection for that very reason. It also deserves special protection for it benefits others and society in general. On the one hand, if what is spoken contains the truth, then that will be of benefit to hearers. It is always good to get at the truth, according to Mill, for we need to operate from the truth – from how things are; from what is right and wrong – in order to flourish. On the other hand, if what is spoken contains falsehoods, then that should stimulate us to challenge what is said. It may rouse us from our dead dogmas and encourage us to defend our views and act on them.

An objection to such widespread toleration is that sometimes the greatest happiness could well be best secured without the disturbing challenges from free speech, without facing the truth. Ignorance can be bliss; many people prefer not to have their views challenged. Once again, Mill's understanding of happiness, as flourishing, with individuals developing their potential, comes to the rescue. In order to flourish, individuals need access to the truth. In order to flourish, individuals should not be docile recipients of people telling them what is best for them and doing what they are told. People should be free to remonstrate with each other about how best to live, but not to compel each other to live in certain ways.

Mill's idea of freedom of speech may be criticized as assuming an impractical ideal, especially when reflecting on his advocacy of a free press. The ideal is that of genuine debate and a search for the truth, both with regard to how things are and how they ought to be. The image is that of enquiring minds, as if at university symposia. In practice, of course, what is published by the media is shaped by commercial pressures and political agendas. In practice, debate is 'dumbed down' to screaming headlines, supported by misleading argument or no argument at all.

Such scepticism of a free press comes to the fore when we reflect on the scare stories run on front pages, about vaccination dangers, paedophiles on the loose, or increased crime statistics, and when, at best, corrections are hidden away, some days later, in middle pages, and hence unnoticed. We may wonder whether a free press is all that desirable when it can amount to advocacy of greater consumerism, be it through the idea that every child should have a playstation or the alleged efficacy of dubious diet plans. It is all very well for Mill to speak of how either we are exposed to the truth or we are stimulated to argue against falsehood; but, in practice, many people simply lap up the latest media reports. Think of the pressure on individuals, through 'free' advertising, to conform to latest fashions, fads and diets.

Harms, offence and sex

There are, of course, some areas where freedom of speech – and freedom of expression more generally – clearly needs to be curtailed. The Liberty Principle takes those into account. Speech that directly incites people to harm others, without consent, deserves no protection. Critics often point out that there are practical questions about where incitement begins, and, for that matter, what constitutes harm. In reply, the principle is valuable for setting the framework for how such matters should be determined. That there are grey areas is typical of much of our life and law – as explored in Chapter 14, *How to live on slippery slopes*. People challenging our beliefs, even angrily but not threateningly, is no harm to us. People bashing our eardrums with loud beat music or road drillings is harmful to many – and being beaten up is harmful to all.

There is the particular question of whether offence counts as a harm. People can be offended by all manner of comment and activities – from seeing people kiss in public to just knowing that 'deviant' sexual practices, or even discussions of such, are quietly taking place next door. Being offended, though, is far removed from suffering physical or psychological harm. In fact, perhaps we can separate out offence from harm.

People usually are offended because they hold certain beliefs about what is morally wrong or just not right or decent. Offence is an indirect challenge to their beliefs rather than a harm to them; and such indirect challenges have the very value that we find in free speech. Beliefs deserve to be challenged – and, ideally, the challenge either corrects the beliefs or leads to their proper justification. This does not mean that we are justified to go out of our way to cause offence come what may. We need to be sensitive. Sexual activity in many public places causes offence, even disruption; but, as such activity can be engaged away from the public gaze, there is a simple solution. Well, there is a

simple solution unless exhibitionistic sex is the requirement. True, some authorities would love to control
what happens in the privacy of the bedroom, but what
happens there is usually between consenting adults, not
directly harming others. As Mill comments, it is a
'superstition and barbarism of the human race's infancy'
to impose restrictions on what people do privately.

A particularly problematic area is that of religious belief.
Even when it is acknowledged that religious beliefs
should be open to public challenge, it is often claimed
that the treatment must be respectful and serious. If
the treatment lacks such features, the believers claim
offence, sometimes on behalf of God: they know how
he feels. That position minimally suffers from an asymmetry, for many believers maintain their right to make
horrendous announcements about what will happen to
unbelievers, yet take offence at provocative claims or
cartoons about their God or gods. A danger that arises
when there is fear of causing offence – and fear of
reprisals – is that of undeclared self-censorship, such
as that which has taken place since the reaction of
certain Muslims to the Danish cartoons of Mohammed.

The intolerable

Toleration requires a neutral state, that is, a state that
holds the ring between diverse experiments of living.
The neutral state is a ringmaster, allowing radically

different acts to play as they wish, rather than being an orchestra's conductor, forcing all its citizens to sing from the same hymn sheet. It does not follow from this that the neutral state is neutral between values. One value it espouses is toleration; another is that there should be laws to prevent individuals from harming others without their consent. Those two values vie with each other. There are, of course, other values, concerning the provision of welfare and education, so that people acquire the relevant abilities to seek to fulfil themselves – to conduct their experiments of living.

Because of the high value that may be placed on autonomy, many people do respect people's freedom to express views, even intolerable views, about important matters concerning how we ought to live. Yet, we return to the puzzle of how far we should go when tolerating views that may influence people to adopt ways of living that are far removed from flourishing. We may puzzle whether we should tolerate views that advocate the enforced veiled life for women and an end to toleration. Perhaps we can rest content with our toleration of people expressing their intolerable views only when we have good reason to think that such toleration will lead to the rejection of those views rather than to a wider acceptance. Otherwise, we may prefer tolerating limits to our easy-going toleration or, at the very least, ensuring that the intolerable views are well met with good arguments against them.

The dangers of tolerating the expression of intolerable views need, of course, to be weighed against the dangers that may result from prohibitions, and also against other values concerning autonomy, welfare, community cohesion, fairness, and so on. The weighing is no fine science, nor fine art: it is, dare we say, some muddling. Paradoxically, the great virtue in toleration of the most intolerable views is only a virtue when we are confident that those views are pretty impotent. Otherwise, why risk tolerating them?

And so, we return to the rational and reasonable, the thoughtful and concerned John Stuart Mill:

> *The only freedom which deserves the name, is that of pursuing our own good in our own way, so long as we do not attempt to deprive others of theirs, or impede their efforts to obtain it.*

CHAPTER 25

How not to be a three-legged frog . . .

in a four-legged world of morality

'It's all relative' is often murmured by way of excuse. We hear of some horrendous laws elsewhere, and we may yield to the thought that the laws, though wrong for us, are right for them. The 'all is relative' mantra has tempting force; after all, we often disagree about right and wrong. Some thinkers even argue that *all* truth is relative. The driving thought may be that the concepts we use for worldly comprehension are human concepts. Yet, what else could they be? The argument is sometimes that all claims are open to interpretation; any interpretation is as justified as any other.

What is true for you is false for me

When Bill argues with Ben, they may seek resolution and reconciliation: 'Well, what you say is true for you, but false for me.' Peace breaks out because what was thought to be a single claim under dispute turns out to be two distinct claims, one about how things are for Bill, the other how things are for Ben. Over that, they agree. Forms of language may deceive. Bill's and Ben's assertions, for clarity's sake, have been revised; they are made relative to the speaker. The approach is that of Protagoras of Abdera, a Greek philosopher, a Sophist, of the fifth century BC. Protagoras understood truth as relative to human beings:

> *'Man is the measure of all things: of things which are, that they are, and of things which are not, that they are not.'*

Yet how may the strategy of relativism be taken?

Bill says that. . .	Ben says that. . .
whisky is nice,	whisky is nasty,
war is wrong,	war can be right,
grass and sky differ in colour,	grass and sky are same coloured,
no one is asleep.	at least one is asleep.

How plausible is it to see the above disputes as relative matters? After all, some relativists do apply their doctrine to all assertions.

In the case of the whisky tasting, we should have no difficulty in reconciling our Bill and Ben. What tastes great to Bill may well taste nasty to Ben. There is no big argument about whether in fact whisky is nice or nasty. We simply revise what is said into 'Bill likes the whisky; Ben does not'. When we move to the sleeping example, the plausibility of relativism radically drops. Whether there are sleepers in the room or not is no relative matter. Either it is true or it is false. Of course, there may be difficulty in telling whether someone really is asleep, but that is a distinct problem. When people in exasperation say, 'Well, it's true for you, but not for me', we should often understand them as saying, 'You believe that; but I don't'. Bill believes something is true; Ben believes otherwise. But that does not show that what is true is relative.

Turning to the colour example, our perceptions of the world are more, or less, discerning. The colour-blind grade the world's colours more coarsely than do others; and when differences in colour are spotted, the differences really exist even if others fail to spot them. There are, of course, further questions concerning quite how we should understand colours as existing independently, or not, of conscious beings. There are no such questions with niceness and nastiness. Objects are not nice or nasty independently of people's taste.

Man is the measure of all things

Protagoras battled with Socrates over whether all truth is relative. Protagoras, as we saw earlier, claimed it was – well, relatively so, we may suppose. Yet what may we say to someone who insists all truth is relative, that whenever people say that p is true, they are really saying that p is true for them? We may try some quick moves concerning consistency, assuming that the claim applies to itself. Perhaps Protagoras is saying that it is objectively (not relatively) true that all is relative; but then he contradicts himself, unless he means all truths apart from the claim that all is relative. However, once we have a grip on non-relative truth in one matter, we may wonder why stop there. Of course, Protagoras may just mean that his claim is true *for him*; but then we ought to question why we should take any notice of it if it is only true for him.

With the whisky, it was a relative matter whether it was nice or nasty; but it is an objective truth that Bill likes it, Ben does not. Any claim that Protagoras makes, according to Protagoras, is true for him; but that seems to carry the implication, as with Bill liking the whisky, that there is still an objective fact involved, namely that something is true for Protagoras. Further, in order for Protagoras to express his claim to us, he must assume that there is a common language – and that that is true, full stop. We may also wonder how anyone would get on in life asserting that it is true for him that he can fly, walk on water or turn himself into a peach. If such are just matters of opinion, maybe relativists should try out life based on such opinions.

Live and let live?

Relativism particularly attracts people when we are in the area of value judgements – of morality and beauty. Here we stick with morality; beauty arises in Chapter 33, *How to see beauty*.

Some people – often sociologists and anthropologists tagged 'cultural relativists' – argue that moral judgements are relative to the culture, the law and the religion. For example, stoning adulteresses and insisting that women should be veiled in public are right within the Iranian Islamic culture, but wrong in ours. Capital punishment is morally right in the culture of the United States, wrong in the current European, and so forth. Once again there is the self-referential dilemma, if we assume that 'all moral judgements are relative' is itself a moral judgement. Here is how. On the one hand, if the moral relativist is maintaining that all moral judgements are relative, then it too must be relative, so why should we take any notice? On the other hand, if 'all moral judgements are relative' is intended as an objective truth, then contradiction is reached.

Maybe we should understand moral relativists as presenting and encouraging a certain attitude to morality:

a shrug of the shoulders and 'it's just your opinion'. That attitude can be infectious; and relativists may be pleased. They may be serious people seeking to promote a tolerant attitude: 'live and let live'. Moral relativism and toleration, though, are different. Toleration is not committed to the crazy idea that all moral judgements are relative – 'true for some, false for others' – or the even crazier idea that all truth is relative. Were that so, there could be no good argument for the objective conclusion that we ought to be tolerant. Were morality relative, then whether one ought to be tolerant would be a relative matter too. And it would certainly not follow that we ought not to interfere in Iran or the United States as a matter of objective fact. Relativism is as likely to lead to intolerance as to tolerance.

Morality is often viewed as relativist and akin to taste because differences in moral judgments can arise with no obvious means of working out who is right. We may reflect how different times and societies prize different values: consider how attitudes towards chastity, self-sacrifice and honour have changed. Some philosophers, emotivists, have as a consequence understood moral claims as subjective expressions of approval or disapproval, of 'hurrahs' and 'boos'. Now, 'hurrahs' and 'boos' are neither true nor false.

We ought not to succumb so readily to those siren voices insisting great differences exist in moral views.

Yes, there are many moral dilemmas, but they often arise against a background of agreed principles and universal human needs. Most people by far in most societies have a sense that promises should be kept, that innocent people ought not to be killed, and that fairness is required. Problems arise when, for example, to keep a promise, someone's life is endangered: which principle takes priority?

Which principle takes priority may vary, depending on circumstances. By way of analogy, consider the mathematical operation of squaring a number. One and the same operation of squaring, if applied to 3 gives the answer 9; if applied to 4, it gives the answer 16. So, one and the same concern for people's overall welfare may, if in a country of poverty, deliver welfare at the cost of freedom of speech, whereas in a wealthy society, the priorities may be reversed.

'Everything is permitted'

When morality is being attacked as merely relative, some claim that as a matter of fact we always act out of our perceived self-interest. Of course, if all morality is relative, then there is no objectivity concerning how we ought to behave. Chapter 31, *How to hear the Sirens' song in safety*, assesses whether our behaviour is always self-interested, but here we ask whether we may choose our values.

'Everything is permitted' – whether the actions be those from self-interest or from other motivations. That is the line often given, once the existence of God is denied. It is a line of Jean-Paul Sartre's, sometimes mixed into his French existentialism, and it sums up the position of Ivan Karamazov in Dostoevsky's novel. Yet, is the line true? The argument relies on the proposition that God and only God can be the source of moral values. That proposition is the heart of the Divine Command Theory of morality. Although it still has adherents, it faces a dilemma that is difficult to resolve. It is a dilemma brought to the philosophical world in Plato's *Euthyphro* dialogue, though the dialogue is oriented to piety and what the gods love rather than morality and what God commands.

The dilemma arises in the following way: does God command the good because it is good, or is the good good because God commands it? Bringing it down to some detail, we probably all accept that torturing inno-cent children is morally wrong. Now, is such torturing only wrong because God condemns it, or does God condemn it because it is wrong? If the latter is correct, then we can see that its wrongness exists independently of what God condemns; hence, it may be argued, God is not an essential part of the story with regard to its (im)morality. But if the torturing is wrong only because God condemns it, then we should be led to accepting, it seems, that whatever God condemns is wrong and whatever God approves is right. Now, many religious believers assert that homosexual relations are condemned by God. If they are right, we should have to conclude that such relations are wicked. Yet many people not tied to particular readings of certain books labelled 'scripture' find it appalling that such private sexual activity could be deemed wicked. Of course, there is the reply that God by his very nature is good, so he would not issue horrendous commandments such as that witches should be burned, or people who leave Islam should be killed or contraception is morally wrong. That suggests, though, that we have a grip on what counts as morally good, independently of godly belief. Many atheists are, in fact, humanists, and they are far from arguing that everything is permitted. Rather, we should pay attention to our fellow feeling and sense of fairness and consistency; those underwrite our sense of what is right and wrong.

Three-legged frogs

Returning to relativism in general, there are different orders and degrees of relativism – and different responses. When considering universal claims – 'all' this – it is worth wondering whether they refer to themselves and the consequences if they do. Concerning self-reference, we wondered earlier whether the relativist claim is itself relativist. As for consequences, if all claims are just matters of opinion, then we should lack impetus to investigate, to do the hard work of discovery. We well know, though, that investigations have led to successful predictions of how the world works: the predictions are no mere matters of opinion.

As for morality in particular, if the true relativist position is that objectively anything goes, then it is saying that someone who kills and rapes and pillages is doing nothing wrong, full stop. Yet most people – including relativists, one suspects – acknowledge that such dreadful deeds are morally wrong. If the reply comes, 'Ah, but Dictator D committed genocide' or 'Thug T tortured and raped those innocent schoolgirls', let us respond in two ways. One response is that sometimes such dictators and thugs know that they are doing wrong. Another response is that even if they do jeer at morality, laugh at victims and mock the courts, this fails to show that human nature lacks moral awareness. That there are some three-legged frogs does not undermine the truth that it is in the 'froggy' nature to have four legs.

Here is one final example. Students are often inclined to be relativist over values – it is all a matter of opinion – yet they would soon complain if their excellent essays were given low marks with the tutor's sole explanation being, 'Well, as you say, it's all just a matter of opinion.'

CHAPTER 26

How not to be squeezed by time

. . . and how to find time for

past and future

The past is past – and the future is, well, future. Therefore, only the present exists. But how can we have memories and hopes if there is no past to remember and no future to anticipate? We cannot, then, dismiss time as an illusion. Further, without time there could be no change. That point suggests that time cannot be just another dimension, akin to the spatial. True, discussion of these matters passes the time; but, as Samuel Beckett quipped, time would have passed anyway. Yet, how does it do that?

The boundary

There is a tendency for people to say – perfectly reasonably – that the future does not exist, well, not yet. And, of course, the past is past, so the past no longer exists. Hence, all that we have is the present. Only the present is real. That is 'presentism'. But now we have an immediate problem, for what do we say of the present? If the present possesses duration however short, then that duration must consist either of some past or some future or both. But those elements of the present are not truly present: they are either past or future – and hence are non-existent. With such reasoning, we are driven to the conclusion that the present lacks duration.

We may conclude that the present is therefore a mere boundary between past and future. But that also is highly unsatisfactory, for if neither the past nor the future exists, then the boundary is a boundary between two non-existent times. How can there exist a boundary between items if there are no existent items to be bound? Further, how could we exist – with our experiences – just in a boundary without duration?

Something has surely gone wrong with the reasoning, so let us consider a typical rebuttal. The rebuttal is that past, present and future all equally exist. This is often known as the 'block universe' view or 'eternalism'. What we think of as present can therefore extend a little bit into the future and into the past without problem. Indeed, we understand our perception of the world as showing us the past. Because light does not travel instantaneously, what we see is how things were – and perhaps, more accurately, how they eternally, timelessly, are in relation to other things, past, present, future.

If past, present and future do all equally exist, we hit fresh puzzles or, at least, consequences that are counterintuitive. For example, our experience is of events changing their temporal location, changing from being in the future to being in the present to being in the past. Whatever that experience is, it cannot be a correct representation of reality if past, present and future all equally exist. Eternalism seems to have lost scope for the idea of changes taking place. Eternalism also makes our special concern about the future unjustified. We fear our non-existence after death, but not our non-existence before birth: recall our discussion of Lucretius in Chapter 17. We worry about the pain at the dentist tomorrow, but not the pain we suffered yesterday.

When it is suggested that past, present and future all exist, that ought not to imply that they all exist *now*, as opposed to in the past or future. Were that the case, we would need another 'super' time in which our ordinary past, present and future are all in the present, the 'super' time's *now*. Rather, on the eternalist view, they all exist outside of time. We have a grip on that in that we consider $2 + 2 = 4$ to be a timeless truth – and we may indeed think of numbers existing, but not as existing at this or that particular time. To exist outside of time – eternally – is not to exist at all times in time. We could, though, try a modified version of eternalism, the 'growing universe' view. Perhaps only the past and present exist: as more events pass from future to past, so the size of the existent past is ever increasing. Our 'present' may then extend a little way into the past. This still has the curiosity of the past existing in the same way as the present for us. To reflect more on the nature of the present, we need to look at how time may be conceived.

The passage of time

Time flows – well, so it is said. Yet it is difficult to make sense of time itself flowing or changing. After all, would we not require a higher time in order to tell how quickly or slowly time flowed? What we surely have in mind when we speak of time flowing is the fact that events come and go, that they may be in the future and then move into the past, and that certain events come after certain other events. In our time talk, we may be focusing on one or other (or both) of two series, each of which captures a characteristic of time, alluded to in the phrase 'the passage of time'. The two series were brought to prominence by J. M. E. McTaggart, who argued that time is illusory. Popping that controversial argument to one side, let us address the two series.

Under the A-series, events change their temporal characteristic – from future to present to past. Consider the natural changes of the seasons. The cherry tree awakens in spring: it blossoms. In due course, the blossom is blown away, then, in autumn, leaves begin to fall. Think of the development of a butterfly, from egg to larva to pupa to the fluttering by of the butterfly, and then the butterfly's demise. We are using the A-series when we make statements with tenses, talking about what will happen and what has happened to the tree or the butterfly. Time, in contrast to space, is the dimension of change. The A-series gives voice to that change. A piece of seaside rock may have different layers of colour; but that alone does not manifest any changes occurring in the rock. In contrast, place a dark metal poker in a raging fire and the heat causes the poker to change to hot redness gradually along its length.

The A-series guides us to another series, the B-series. The B-series is the sequence of events, standing in the relation of before, simultaneous with, and after. In the B-series, Purcell's birth and death occurred before Mahler's birth and death, which occurred before Benjamin Britten's birth and death. Events as ordered by the B-series never change their position. The B-series, it seems, fails to manifest change: it is static and radically differs from the A-series. Hence, as change is real, we need to make sense of time's A-series and not rely solely on the B-series. Let us look more closely.

The reality of the present

Presentists are those who believe that only the present exists. We have not, of course, sorted out how they can make sense of that, bearing in mind that the present requires some duration, but whether or not only the present exists – or whether past, present and future exist – what reality is there to the present? We approach the question by asking what temporal characteristics would exist were there no conscious beings.

We assume as true that many years ago, the Universe existed without any sentient creatures. Presumably we accept that in the future, there will be times when no conscious beings exist. If we flip back to many years ago, we surely accept that the Earth orbited the Sun, that trees were blown down, that the oceans' waves ebbed and flowed. So, the B-series applied those many years ago: certain events came before others; certain events came after others. Yet did any events happen in the present? Was there the 'now' of the A-series from whence some events were future and not yet now, and other events were past and no longer now?

Those who answer yes to the above question are committed to the A-series applying even without conscious beings. Indeed, they make the point that time essentially involves change, and change requires events to have the A-series characteristics. With regard to space, if there are no conscious beings, then there is no particular place that is 'here'. In contrast, with time there is a 'now', it seems, even if there are no creatures to perceive it as now.

How may those who reject the A-series reply? Well, they understand the concepts of the A-series – the tensed talk; the concepts of past, present, future – as being relational: they relate events in the world to the perceivers' utterances or thoughts. When you say that the Sun is shining now, all that is being said is that the Sun is shining at the same time as your utterance. There is nothing more to 'nowness' than that. When you rightly argue that there will be more economic chaos next year, economic chaos stands in the relation of 'after' with regard to your arguing. There is nothing more to the future than that. The rejection of the A-series as holding in reality independently of observers is an eternalist rejection. Time is but another dimension. It is akin to space for, when you say that the explosion took place *here*, you are merely saying that it took place in the same location as your utterance. Were there no observers, there would be no 'here'.

Global freezes

Despite the above, we may insist that changes do occur, requiring time as per the A-series. We may, though, now ask whether time requires changes. Can we make sense of items persisting through time – of time passing – if no changes occur at all? Can time just pass, with nothing else happening? Probably the natural answer is 'No', but Sydney Shoemaker, a US philosopher, offered an ingenious thought experiment.

Suppose the Universe consists of three distinct zones, A, B and C. Each zone regularly freezes for an hour, with no change taking place at all, but then everything carries on just as before. Although the freezes are regular, they occur at different times, depending on the zone. The local freezes can be readily spotted from the unfrozen zones. Maybe no light escapes from the frozen zone; perhaps all is blackness.

Zones B and C can tell that zone A freezes for its hour every three years. Zones A and C can tell that zone B freezes every four years. Zone C freezes every five years, A and B note. So, the scientists throughout the zones have good evidence for the theory that all three zones, A, B and C, regularly freeze together every 60 years. Every 60 years, there is a global freeze, with time still passing for an hour. Of course, the scientists have no direct way of telling that such global freezes happen. They could resist the theory of the global freeze; they could argue that the regular local freezes occur, except at the 60th year; but that feels ad hoc. The example at least seems to establish that there could be evidence for global freezes and that it could be rational to accept that they occur. Of course, there is no reason to think that they occur in our world.

Back to the present

If only the present exists, then, according to some, it is a mystery that we are able to talk about items that are not present, items such as historical characters – Socrates, Shakespeare, and Spinoza – and future events concerning comets, catastrophes and coronations. Yet, if the eternalists are right, our common-sense understanding of change, and of the past and future being intrinsically different from the present, is deeply mistaken.

The above difficulties suggest that we need to take a fresh look. There is a widely held belief that if a proposition is true, then there needs to be a truth-maker. It is true that Plato admired Socrates. What makes that true? Presentists seek something in the present. In contrast, eternalists have the past fact of Plato's admiring Socrates as possessing as much existence as the present existence of you the reader reading right now. Resisting both approaches we make the simple point that what makes it true that Plato admired Socrates is the fact that once was present, namely Plato's admiring Socrates. What makes it true that there will be an American presidential election in 2020 is the fact that in so many years the election will be present.

Returning to how we should avoid being squeezed by a duration-less present or 'now', maybe our opening puzzle results from a bewitchment by abstract finer and finer divisions being applied to the world. We encountered such bewitchment with infinite divisibility in Chapter 20, *How to be a monkey endlessly typing*. When discussing 'now' and the 'present', we have different durations in mind, depending on the context. Our present century is the 21st, but that does not mean that it is squashed into an instant. When we hear a musical theme unfolding, we do not hear it 'at an instant'. Right now you are reading this book. That does not mean that your reading of a book or a chapter or a sentence or even a word can be squashed into a moment. True, we live, love and lust in the present, but not in a squashed present – and not without genuine memories of what once was present and genuine anticipations of what will be present. Arguing about time does, indeed, take time.

CHAPTER 27

How to outdo artificial intelligence

. . . and choose where to sit

Human beings show intelligent behaviour – well, sometimes. Human beings can think, deploy concepts, and assess and judge happenings in the world. And with that simple reflection in mind, we may head off to chimps and gorillas, pigs and dolphins, seeking to discover the nature of their intelligence and what understanding they may have. Here, though, we head off in a different direction, one of equal fascination to philosophers. This direction takes us to machines and computers, robots and automata.

Thermostats and chess-playing computers

People respond to the world, and their responses manifest an understanding of what is going on, what is likely to go on, and what they want to go on. The understanding could be a misunderstanding; the wants could be foolish. Whether mistaken or not, the psychological states have direction and content. For example, your thought may be directed towards the

man on the windowsill, the content being 'Don't jump!'
– or perhaps even 'Jump!'

A person peers out of the window, stares up at the black
cloud. A few minutes later, she is picking up an umbrella
and leaving the house. We, her observers, conclude that
she believes it will rain and has no yen for wetness. She
has an understanding of the world and a desire by way
of outcome. Indeed, we have an understanding of her
understanding, though we could be mistaken. Perhaps
she believed the sun would soon appear and so she
wanted the umbrella as a shading device. Either way,
all we saw were bodily movements resulting from her
environment; we interpreted them as conscious activities, as intelligent behaviour. Contrast with thermostats.
Thermostats respond to the environment; but we have
no inclination to consider the thermostat intelligent.
The thermostat is not judging and reflecting upon the
local temperature. It has no desire to ensure a constant
temperature by switching the boiler on and off. When
it goes wrong and leaves the temperature rising, we may
be annoyed but not at its misunderstanding.

Perhaps thermostats are too simple. Chess-playing
computers can respond to numerous chess formations
and win games even when playing grand masters. Yet
we rightly doubt whether computers understand the
game of chess, possess beliefs about the current state
of play, with the aim of winning. Perhaps chess-playing

computers also are too simple. The question now arises: what type of behaviour should lead us to believe that a machine understands what is going on, possesses aims and desires? What would show a machine to be 'minded', to be artificially intelligent?

Alan Turing – the British mathematician who broke the Enigma code, a kindly man driven to suicide because of repressive laws against homosexuality – suggested an approach. Suppose a computer, or thermostat for that matter, could engage in conversations with human beings and, as a result, be taken to be human. That would show the computer to possess intelligence as humans do. Going further than Turing, maybe it would reveal the computer as having beliefs and desires; and, further still, perhaps that just is what it is to be in such states. Of course, we assume that the computer cannot be seen: that would give the game away. We need also to restrict the conversations, to avoid other give-aways, such as the computer asking to be oiled (well, whatever computers need), yet not restrict ourselves to remarks about which chess piece to move next.

The above is the rough idea of the Turing Test in which the same questions are put to A and B, both hidden behind a screen: one an intelligent human being, the other the computer. If, by their answers, we cannot assess which is which, then we should conclude that the computer is as intelligent as the human. If we do not so conclude, we should be guilty of a preference for biology over silicon chips. We should be, so to speak, biochauvinistic. Indeed, Turing writes:

> *Machines take me by surprise with great frequency . . .*
> *A computer would deserve to be called intelligent if it*
> *could deceive a human into believing that it was human.*

So, according to defenders of artificial intelligence, if a machine manipulating symbols passes the Turing Test, perhaps that is even sufficient to show that the machine is thinking and believing. The slogan is: the mind is to the brain as the program is to the machine, the computer, the hardware.

The Chinese Room

With the Turing Test in mind, the American John Searle produced a much discussed thought experiment. What happens in Searle's Chinese Room tale is meant to be analogous to what happens when we use a computer; it is meant to be analogous however 'intelligent' our computers may become, if they work by manipulating symbols. There are three components to computers and to the Chinese Room – and, for that matter, to a thermostat: an input, an internal process, and an output. The argument is as follows.

Chinese speakers outside the room push slips of paper under the room's door; on the slips are written Chinese characters. Let us call the slips 'invites'. In the room is an English, non-Chinese-speaking person: let us call him 'Hermit'. Hermit is surrounded by reply slips in Chinese, piled up in baskets – or, better, neatly filed. He possesses a highly complicated rule book, written in English, which tells him which reply slips, which symbols, to put together to push out of the room, depending upon which invites he has received and their structure. Those replies form the output. As the invites come in, Hermit consults the rule book, shuffles through the baskets and files, and finds the symbols to send as replies.

The Chinese speakers outside the room receive replies that make sense, given their invites. They are impressed. The invites could in fact be simple questions about the world or about a story that has been set out (also in Chinese) or they could be reflections on political matters. What is clear – at least to Searle – is that Hermit does not understand Chinese: he neither understands the invites nor his replies. He neither recognizes the symbols as Chinese, nor the meaning of the invites and replies. He is merely processing symbols in accordance with certain rules: he is handling the syntax, but lacks a grasp of what is meant, of the semantics.

Any Hermit-like figure in the Chinese room would pass a Turing Test for understanding Chinese, yet clearly he lacks all such understanding. If we accept that conclusion, we should then agree that computer programs that operate solely by symbol manipulations, whatever the details of their architecture and even though they are churning out answers that make sense to recipients, are not thereby understanding anything themselves; they have no grasp of the meaning, no understanding of what is being said. Symbol manipulation is insufficient for understanding, for intelligence.

Maybe the room thinks?

The Chinese Room story focuses on the individual, Hermit, in the room. Hermit does not understand Chinese, but that does not establish that the combination of Hermit with rule book and potential invites and basket of replies does not understand Chinese. This reply to Searle takes the daring pathway of saying that the room and its contents overall understand Chinese. Yet there is a reply to that reply. Suppose Hermit has an amazing memory: he remembers the rule book in detail and remembers all the different symbols in the replies' baskets. In other words, all the symbol information is present in Hermit – and when the invites come along, he writes out the replies, following the rule book. Once again, we should surely be inclined to say that Hermit lacks any understanding of what is being requested and what his answers mean.

Of course, there is a brave reply to the modified Chinese Room such that Hermit becomes the room. The brave reply is that Hermit understands Chinese, but fails to realize that he does. Bravery, though, does not secure truth. Why should we believe he has such understanding, yet be unaware that he does? For us sensibly to believe that some understanding is going on, we need to refer to more than the mere distribution of symbols. A basic criticism of Searle's story remains, though, namely, that it it is operating at too simple a level. Searle's model is no more interesting than that of a chess-playing computer. Once we build up some greater complexity, it may be that we should lack the intuitive response that 'obviously Hermit does not understand'.

Certain properties only emerge once a system is sufficiently complex. A pile of grains of sand illustrates emergence. So long as the pile does not pass beyond a certain size, it remains static. However, at a certain point the forces cease to cancel each other out, and as more grains are added we find ourselves confronted by a sand-swept avalanche. Dynamism has suddenly emerged as a result of increased complexity. So, flows the speculation, using the sands as an analogy, if the baskets of symbols build up, with the rule book becoming more complex, maybe understanding emerges.

Getting Hermit to the dance

Do we have any good reason to believe that understanding can emerge in the above way and so is just a matter of symbol manipulation? Let us see why 'Yes' remains implausible, assuming that we are talking solely of symbol manipulation, however complex. We return to Hermit. The initial Chinese Room probably led us to think of answers to questions without any behavioural implications save for outputs by way of symbols. When a system is isolated in that way, as it is for Hermit, we have a system akin to the unthinking chess-playing computer or even the more minimal thermostatic way of life. There is, so far, no reason to think understanding is taking place.

Suppose the invites in Chinese are, though, invitations to a dance, to wine and dine next week, even to join someone in bed tonight. Suppose the rule book – true, the rule book is now becoming a very curious rule book – leads to answers, some 'Yes', some 'No', with various caveats about time and place. Hermit gives those answers, but has no idea what they mean. It would be sheer serendipity if he turned up at the dance, the restaurant, the airport or the bed. Were Hermit to understand what he said, he should be disposed to behave accordingly – or at least be aware that he is not going to do what he said he would do. Yet, as he lacks any idea of what he has said, he neither behaves accordingly nor possesses awareness of misleading his audience. Before there exists any plausibility in the suggestion that Hermit is understanding Chinese, the symbol manipulation of artificial 'intelligence' must be linked with appropriate behaviour. That leads, of course, to the question of the nature of that linkage – and it is but a speculative thought that greater and greater complexity in the symbol manipulation could lead to the emergence of appropriate behaviour. The speculation is all the more pronounced if we contrast the 'intelligent' desk-bound computer or a clanking robot and the embodied human heading off to the sea for a swim.

Know how

Human understanding, intelligence, requires knowing how to handle things in the world – and that 'knowing how' is involved in our possession of concepts. Knowing how to cycle, how to swim, how to caress a lover, is not just (or even) a matter of grasping a sequence of propositions saying that you do this and this, and then that and that. Knowing 'inside out' the instruction manual on how to ride a bicycle or do the breast stroke is no guarantee at all that you know how to ride the bicycle or do the breast stroke – or indeed caress the lover's breasts. Furthermore, numerous concepts that we use every day require awareness of what it is to live a life as a human being, what it is to find certain items beautiful, to find certain events disturbing.

Consider the concept 'bed'. Our understanding of it requires an awareness of what it is to feel tired, of how sofas and even floors can be used as beds, of how beds are part of the furniture, and so on. Understanding seems necessarily linked to our biological state and the fact that typically we can move around the world, generating hopes and fears. That is how we are more than a thermostat, how we outdo 'artificial intelligence'. Perhaps the concept of understanding as an emergent property can still enter the story. Understanding emerges from the increased complexity of our interactions with the world. We are part of the moving and movable furniture.

CHAPTER 28

How to deceive yourself . . .

by leaving a hand behind

When I deceive you, I am in the know and you are not. But when I deceive myself I am in the know and not in the know, which sounds contradictory. Yet self-deception exists, or so it seems. A lover may be all too aware of the tell-tale signs that his partner is having an affair, yet somehow he blots that awareness out: how else can he cope? Another, with jealousy at heart, may know her partner is faithful, yet 'see' evidence everywhere of infidelity. So, how can philosophy make sense of such curious states of psychology?

A young woman sets the scene

A young woman senses the romantic intentions that her companion cherishes towards her. It is a café scene and, as they talk, the man takes her hand for the first time. The young woman is all intellect, talking of lofty matters, of philosophy, of life; and she leaves her hand in his, as if separate from her awareness.

Her hand left thus will assuredly be read by the man as encouraging some sexual advance. Although she knows that, she 'does not notice' her hand left there. She certainly is not encouraging him – or is she? Jean-Paul Sartre presents the scene as self-deception. The woman, at some level, knows what she is doing; yet she disguises the fact from herself. We shall return to the scene; but first we review typical philosophical analyses of self-deception. For simplicity's sake, we stay with the fidelity concerns.

Deception, when of another, is no puzzle at all. When Daniel deceives Edward, he intentionally misleads. Dan knows, for example, that someone (not Dan) is having an affair with Ed's girlfriend. Ed also knows. Dan, though, with a silver tongue or the brashness of pretended conviction, makes Ed see things differently. Ed becomes convinced that all is well with his relationship. He has been deceived by Dan. He may one day meet the truth again, or he may remain deceived. A serially unfaithful wife may convince her husband for all his life that she is sexually faithful.

Puzzles in self-deception

In self-deception, using the above example, Dan and Ed become one and the same individual. Ed knows his girlfriend is unfaithful, but convinces himself otherwise. The knowledge disturbs him, stimulating him into a comforting belief, which is inconsistent with the disturbing facts of which he is aware.

Knowledge forms no essential component of the story. Self-deception may occur when the starting psychological state is merely belief. Ed firmly believes that his girlfriend is unfaithful; but, because of the resultant distress, he convinces himself that all is well on the fidelity front. Of course, if in fact all is well and Ed's manoeuvres end up with his holding a true belief, then Ed is not being deceived; but he has still, puzzlingly, managed to move from a distressing belief to its opposite and the resultant emotional calm. In fact, sometimes the deceptive switch may move the believer from calm to distress. A jealous character may know, at some level, that his girlfriend's behaviour is genuinely faithful and loving, yet, for reasons unknown, he is impelled to read things otherwise, with the consequent misery of holding a deceptive belief, namely, that she is having affairs.

How can the knowledge or belief that p lead to belief that not-p such that the outcome is understood by outsiders as a case of self-deception and not mere wishful thinking or change of mind? Others can tell that Ed's knowledge of his girlfriend's infidelity has somehow been blotted out. They may have seen Ed's shocked face when he found hotel receipts, new earrings and his partner's newly found interest in poetry;

yet now they see how that evidence is explained away by Ed as innocent – or is never mentioned again. Did Ed intentionally manage to blot out the truth about his girlfriend? Does he – somehow – hold contradictory beliefs? Ed surely knows his girlfriend is unfaithful, yet believes otherwise. Or so it seems.

Sensitivity to evidence

Beliefs about how the world is cannot just be decided at will. People may tell us that it is up to us what we believe, but it is not really up to us – it is up to how the world strikes us. You are on African safari, unconcerned; but then, surveying the scene, you spot an elephant charging in your direction. You cannot readily choose not to believe that there is an elephant en route. What you believe is sensitive to evidence – in this case, seeing an elephant charging towards you. Our beliefs necessarily are beliefs about how we take the world to be. It would be magical were we able deliberately to conjure up beliefs whenever we wanted. It would be as if we could choose to make the world in an image of our own wants. Maybe a god could do that but mere humans cannot. The slogan is: beliefs aim at truth. Our aim may be poor. The slogan implies that if we believe that *p*, then *we believe* that *p* is true. It does not imply that *p* really is true.

Despite the above, we may sense truth in Caesar's observation: generally people willingly believe what they want to believe. And without resort to Caesar, we may reflect how people often buy newspapers that hold their preferred political stance – to reinforce that stance. Our existing beliefs and attitudes determine, in part, the evidence to which we expose ourselves. If we select the 'right' evidence – change our newspapers – we may find ourselves with changed beliefs. A mere belief change, though, is insufficient for it to be self-deception. Self-deception requires more – and maybe less. The more is by way of either the self-deceivers' motivations in selecting the evidence or their intentions to form the new belief. The less is that the original belief, it seems, continues to be held as well as the new, usually benign belief.

Now, when one person is deceived by another, the deceived state is often intended, but not always. We may be careless about the evidence or focus on certain facts rather than others; as a result we unintentionally misinform. Such non-intentional cases may form a better model for self-deception than the intentional. The non-intentional model frees us from working out how a person can intentionally self-deceive. Instead, the model has the person possessing certain desires, hopes and fears – certain motivations – and they guide his reading of the evidence, leading to the deceptive belief.

Motivation or intention

Ed, as described above, is deeply distressed by the hotel receipts and so forth. They carry the news that his girlfriend is unfaithful, news that he cannot bear. Without conscious intent, he sees the evidence anew. Perhaps the receipts belong to a female friend – after all, they are not in his girlfriend's name and 'Lesley' could be female. And are not the earrings from ages ago? With selective attention and renderings, Ed comes genuinely to believe that all is well. This motivational approach to self-deception requires no reference to conscious intentions. The self-deceivers' psychological states are such that the self-deceivers genuinely review the evidence and reach the happier conclusions, the disturbing beliefs now abandoned.

The above may well be how self-deception often works, but we may sense that there are cases where it seems as if the individual has deliberately and intentionally set about to move himself into a deceived state. Intentions, though, cannot be successful if they aim at switching on new beliefs, 'just like that'; but they may be successful if setting procedures in motion that work slowly and indirectly, procedures relying on poor memory, hypnosis or even drug-induced states. Ed may ask friends to reassure him of his girlfriend's love, whatever they really think, confident that after a while he will have forgotten about how that reassurance came about. A classic example of intentions generating a belief is through use of Pascal's Wager.

Pascal argues that it is prudent for an atheist to believe in God 'just in case'. The trauma in attending church and confessing sins is nothing compared to the eternal rewards possibly reaped and the dangers of eternal damnation. Pascal's argument, a probability argument, has defects. After all, which religion's God should an atheist seek to back? Our atheist, though, falls for the argument; but he cannot simply switch on a godly existential belief.

Our atheist, given his prudence, may place himself in circumstances where the required belief is likely to be gained. He may regularly attend church, mingling with believers whom he respects, reading the scriptures and so forth. Beliefs are contagious. Sure enough, he ends up believing. In this case, there is no problem in his remembering that he took a cynical calculating route to godly belief. The route need not undermine the sincerity of his new belief. Pathways to God are multitudinous.

Partitions, contradictions and the Hard Puzzle

In the self-deceptions just discussed, the deceived individuals do not end up holding contradictory beliefs at the same time. The threat of contradiction is avoided by means of a 'temporal partition': the threat is avoided because, in more usual language, our beliefs change over time. What we once believed, we no longer do. The self-deception puzzle has reduced to that of how the individual engaged in self-deception moves from what he once believed to the new replacement belief. And that puzzle is dissolved by stressing how his desires lead him to select or reinterpret evidence, or how his intentions place him in new evidence-gathering circumstances. The bite in self-deception returns, though, when we reflect on cases where it seems both that there has been a conscious intention to move into a deceived state and that the original belief is held as well as the new and deceptive one. That is the Hard Puzzle of self-deception. It rests upon the seeming intention to accept contradictory beliefs.

Now, we often unwittingly hold contradictory beliefs. We arrive at two opposed beliefs via different routes: we fail to spot the beliefs as contradictory. This may be because we have not brought them together, transparently, in consciousness; or it may be because, even if consciously considered, we fail to see how one contradicts the other. We may know what a prime number is, yet also consciously believe (wrongly) that the number 511 is prime. To sum up, Ed can believe that p and also believe that not-p, but arguably not transparently in consciousness at the same time. That Ed can hold contradictory beliefs is different from the following impossibility: that Ed believes that p and also it is not the case that Ed believes that p.

The Hard Puzzle in self-deception remains. The Hard Puzzle typically has the individual, because of his distress at the truth, consciously intending to let himself hold and live under a false, but more blissful belief. Philosophers who acknowledge the puzzle's existence seek to soften it by partitioning the individual's psychology. Tripartite divisions may be introduced, as by Plato or, more recently, by Freud. Yet in breaking up the individual's psychology, puzzles do not vanish. They appear in the question: which part of the 'soul', the person, is doing quite what to which other part? And with which part does the individual identify? The problems in answering those questions may explain why many other philosophers flip back to the non-intentional model as the only one that may cope with self-deception.

The young woman's bad faith

When Sartre discusses self-deception, he focuses on its morality. Such deception is *mauvaise foi*, bad faith. To return to Sartre's young woman at this chapter's beginning, whatever she is up to, she cannot be representing her actions to herself as deception. As Sartre writes, the project of *mauvaise foi* must itself be in *mauvaise foi*.

Of course, we may challenge Sartre's understanding of the scene: perhaps the young woman is consciously keeping her options open: to withdraw the hand may be seen as an outright rejection of the man. But how may we make sense of the scene if taken as one of genuine self-deception? Sartre gives an example of counting cigarettes – splendidly politically incorrect these days. Astonishingly, indeed, public images of the chain-smoking Sartre often now have the cigarette in hand or mouth erased. Still, in counting his cigarettes, Sartre need not be reflecting that he is counting, even though if asked what he is doing, he would immediately be able to give the correct counting answer. Now, the young woman is not reflecting that she has left her hand in the man's hand, but, if asked, how would she answer? 'I didn't notice' – yet that is a denial of what she surely must have noticed.

When going to sleep, we may act with purpose; yet, if wise, we avoid reflection on that purpose. The young woman certainly has purpose in leaving her hand in the man's, yet her lofty conversation prevents her from acknowledging that purpose. 'We put ourselves into *mauvaise foi* as we put ourselves to sleep.' Well, as this chapter has failed to explain how intentional self-deception is possible, at least the puzzle may keep readers awake instead of falling asleep. How we deceive ourselves remains a hard puzzle.

CHAPTER 29

How to love what does not exist . . .
what does not exist at any time

There are possible worlds in which pigs are flying and your
neighbour owns up to being madly in love with you. There
are possible worlds in which living creatures do not exist.
Yet talk of possible worlds concerns mere possibilities.
What is their value for our understanding of this, the actual
world? After all, why should 'might be's and 'might have
been's be relevant if they are not really and have never
really been? Intriguingly, though, our very understanding of
the world hangs heavily on possibilities, even those never
to be realized.

Opera, running and conditionals

Ludmilla is a frequent opera goer. You would love to
accompany her to her favourite opera, performing later
this week. Obviously, you need to know whether she
is going. Or is that quite right? She may be going, but
she goes only if she knows you are not. Who can be
sure how she feels about you? What you need to know

is: if you ask to accompany her, will she go? That is a conditional proposition about the future; you need to know if it is true.

You see the bus approaching the bus stop. You could run for it. Obviously, you need to know if the bus is going to stop. Or is that quite right? It may be going to stop, but not if the driver sees you running for it. He may put his foot down on the accelerator; he could be that kind of driver. To tell whether a run is a wasted run, you need to know whether, if you run for it, the bus will stop: that is another conditional proposition about the future.

We rely upon countless such conditional propositions daily. Yet they concern possibilities, and they concern possibilities that may never become actual, may never be realized. To use our examples, perhaps you do not pluck up courage to ask Ludmilla or you do not bother to run for the bus. In such cases, the conditionals concern unrealized possibilities; they are counter to how the facts turned out – hence, they are *counterfactuals*. Had you asked Ludmilla, would she have agreed? Had you run for the bus, would it have stopped? Surely there are true answers, one way or another, to those questions. Perhaps it is false that, had you asked Ludmilla, she would have agreed. Perhaps, had you run for the bus, it would have stopped. Maybe the bus did not stop, but would have done so, had you run. Maybe

Ludmilla did attend the opera, but had you asked, would have resisted attendance.

Our examples illustrate the point that we certainly do reflect on such possibilities – and those counter to fact – in order to decide what to do. It looks, therefore, as if we do need to consider many counterfactuals as being true or false, as having a truth value. We may, though, rightly wonder what makes them true or false, assuming that they should be treated as such, and how we can tell, if we can, which truth values they have.

Bows and arrows and more

Before we spin the possible worlds, let us tiptoe a little further into counterfactuals. Hitler was anti-Semitic. Consider: had Hitler been Jewish, then he would have been anti-Semitic. Presumably, we think it is highly likely that that counterfactual is false. Hitler sought to conquer Europe. Consider: had Hitler possessed nuclear weapons, then he would have threatened to use them. That counterfactual, we probably suspect, is true. In contrast to those examples, we engage many counter-factuals upon which we lose grip. Had Hitler been a non-Jewish Austrian born in Israel, he would not have been anti-Semitic – or would he? Had Julius Caesar been the American President who ordered the invasion of Iraq, he would have encouraged use of nuclear weapons. Well, maybe – but maybe instead – had Julius

Caesar been the American President, he would have preferred use of bows and arrows.

In assessing counterfactuals' truth values, we need to judge what we hold constant in the background. With our suppositions about Julius Caesar, we are holding firm his character of ruthlessness. In one supposition we pop him into the American presidency with nuclear weapons available. In the other supposition, perhaps we are thinking of him with only his primitive technology available, or perhaps we are thinking of him as so wedded to his familiar fighting technology that he dismisses the newfangled nuclear.

Here is a down-to-earth example. Silvana is feeling sick. Probably the strawberries were the cause. Had Silvana not eaten the strawberries, she would not now be feeling sick. Or maybe the sickness resulted from the glass of champagne. Had Silvana not eaten the strawberries, she would still be feeling sick – but had she resisted the champagne, she would have been fine.

Silvana's strawberries and possible worlds

'Possible worlds' can be useful in understanding counterfactuals. We need, though, to avoid some worldly confusions. The great 17th-century German philosopher Gottfried Leibniz promoted the use of possible worlds for dealing with logic and metaphysics. We have already met Leibniz through his identity of indiscernibles and apex of rationality.

When philosophers speak of the Universe, they usually have in mind everything that is actual (apart from a God, if discussing the Universe's creator). Physicists sometimes speak of there being other universes, maybe ones that we cannot access, but they are still actual universes, as ours is an actual universe. The philosophers' universe, or world, covers the whole lot. Possible worlds are, therefore, usually understood as distinct from the physicists' other existing universes. The caveat 'usually' is added because an influential philosopher, David Lewis, did think of possible worlds as existing just as our world exists. Lewis was a modal realist, considering some possible worlds to contain counterparts of us. Here, though, we need to treat all possible worlds as merely possible, except one, namely, this world in which we live; this world is also actual.

In this book's introduction, we spoke of how it is contingent that Barack Obama is President in 2012. He might have lost the election. He might have gone in for pig farming instead of politics. There are possible worlds which contain Obama, yet in which he is not President, but is pig farming. There are possible worlds in which he became a Republican and not a Democrat, and so forth. Necessary truths, in contrast to contingent truths, are ones that are true in all possible worlds. There are possible worlds in which the word 'nineteen' might have been used to designate an even number. However, in all possible worlds, the number 19 is an odd number.

Now, what makes it true (assuming it is) that, had Silvana not eaten the excess strawberries, then she would not now be feeling sick? Well, reflect on those possible worlds in which our Silvana resisted the excess. Certainly, there is at least one possible world – no doubt, there are many – in which Silvana resisted and did not fall sick. It is true that, had Silvana not eaten the strawberries, she would not now be feeling sick, because at least one of those possible worlds is far more similar to the actual world than the possible worlds in which she resisted the strawberries, yet still felt sick.

Disappointment, causality and circularity

Our experience tells us that an excessive quantity of strawberries is more likely to cause illness than a single glass of champagne. Of course, there are possible worlds in which the constitutions of human beings and strawberries are so different that harms never result, but those are possible worlds far removed from the actual world. There is a possible world in which Silvana ate no strawberries, but ate instead the mud on the seashore and was ill; but that is a world very distant from the actual world of Silvana's behaviour. None of this tells us for certain what caused Silvana's sickness. 'Possible worlds' talk is exciting, yet – once we reflect – we may see that its value is merely that of the picturesque. The talk alone does not tell us which counterfactuals are true. The idea of possible worlds makes us reflect on what we hold firm as background. One background firmness consists in the laws of nature. There is a possible world in which Silvana turns into a strawberry, but that is remote from our actual world with its laws of nature.

There is danger of circularity above. Consider the causal relation and how it differs from, if we may so say, a casual relation. Silvana sneezes; the dog nearby barks. That may well have been a mere casual coincidence – or the sneeze may have been the cause, startling the hound. For Silvana to have been the cause, the following needs to be true (it seems): had Silvana not sneezed – and all other things compatible with that remain the same – then the dog would not have barked. In judging which possible worlds are closest to ours, we need a grasp of which occurrences are *causally* related and which are *casually* related; yet our grasp of that distinction is in terms of certain counterfactual conditionals picturesquely displayed by possible worlds.

Counterfactuals lurking

The grasp of A causing B requires a grasp of counterfactuals. Let us emphasize this through a general example. First, suppose that the following is true: if A occurs, then B occurs. Further, A does occur, so B also occurs. That could still just be a casual coincidence. *Post hoc ergo propter hoc* – after this, therefore because of this – is the fallacy of treating a casual connection as sufficient for a causal. Secondly, then, we need the counterfactual: had A not occurred, then B would not have occurred. Counterfactuals are hence also important in distinguishing between regularities that are mere coincidences and those that are laws of nature, seemingly built within the world's fabric. Consider: all copper expands when heated. That feels like a law of nature. It supports the counterfactual: had this ring been made from copper, then it would have expanded when heated. In contrast, consider: all the coins in that room are made from copper. So, were we to place this (silver) coin in that room, it would be made from copper. That is obviously false – unless that room possesses powers that turn all coins to copper.

Counterfactuals also lurk in our understanding of people's characters, dispositions and states of knowledge. If Silvana is loyal, then she would have behaved in certain ways had she been in such-and-such challenging circumstances. In Chapter 6, *How to know what knowledge is*, the analysis of knowledge led us to think of someone knowing that *p* – for example, Sophie's knowing that Istanbul is the capital of Turkey – as possessing a certain stability in being right about the matter. Minimally, we need the truth: had Istanbul not been the capital, then Sophie would not have believed it to be so.

We have seen how we rely on what does not exist, but is only possible, and we have spoken freely of counterfactuals as possessing truth values. Yet many philosophers demand 'truth makers' if there are to be truths. They then point out that there is nothing about the actual world to make counterfactuals true (or false), just as they point to difficulties in finding truth makers for the past and future, as seen in Chapter 26, *How not to be squeezed by time*. That suggests that counterfactuals need to be accepted or rejected in some way without treating them as true or false. Let us, though, swing back round to whether you should bother to run for the bus.

Suppose you do run for the bus and it stops. Now flip to a near possible world in which you do not run. From that world, you consider the counterfactual 'Had I run, it would have stopped'. It looks as if you are considering something true. To misquote Shakespeare, 'There are more truths in heaven and earth – and in possible worlds – than are dreamt of in some philosophers' philosophy.'

CHAPTER 30

How not to be left looking after the clothes . . .

and be regimented by logic

To learn that Pamela was left in a pickle would be challenging, if you were unaware of the 'pickle' word's metaphorical use. A picture could come to mind of Pamela floating in an urn of vinegar. That would be a right pickle for Pamela in both senses of the word. Plights, of course, are very different from pickled vegetables. Our language can mislead – and so can logicians' attempts at regimentations of language into fixed logical structures.

What a pickle

Pamela was in a pickle; but if we then do something for Pamela's sake, we ought not to search for a 'sake' as an entity additional to Pamela. Gilbert Ryle (whom we met in Chapter 8, *How to be a ghost in the machine*) tells a tale almost as trivial as our 'sake' and 'pickle', yet one that made a point of some influence. A visitor asks to see the university; so, we show her the senate building, the library, the colleges, the research laboratories and so forth. She is very impressed; but then she asks, 'But may I now see the university?' She mistakenly thinks of the university as a building in addition to the colleges, the library and so on. She commits a 'category mistake'. She pops 'university' in the same category as a component of the university. To go home in tears and a taxi – well, that mixes categories – as do the two meanings of 'pickle' above.

Ryle attacked Descartes for treating the mind as a 'thing' just as the body is a thing, except that the mind is immaterial. Earlier, Wittgenstein drew attention to misleading features of language, to how we may, for example, mistakenly think of the word 'I' as a name. Earlier still, Bertrand Russell had analysed sentences containing expressions such as 'The Golden Mountain', 'The author of the Universe' and 'The King of France' in such a way that no commitment to such entities in some odd realm of 'being' – a realm somewhat less than existence – was required.

Wittgenstein wrote that philosophy is the battle against the bewitchment of our intelligence by means of language. He was not suggesting that philosophical questions were trivial. Far from it – for our language expresses our deepest concepts, attitudes and way of life. True, misunderstandings through language may issue in trivial yet enjoyable humour. The barmaid asks what the customer wants: 'Bitter?' 'Just tired,' he replies. If a sequence of jokes has been of the 'Man walks into a bar' ilk, the final laugh may arise from the simple, 'Man walks into a bra. He was dyslexic.' Philosophical puzzles, though, come to the fore when we attend to quite what is said and what information is conveyed in view of context and common assumptions.

How to mislead with the truth

Zeki helpfully tells you that someone was rifling through your underwear, love letters and store of chocolates. Sure enough, your possessions have been disturbed. You thank Zeki for the alert. Later on you realize that the searcher was in fact Zeki. Did Zeki lie to you? Not at all. If challenged on the matter, you would have to agree that Zeki spoke the truth: someone had indeed been rifling through your possessions. With lies, speakers assert something to be true that they believe false; and they make the assertion intending to deceive the hearers by the content of that assertion. Zeki escapes the description 'liar' for he told you the truth and you grasped that truth, yet he certainly misled you and arguably deceived you. The distinction here between lying and misleading rests on a distinction between what an assertion logically entails and what hearers may reasonably end up believing as a direct result.

Zeki said that someone was rifling. That does not logically entail that the someone was other than Zeki. Given the context, though – Zeki was seemingly helpful in informing you – you reasonably took it that Zeki was not the culprit. In the terms of Paul Grice, there was a conversational implicature that the someone was other than Zeki. Many complexities arise once we take into account implicatures as well as what assertions logically imply – once we throw into the conversational pot the context, background assumptions and the literal/metaphorical distinction. 'No man is an island' is literally true, yet is a metaphorical truth too. Surely you may speak the unvarnished truth when you say that you are near breaking point, yet not when you say that you are literally near breaking point. 'Literally' cannot, it seems, be taken metaphorically.

Philosopher logicians, seeking to bring order to language, offer regimentations of underlying structures. One simple regimentation is the following: the combination of two propositions 'p and q' has the same logical implications as the reverse combination 'q and p'. Yet such regimentation needs to handle the everyday distinction between saying, for example, 'She had a swim and took off her clothes' and 'She took off her clothes and had a swim'. The order of the component propositions, irrelevant in the regimentation, may suggest a temporal order: there may be a conversational implicature of that order. The time has arrived, though, given the chapter's title, for some complexities when conditional propositions are in play.

'You're not very good at logic'

When Dim Dave goes to the beach with his girlfriend Silly Sally and his male friend Clogs so Clever, Dim is always the one left behind on the beach guarding the clothes, despite being as keen as the others to swim. How can this be? One of the others could surely sometimes stay behind. But that man Clogs has been spinning a yarn to poor Dim. Things start off fine with the spinning. One simple constraint on their circumstances is that at least one of the three must guard the clothes and bags on the beach when the other or others swim. The additional constraint is that Silly will only ever go in the sea if with Clogs.

The constraints set surely permit Dim sometimes to be in the sea, be it alone or with Clogs. When we put this to Dim, he sighs. 'You're not very good at logic,' he says. 'Clogs has explained it all to me, muttering something about how Lewis Carroll would be proud of him.' And the tale does, indeed, derive from Lewis Carroll's Barber Shop. Here is Clogs' reasoning.

Given the constraints mentioned, the following conditional is clearly false: if Silly is in the sea, then Clogs is not. Now, let us suppose that Dim is in the sea.

After all, that initially seems to be a possibility. Well, on that supposition, if – *if* – Silly is also in the sea, Clogs would have to be beach-bound, minding the clothes. But it is never true that Silly is in the sea while Clogs is on the beach.

The supposition that Dim is in the sea leads to the following falsehood: if Silly is in the sea, then Clogs is on the beach. But there is one feature of good arguments upon which logicians are agreed: in good arguments truths cannot lead to falsehoods. So, it cannot be true that Dim is ever in the sea. That is because supposing that he is in the sea, we reach a falsehood, namely that if Silly is in the sea, then Clogs must be stuck on the beach. Hence, the supposition must be false: Dim must always be on the beach, minding the clothes. Such is the power of logic. Such is the power of logic, unless Clogs has tricked Dim – and surely he has.

Spelling out Clogs

If you are arguing well, and if you start with truths, then you cannot reach falsehoods. That basic principle sets a minimal condition. So, we must look at the other steps in Clogs' dubious reasoning that lands poor Dim always stuck on the beach. One condition is that at least one of the three remains on the beach; but that condition is fine. What do we have left? Well this is where we meet some conditional propositions, as encountered in the previous chapter.

T1: If Silly is in the sea, then so is Clogs. *[True]*

There is no problem with that. Someone might well only go in the sea with a certain other person. So, there is indeed nothing odd about T1. Clogs' argument, though, then assumes that therefore the following conditional proposition must be false:

F1: If Silly is in the sea, then Clogs is not. *[False]*

Yet how does the reasoning go? Well, it supposes that Dim is in the sea; and that supposition allegedly leads to the falsehood F1. Hence, given the simple principle of good reasoning, the supposition that led us to F1, the supposition being that Dim is in the sea, must itself be false. What can be done? The puzzle's heart is its treatment of conditional propositions, such as F1. We have casually treated that as false. But is it? More pointedly, is it false, *whatever we suppose*? Before we address that question, let us reflect a little on how to understand straightforward conditional 'If . . ., then . . .' propositions such as F1 and T1.

'If it is sunny, then the beaches are crowded.' That, according to logicians' typical regimentation, can be treated as saying the same with regard to truth and falsity as 'Either it is not sunny or the beaches are crowded.' The use of 'or' allows for both to be true. On this regimentation, 'If Silly is in the sea, then Clogs is not' is the same as saying 'Either Silly is not in the sea or Clogs is not in the sea.' Now, on the supposition that Dim is in the sea, Silly certainly is not – for if she is, then so is Clogs, and hence no one is left minding the clothes. In other words on the supposition given, of Dim being in the sea and hence Silly being on the beach, the 'Either Silly is not in the sea or Clogs is not in the sea' must be true – simply because Silly is not in the sea. Hence, on the supposition of Dim being in the sea, F1 'If Silly is in the sea, then Clogs is not' is true, not false as Clogs maintains. Hence, Dim's being in the sea does not lead to a falsehood after all. Dim was trapped into thinking that F1 'If Silly is in the sea, then Clogs is not' is always false, but on the supposition given in Clogs' argument, that conditional proposition is true. So, all is well – as far as resolving the puzzling reasoning is concerned.

Regimentations

All has been made well for the puzzle, but does the regimenting medication have unfortunate side-effects? We have treated conditional propositions such as 'If it is sunny, then the beaches are crowded' as either/or propositions: 'Either it is not sunny or the beaches are crowded'. It follows that when it is not sunny, the either/or proposition is true – and hence the conditional 'If . . ., then . . .' proposition is true. More generally, with conditional propositions 'If such and such, then so and so', whenever the 'such and such' part (the antecedent) is false, the whole conditional is deemed to be true.

Treating conditionals as true whenever the antecedents are false is somewhat unfortunate. Suppose it is raining heavily now, but you have not noticed. You remark that, 'If it is sunny, then the beaches are crowded.' That is plausible and true – but think of all the other conditionals that are deemed true, just because the antecedent is false. If it is sunny, then the beaches are empty. If it is sunny, then the moon is made of cheese. Regimenting conditional propositions as equivalent to 'either/or' propositions has its dangers. That does not mean we must pop Dim back onto the beach; it does mean that conditionals need sensitive handling.

In the previous chapter, we met counterfactual conditionals: conditional propositions in which the antecedent, the segment immediately after the 'if', is false. So, on the either/or analysis, all such propositions must be true. That strongly suggests that counterfactuals ought not to be squeezed into that either/or logical category. To squeeze so would be a category mistake. Regarding Dim, Silly and Clogs, we suppose first that someone must always be on the beach guarding the clothes, and then suppose Dim is in the sea – and then, on top of that, suppose Silly could yet be in the sea. Maybe we could run the suppositions in terms of the previous chapter's closeness of the possible worlds, but at their suppositional heart, it seems, lies contradiction. Small wonder that we hence become baffled by the suppositions, baffled both by what is logically implied and by what may be the conversational implicatures; yet at least we now know one regimented way of not being trapped into always looking after the clothes.

There is a moral to be drawn, one expressed in the early twentieth century by Frank Plumpton Ramsey. Ramsey, a Fellow of King's College Cambridge, died aged 26; yet in his short life, as is now seen, he made major contributions to mathematics, economics and philosophy. He was also influential in Wittgenstein's rejection of his earlier work that sought to uncover an exact logical form underlying language. The moral is:

The chief danger to our philosophy, apart from laziness and woolliness, is scholasticism, the essence of which is treating what is vague as if it were precise, and trying to fit it into an exact logical category.

CHAPTER 31

How to hear the Sirens' song in safety . . .

and how not to be bound by reason

You want another drink, but your reason advises you against it – despite that, you drink. At a party, you wisely ask the hostess to hide your car keys. Yet, of course, a few drinks later, you are demanding the keys. Does your hostess obey your earlier command or your demand right now? We need, then, to be able to determine what makes an action rational and how reason may tie us down over the future. Indeed, we shall see how it can be rational to bind ourselves to doing even the irrational in the future, however distant it may be.

Where lies irrationality?

We often act with reason, but that does not thereby make our actions rational – for the reasoning may be bad. If you want a sunny holiday by the seashore, with fine wine and food, practising your French, then it would be wildly irrational to set off to Berlin in the winter. Even so, we need some caveats. It would certainly be irrational if you knew about Berlin and its location. An external observer would see your action as irrational; and from your own perspective it too would be irrational. If, though, you sincerely believed that Berlin was on the French Riviera, then you acted rationally given your radically mistaken belief. From our external observers' viewpoint, your behaviour was still irrational; but, were we to imagine ourselves in your position with the false belief, we should understand how your Berlin choice would appear rational. Of course, that you came to believe that Berlin is in France may be manifesting earlier irrationality.

We have complexities enough, but here are some more. Despite your knowing about Berlin and your desire for a French coastal holiday, there may be other factors that lead you to the German capital. You may have been offered £100,000 if you behaved irrationally with regard to your holidaying; and so, setting off to Berlin manifests such irrationality, though not irrationality with regard to wealth acquisition. Paradoxically, however odd your behaviour, you cannot win a prize for being irrational if performing odd actions in order to win makes what you perform rational.

Having reasons is not sufficient for actions to be rational. Flipping the relationship round, we ought not mistakenly to draw the conclusion that a rational action must therefore be one that is done for reasons. Sometimes it may be rational to act without reason. There need be no reason why we yearn for happiness, yet it can be perfectly rational to yearn for such. We have reason to scratch an itch: an itch itches and we want relief; but we have no reason for wanting relief – we just want that relief.

A tragic but true story is reported of a mentally ill man who thought he had two heads, one of which tormented him. He wondered what to do and, given his beliefs, he acted in the end with good reason – from his perspective. He pulled the trigger of his revolver and shot the alien head, his head. From an external perspective, he was acting without good reason; but once we place ourselves in his mindset, we see the rationality of his desperate shooting.

That example leads us to the paradoxical thought that, in trying to understand aberrant – odd, bizarre, irrational – behaviour, we are endeavouring to make it rational, from the agent's perspective. Thus it is that psychoanalytic explanations draw on unconscious elements in the agent's motivations, thus making the resultant behaviour rational, given the agent's perspective. Any successful account of behaviour would seem determined to read that behaviour as rational: irrationality gets ruled out.

Reason as slave

Rationality – and reason more generally – is often thought of as opposed to desires, passions, emotions. The picture is of our reason sometimes holding our passions in check. Were that right, we should also be able to conceive of reason urging passions upon us. Miriam wants to run away with the milkman, but her reason, her rationality, holds her back. Her reason tells her that they would have no money, she would miss her children, and it would all end in tears. Yet is her reason really preventing her from joining the milky runaway kid? David Hume's answer would be 'No'. Hume writes:

> The principle, which opposes our passion, cannot be the same with reason, and is only called so in an improper sense. We speak not strictly and philosophically when we talk of the combat of passion and of reason. Reason is, and ought only to be the slave of the passions, and can never pretend to any other office than to serve and obey them.

Thus Hume asserts, no doubt with an eye-catching twinkle, that it is 'not contrary to reason to prefer the destruction of the whole world to the scratching of my finger'. We have our desires, our passions, but they can only count as unreasonable, as irrational, if accompanied with some false judgement. Properly speaking, it is not the passion, the desire, that is unreasonable, but the false judgement. Miriam's reasoning is not holding her back from the milkman. It is Miriam's desire for her children, her desire not to be impoverished and ending in tears, that hold her back. Her reasoning merely displayed the likely consequences of her possible milkman jaunt.

What we aim at achieving – the ultimate ends of our human actions – is determined by our feelings, our sentiments, our desires; they and they alone have the power to cause actions and to prevent actions. Reason is deployed in working out the means for securing the chosen ends. 'Reason' here includes investigating the world, discovering the truth about which means secure which ends at minimal cost. As seen earlier, if you desire the sunny beach, an opportunity to practise French and some fine wine, then you investigate the world and end up somewhere in coastal France. Reason has helped you to achieve your end.

How quiet is reason?

With regard to the man who prefers the destruction of the whole world over some trivial matter, our reasoning may reveal to him how the destruction would lead to his death or how, if he alone survives, life would feel mighty empty – or how, indeed, he may prefer to be surrounded not by destruction, but by a world of flourishing flowers, blossoming beauty

313

and philosophers pondering on passion. Reason may guide him to reflect on consequences and what he truly wants; but, in the end, what he does is not determined by reason but by passion. So the Humean story goes.

We may challenge Hume's approach by suggesting that some chosen ends just are irrational. Surely, to spend your life running along a main street, clapping your head, singing 'I'm a mango', clad in bananas head to toe, is no way to flourish. And, no doubt, it is no way to flourish for most people. Our mango man, though, may insist that that is what it is for him to flourish – or he may be dismissive of flourishing, desiring instead to follow the little voice in his head that recommends the singing, the clapping and bananas.

Yet some may argue – and Immanuel Kant would be one – that reason can direct us to what we morally ought to do. Just as reason shows us how there are certain universal mathematical truths, so reason can lead us to see that we ought not to break promises, that we ought to be honest, that we ought to be just. In short, reason can disclose moral duties, and such duties can motivate us into action, into doing indeed what we may not want to do. One challenge to this is that it is perceived self-interest and perceived self-interest alone that motivates us. We consider self-interest in the next chapter, but here, whether the motivations be of self-interest or of morality, how do they stretch forth into the future?

The Sirens' song

Homer tells of Odysseus wanting to hear the singing of the Sirens, their melodious and, no doubt, sensual song. Odysseus knew that the song beguiled. Sailors were unable to resist its sweetness; their lack of resistance led them to watery graves. Odysseus' solution – what he reasoned to – was to have his sailors bind him to the ship's mast with instructions not to release him, however much he showed himself to have changed his mind. Their ears were stopped with beeswax so they would not themselves be tempted by the song. Now, as Chapter 2, *How to awake as a gigantic insect* explored, it is difficult to understand quite what constitutes a person remaining the same person over time, but without a doubt we can understand the rationality of Odysseus' actions. He puts his plan into action in order to get what he now wants for himself in the future, namely, hearing the Sirens but without yielding. Yet paradoxically, that means he is making a pre-commitment, binding himself to a future commitment, namely, not getting what he genuinely will be wanting later on.

Samuel Coleridge apparently hired porters and hackney-coachmen to oppose by force his entrance into any druggist shop. But as the authority for this was derived from Coleridge, the hapless guardians found themselves in a metaphysical fix. When they tried to prevent his entrance, Coleridge, then desperate, could point out that his authorization *now* was that they should let him through, otherwise there would be grounds of action for assault and battery. What, though, should count as the 'true' Coleridge position, given his changes of mind? An asymmetry may sometimes suggest an answer.

Coleridge, when un-drugged, sought to bind himself to make ineffectual his urgent quests for drugs, whereas Coleridge when on such urgent quests paid no attention to binding the sensible Coleridge when not desperate for drugs or under their influence. Whether or not the asymmetry is relevant, when we tie our future selves down, we believe that what is in our long-term interests – or what we ought to do or what sort of life we should lead – involves overcoming some future desires, however genuine and powerful those desires at that later date may be.

There are various ways in which we do bind our future selves down – or allow ourselves to be bound. We can hide car keys or bottles of whisky, knowing that we shall forget where they are when we are no longer sober. We may leave it too late to reach the weekend party of wine, women and song – hence avoiding unwelcome tiredness the following Monday. We sometimes make promises of fidelity in the hope that they will carry weight, *being promises*, when subsequent flirtations arise. All such planning can be rational – and, furthermore, avoiding the drunken driving and the seductive temptations itself may well be highly rational. Yet sometimes the rational plan involves commitment to the irrational – as we shall now see.

Deterrence: binding to madness

In the Cold War, the USA and USSR threatened mutual destruction. To update matters, let us suppose that in a few years' time a nuclear Iran and a nuclear Israel are in a similar relationship – both fearing a first nuclear strike by the other. Israel threatens a massive retaliation, were a first strike to occur. That may seem immoral, yet its moral defence is clear: it should prevent the Iranian first strike and subsequent harm. Of course, Iran threatens in a similar way. All may go well – the mutual threats may deter first strikes – but suppose that, because of some crazy generals or some mistaken communications, the Iranians launch a nuclear missile at Tel Aviv. Should the Israelis now bomb Tehran in retaliation as threatened?

Well, suppose that it is known that the Iranians cannot bomb any more Israeli cities. In such circumstances, what good can come out of the Israelis keeping to

317

their threat? There would be further devastation – pointless devastation as it would prevent no future attacks and harms. So, it would be irrational and immoral to go through with the retaliation, even though it was rational to threaten it. Paradoxically, it can therefore be rational to threaten what it would be irrational to carry out. The irrationality would be strengthened were the retaliation to involve the obliteration of both countries.

There are more paradoxical twists. If the Iranians know that at heart the Israelis would not do anything so stupid as to destroy cities pointlessly, then they can calculate that they will get away with a first strike. A further twist now comes: the Israelis themselves go through such reasoning, so they realize that they cannot really intend to do what they threaten to do because they know they would not carry out the threat. And they may reason that the Iranians will be reasoning likewise. What both parties need is the strong suspicion that the other party may well act irrationally, crazily, if victim of a first strike. For certainty, though, parties need to put systems in place that automatically retaliate and cannot be overridden – but then, of course, it would be irrational to do that, knowing that later on it may be regretted. So it is that even rationality itself, in binding us down, can tie us in knots.

CHAPTER 32

How to think like a bat . . .

or how far science may go

From high in the chapel's rafters, we look down on you humans and wonder, 'What is it like to be a human being?' We can try walking on two legs. We may attempt to sleep on beds – oh for a lovely rafter! – but that would only tell us what it is like to be a bat pretending to be a human. You humans lack our echolocation faculty. Your experiences must be most limited and utterly bizarre. We could investigate your brains and see how you respond, but we should still miss out on how you humans experience the world.

Pushing the limits

There are, of course, no philosophical bats, but philosophers raise questions, sometimes seemingly bizarre questions – usually from the comfort of the study, the armchair or even the bed, with a sip of wine, port or some further delight. In this book we have already encountered many thought experiments – though maybe not the wine, port or further delight. 'What is it like to be a bat?' How could we know what it is like? The question leads into big conceptual areas concerning how we grasp the world around us – indeed, how we can and how we should grasp the world around us. With our earlier discussion of the mind-brain identity theory, we saw how scientific analyses must miss out on how things are 'from a first-person perspective'.

The bat question, made famous by the American philosopher Thomas Nagel, encourages us to accept that a scientific understanding of the world cannot capture everything. That is so because scientific understanding abstracts from our peculiar subjective views, seeking an objective viewpoint – one that is bound to lose features of the subjective. The sea feels cold to you, tepid to me; yet chemists and physicists may tell us that 'objectively' the water's molecular motion is so and so, with the kinetic energy at a certain level. Those latter features are independent of our sensations. The motion, the energy, interacts with our nervous systems – and then we have the experiences, in this case, different sensations of heat.

The batty question runs the risk of getting out of control. Once we feel that there is something there in the bat's perception of the world, something that is necessarily unavailable to us, we may take things further. Religious believers may insist that they undergo experiences that atheists simply cannot. Being a male, I may wonder whether there is something essentially elusive about the way women grasp the world.

Taking such thoughts yet further, I may question whether I can ever know what sort of experiences anyone else at all has of the world. 'I have, and can have, only my experiences.' Now, that comment may appear as a deep and troubling thought. Arguably, though, it amounts to nothing more than a piece of grammar or logic such as 'One plays patience with oneself', a suggestion of Wittgenstein. After all, what would it be for me literally to have your experiences and yet for those experiences to be mine?

Scientism

There is a tendency to believe that a scientific under-standing of the Universe can tell us everything about the Universe. That is scientism, the view that there can be a unified scientific understanding of every aspect of the world, including human beings and bats. As seen, the seemingly batty 'bat' question challenges that tendency. However much we may learn about the neurology and behaviour of bats there is, it appears, something that will forever elude us — namely, what it is like to have the bat's perspective, its sensations, of the world. Were the bats truly philosophical, they would find human experiences.and life elusive. Even if on further reflection the batty question is incoherent – a suggestion made by some – we may yet resist the collapse into scientism. In previous centuries, scientism was on offer as a crude mechanical materialism. In the mid-18th century, La Mettrie wrote his radically materialist *L'Homme Machine*. Today many scientists would have us believe that descriptions of human values and activities can be reduced to talk about molecules, genes, neural circuits – or whatever will later be within the scientists' vocabulary. That last caveat may be a valuable escape clause: who knows the scientific concepts of the distant future?

There is, though, no good reason to believe that human life – which involves interpretation, meaning and the individual's viewpoint – can be fully grasped by a scientific understanding. Whatever the causal explanations of individuals' movements of tongues and lips, of sound waves generated, they would not be explanations of the movements' significance – of what the individuals were saying. Awareness of the physical changes of Jesse in the terms of chemistry and physics would not thereby show that Jesse was promising to meet her lover later that evening and loan him her grandfather's watch. Physics and chemistry do not present laws that deploy concepts such as 'promise' and 'loan', 'lover' and 'grandfather's watch'.

The above does not deny the hugely beneficial significance of scientific successes in all our lives. Further, the above is no assertion of a mysterious supernatural realm forever inaccessible to scientific understanding. Human beings – biological beings, not ephemeral souls – give loans, make promises and treasure heirlooms. No doubt, when human beings engage in such activities, numerous changes occur in cells and molecules, in atomic and subatomic structures; but understanding such changes is not to understand the many features, activities and relationships of humans. The position herein endorsed is a rejection of eliminativism (see Chapter 9, *How not to have feelings or beliefs*).

'Just' this

Evolutionary psychology, in particular, may mislead us. Evolutionary psychologists have a tendency to use the word 'just'. Beautiful features of humans are *just* those indicative of health; moral awareness is *just* disguised self-interest. Even if there are evolutionary explanations for such features and awareness, we should baulk at the 'just'. Probably there are good evolutionary explanations of why human beings have flourished; maybe the explanations rely on the survival value of the ability to distinguish the different colours and spot differences between mountains and molehills, yet such worldly differences are not, of course, constituted by evolutionary utility. Our survival success, courtesy of our biology, depends on our awareness of the surrounding world's features; but the surrounding worldly features do not depend on our biology.

In contrast to bats – unless they are philosophical – human beings are aware of a distinction between what they desire and what is morally worthy of desire. We possess a sense of right and wrong, of what we morally ought to do as opposed to what we want to do. Yet, with evolutionary psychology to the fore, some argue that, even if we can make sense of an objective morality – see Chapter 24, *How not to be a three-legged frog* – our motivation is always that of perceived self-interest.

The Ring of Gyges

To assess the claim of universal self-interest, let us suppose that people are often aware of what morality dictates. People act morally, it may then be claimed, because they fear punishment by the state or God, were they to act otherwise. The claim is picturesquely shown and questioned by Plato, who tells of Gyges' Ring, a magical ring that makes its possessor invisible. Suppose two rings, one worn by a just person, the other by an unjust – and for our discussion, let us read 'just' as the wider 'moral'.

No man would keep his hands off what was not his own
when he could safely take what he liked out of the market,

or go into houses and sleep with any one at his pleasure,
or kill or release from prison whom he would, and in all
respects be like a god among men. Then the actions of the
just would be as the actions of the unjust; they would both
come at last to the same point.

People are only moral because of the consequences if
discovered to be immoral. We may, though, challenge
that claim, as does Plato; in doing so, we recall Chapter
11, *How to be a philosophical scientist*, and the need for
possible refutation. When told that everyone acts from
self-interest, we may picture the self-interest of certain
Wall Street types, of businessmen driven by profit,
and, surprising as it may seem, philosophy lecturers
seeking advancement. The claim is, then, an empirical
claim; but is it true? We see a good Samaritan rushing
to help people crushed in a car accident. We observe
the elderly lady giving her last pound to a beggar. We
see a man running into a burning house to save a
child. They are surely counter-examples to the 'all is
self-interest' position. Proponents of self-interest should
argue more calmly that maybe *often* or *typically* people
act out of perceived self-interest. Yet this is where a
sleight of hand may occur.

Defenders of 'all is self-interest' ask us to look more
closely at our seeming counter-examples. Really, they
tease us, such people are motivated by self-interest; they
were doing what they wanted to do – perhaps for the

inner glow or for the pleasure of impressing others. Yet what is the evidence for that self-interest interpretation? Well, that they did what they did.

The judgement that everyone acts out of self-interest is now no longer open to refutation. It has been made true by definition. But nothing is achieved by that manoeuvre. If we stick with the new understanding of 'self-interest' such that everyone always acts out of self-interest, we should need to mark, in some new way, the distinction between self-interested acts that help others and those self-interested acts that do not. In the mode of a quip, we should need to distinguish between helpful acts that arrive free and those that arrive with demands for a fee.

Returning to how things are

We reflect on regularities in the world. Presumably bats have no such reflection, but their survival depends on worldly regularities to which, in the main, they regularly respond. Bats would have a bad time, in fact no time at all, if their dispositions to behave typically failed to fit the way the world runs. And so it is that, in our thinking, we quite naturally accept the existence of a world with features that are independent of bats, of human beings and – were they to exist – of Martians. Yet can we coherently conceive the world as so independent, as so mind-independent? Think of the patterns that we notice in the world. We notice faces in the clouds, in frosty windows, in dust shimmering on the polished table, yet we have no inclination to judge that those faces exist as faces independently of our seeing them as such. We classify groupings of stars as constellations, yet those groupings depend on what we humans naturally bring together in thought. No doubt, if we thought like a bat we should have grouped and described differently.

What of the stars themselves? What, indeed, of any objects or groups of objects? Classifications of them – and how we consider them as being the same objects or as having changed or dispersed – all seem to depend on us, on our perceptions, and on what matters to us.

The world has joints. Were those joints ready-made or were they carved into the world by us? Immanuel Kant spoke of the unknowable noumena, things in themselves – things which we know of only through the imposition of our human concepts, of, indeed, concepts of space and time. Some may conclude that, therefore, there could be no animals, oceans and solar systems before humans existed, for their existence, classified as such, depends on our human concepts. Such thinking may drag us down into the mire of relativism or scepticism – maybe as if there is something that forever eludes us. Yet is there something elusive? If we step outside our concepts, it should not surprise us that we then lack all conception of the world. Perhaps that is the way of the bat.

The picture of humans imposing their concepts may already mislead. After all, were it well motivated, then I may question the existence of other people prior to my own existence. Recalling Descartes' evil genius, if I can really doubt away everything other than my own experiences, well, what sense can there be in the idea of others' experiences? We are being held captive by a picture that separates us, that separates 'I', from the rest of the world; yet, as highlighted in Chapter 27, *How to outdo artificial intelligence*, we are part of the world's furniture, its movable furniture. I am embedded within the world – and if I seek to think of my *self* as an item distinct from this embodied creature, I am bound to tie myself in knots. That comment is not to imply that all is clear. Philosophers remain in business not least because mistaken pictures captivate and not least because it is terribly difficult to find the right picture. Philosophy is indeed a battle against bewitchment, a bewitchment that can arise when thinking about bats.

CHAPTER 33

How to see beauty . . .

beyond the eye of the beholder

'Beauty is in the eye of the beholder.' But if we truly think that beauty is but a matter of eyed taste, then why is there ready acceptance that a sunset is more beautiful than a car park and music by Mahler more ravishing than the beats of the all-night bar's techno? To judge that the music is rapturous is not to say that majority ears are open to such beauty; but they may be opened. Once opened, the experience of beauty can stretch the imagination. A sense of beauty may liberate us from the ugliness of the mundane.

Discernment

In *Don Quixote*, Sancho Panza tells of his two kinsmen who were asked their opinion of a hogshead of wine, supposedly excellent, being aged and of good vintage. One takes a sip, reflects and pronounces the wine to be good, were it not for a small taste of leather that affects it. The other, after tasting and mature reflection, gives his verdict also very much in the wine's favour, but he too has a reservation: the wine's nose carries an unwelcome hint of iron. As Panza goes on to relate, the two were ridiculed for their judgement – as if they could be so discerning. Yet who had the last laugh? On emptying the hogshead, there was found at the bottom a leather thong tied to an old key. The story is brought to us by David Hume, who stresses the importance of taste in determining what is beautiful. For Hume, taste is all that beauty is based upon, though, of course, some may be more discerning than others.

What is beautiful by the lights of Hume is simply what is pleasing to the beholder. Yet there is surely misperception in those lights. As we have seen, people readily recognize that disagreements over whisky's niceness or nastiness are mere matters of taste, of what some find pleasing and others not. We do not usually grow argumentative when disagreeing about the delights, or otherwise, of green tea, *steak bleu* or the latest blend of mongoose tart. In contrast, where beauty and ugliness are concerned, if there is disagreement, we may not be content to leave it at that. We may point to features that we admire or those that jar. We may remain in disagreement, yet finally manage to see something in what the other says.

When Camilla announces 'I know what I like', saying no more, that reflects badly on her appreciation – and things get even worse if, without further comment, she insists that the local supermarket is as beautiful as Botticelli's *Primavera* and the roadwork drillings as astounding as a Wagner opera. Preferring the taste of jasmine tea over camomile tea is no reflection on sensibility; but considering a Mills and Boon romance to be as fine as Nabokov's *Lolita* is very much a reflection. It may be such a reflection that people in those disagreements, as with fundamental disagreements in religion or politics, may be unable to live with each other.

Good taste

There is such a thing as good taste, yet that sits unhappily with the thought that it is but a matter of taste. If it is no mere matter of taste, we may look for something – 'out there' – that makes beautiful items beautiful, regardless of our tasting treatments. Features 'out there' have been proposed. From Pythagoras onwards, a suggestion has been that of proportion, of a harmony between the parts, and where furniture and buildings are concerned a harmony between form and function. The understanding of beauty in such terms has been viewed as comprehensive, bringing together the forms of music, painting and architecture and of the human soul in recognition of that harmony.

There is a mysticism in understanding beauty as purely form and function, and also a glaring mistake. While it is true that certain classically beautiful buildings may exhibit the harmonized geometrical forms proposed, there are many beautiful items whose beauty does not rest on a specified geometrical form or analogy to such. Consider the beauty of a raging ocean or the elegance of Modigliani's *Reclining Nude*. Further, there are items that may have an appropriate form, yet generate no beauty: some lines drawn in the 'right' proportion may simply cause a yawn.

Being of a certain form is neither necessary nor sufficient for an object to be beautiful. Were there rules for beauty – proportions to be followed; clashes to be avoided – creators of beauty would be efficient technicians; yet significant artists, be they painters, writers or composers, have no fixed rule books. They are imaginative and – well – creative. To think otherwise is to be guilty of a Procrustean mistake. Procrustes' bed was a perfect fit for one and all. It was true to its label, but only because Procrustes stretched or chopped those heading to bed to ensure the right fit.

Suppose you are told of a painting that it exhibits harmony in form. Its proportions are explained in detail, but that is insufficient for you to grasp the work's beauty. You need to experience it directly yourself. True, you may have confidence in another who tells you of the beauty; but that is first-hand knowledge of a report, only second-hand knowledge of the beauty.

You have no appreciation of the beauty until you delight in the object itself.

Would a syringe produce these effects?

Let us not, though, be misled by the above emphasis on experience and delight. As Wittgenstein wrote, when considering artistic works praised for their effects, 'Would a syringe which produces these effects on you do just as well as the picture?' Such a comment has wider significance. When musing upon sexual desire, for example, we saw that it was not desire solely for sensations. What we value, what is important, is not solely experiences, not just how things strike us, but how the world and our relationships are, even though, in a sense, all we have are our experiences. The underlying point was well made by Robert Nozick's Experience Machine, a thought experiment. Perhaps the machine is in some grubby basement in a run-down part of the city; but once you are plugged into the machine, you will receive whatever experiences you chose before the plugging.

You are lazy and a coward, but you would love to be fit, courageously battling with the elements, reaching the South Pole. The machine will give you all the relevant experiences and, while on the machine, you will genuinely believe that you are battling through blizzards and not asleep in a basement with your brain wired up. Yet can the machine give you what you want?

It gives you experiences *as if* reaching the South Pole, *as if* being fêted on your return, but it cannot give you the reality of your trekking and achieving your goal. It pumps you with the experiential side of experiences, but it does not make real what those experiences are experiences *of*. This harmonizes with the thought that what we find valuable cannot usually be cashed out solely in terms of experience, ignoring the source. Let us reflect further, by considering some particular cases of what may have aesthetic appeal.

We need to turn to the *elegant* wine glass, the *haunting* melody, the *graceful* nude. They are described as such because their features generate a certain type of response in us. A way of seeing this is to reflect on the alleged distinction between the nude and the naked, a distinction made by, for example, Kenneth Clark, using Kant's notion of the disinterested aesthetic.

Nude or naked?

A painting is of a female nude, of a de-sexualized figure. It may be approached with disinterest. That contrasts with approaching an individual who is naked and may be huddled and defenceless, or with approaching an individual as an object of sexual desire. Classically, indeed, the distinction would be manifested by the nude's absence of pubic hair. So it is that Eakins' painting *William Rush and His Model* offends the distinction not merely because of her pubic hair on display, but because she is a vulnerable naked woman being helped off the dais by the artist, a clothed authority. The nude/naked distinction is impossible to uphold so rigidly when considering beauty. First, there can be beauty in defenceless naked figures. Secondly, it is absurd to suggest that the delight taken in the beauty of a nude necessarily has nothing to do with sexuality. We engage with beautiful objects and that engagement requires that we have pleasure in their presence, a pleasure that cannot be divorced from our biology, our desires, our interests. For an artificially intelligent robot to appreciate the beauty of a natural wilderness or of a nude drawn in charcoal, it would surely need a sense of isolation, and an awareness of sexual desire.

There is a good minimal truth to the disinterested gaze. When we gaze at the beautiful glass, the temple's columns and the painter's portrayal of innocence, we may be moved respectively by the investment value, the commitment of the builders and the morality implied. Factors such as the motives of artists and political context can colour our view of the works; such factors are external factors that threaten domination of our interest. In assessing the beauty of objects, though, we need to bracket off those factors; yet still, beauty is no simple truth and truth is not beauty. Many fine buildings have been built on slavery's ugly truth. A 'bracketing' is needed when we encounter forgeries.

335

Over the years, many forgeries have come to light. Where a forgery is crass and poor, we can see why it may be dismissed; but when it takes years for a forgery to be uncovered and then only through some chemical analyses unnoticed by the naked eye, it is surely not a disinterested gaze that now rejects the beauty of the work. Beauty is to be found in the object directly apprehended, not in the causes it promotes or the artists' intentions, deceptive or otherwise.

Music in the soul

Economic impact, career advancement, usefulness; profitability, property values and paying minimal tax – these are concerns uppermost in many people's minds, concerns promoted by business, government and even today's universities. Proper appreciation of the painting, the poem, the string quartet lifts us away from those concerns. Gazing at the sunset, feeling the emptiness of the wilderness, catching sight of the skylark – these natural beauties experienced are, of course, as important as the man-made. In *Principia Ethica*, a highly influential work of 1903 – it was the 'bible' for the Bloomsbury Group – G. E. Moore writes:

> No one, probably, who has asked himself the question, has ever doubted that personal affection and Appreciation of what is beautiful in Art or Nature, are good in themselves.

Appreciation of the arts, though, can so easily be corrupted, when mingled with artists out to make a fast buck by some gimmick with no beauty at all. Appreciation of nature can be undermined when its setting is sponsored – when observers of the sunset are battered with advertising hoardings.

There is a tension here. For the arts to flourish, for nature to be accessible – for people to have the means to visit galleries and encounter raging seascapes – some economic success is required. It is a matter of striking the right balance, a muddling matter indeed. Also, of course, not all good art is seen as immediately beautiful. Paintings can represent horrors of war; music may gently glide through sorrows of lost love and despairs of death. Yet paradoxically in great art, beauty may be found in the ugliest of themes.

Let us not forget, though, the reality of suffering, a reality that threatens to tarnish our appreciation of beauty. The beautiful red sky has the sun setting over millions living lives in poverty, pain and hopelessness. That incongruity can itself collapse us into despair. Beauty may yet lift us out.

An appreciation of beauty matters for other reasons. The beauty is beautiful – and that draws us away from life's utility. We must mention here that philosophers known as utilitarians are not thereby concerned only with utility as usefulness. As seen in Chapter 15, *How to judge whom to save*, utilitarians such as John Stuart Mill promote the flourishing fulfilled life – and that essentially involves the disinterested values of aesthetic appreciation as well as the values of compassion and helping others. Appreciating beauty – be it listening to Britten's *Death in Venice* or being carried along by Cavafy's poems – not merely draws us away from our 'self' interests, but also opens eyes to free plays of the imagination, to the music in the soul. In beauty we can, in a sense, lose our 'selves': we are lost in its music.

Appreciations, imaginations of the beautiful may also cast everyday lives in new lights. We may value the beauty of simplicity, transience and imperfections as in the Japanese *wabi-sabi*. We may understand our own relationships afresh. It is no accident that lovers often find their love enhanced through a shared poem, through music that enraptures – a shared recognition of the beautiful.

CHAPTER 34

How to know when to stop . . .
and to come to an end

'Explanations must come to an end.' Somewhere along
the line, we need to learn that certain beliefs, certain
modes of behaviour, are simply what we accept, simply
what we do. Philosophy encourages us to justify actions
and reveal reasons for beliefs; and justifications and
reasons beget more justifications and reasons.
Somewhere, though, we have to recognize the end, but
that does not mean that the end is fixed for all time. . .

Why and how

We look for explanations of how and why events happened or will happen. On the grandest of scales, many
people are in awe of the Universe; and they often
exclaim that while scientists can explain 'how' things
happen, they cannot explain 'why'. As it stands, the
exclamation is false. Scientists often explain why events
have happened – by giving causes. Exclaimers of 'Why?',
though, are seeking a purposive explanation, a teleo-

logical explanation, of the Universe. As we saw in this book's introduction, Joanna's jogging may be explained (or seemingly so) teleologically in terms of her aim – to improve her health – or in terms of causes – the neurological events that get her legs moving. Teleological explanations were once given for earthquakes: maybe the gods were punishing humans so wicked. Such explanations were given for the existence of different species, which formed part of God's design. Geological causal explanations have now overtaken the one, evolutionary explanations the other. Yet such natural explanations rest in the end on 'this is what things do'. Strain energy accumulates; certain molecules replicate.

It is difficult to comprehend how scientists could ever give an explanation of the whole Universe that does not itself raise further questions. That difficulty gives licence, it seems, for people to look for purposes, for design, outside the Universe. Such people are astonished that our Universe possesses features that give rise to conscious life. If the basic forces and texture of this Universe were even slightly different, there would, so it is said, be no conscious life. How unlikely, then, that this Universe should exist – unless designed.

A mystery is no explanation

Spinoza, writing in the seventeenth century, despite being the 'god-intoxicated philosopher' points out that:

. . . there is no end to the questions which can be asked: but why was the sea tossing? Why was the man invited at just that time? And so they will not stop asking for the causes of causes until you take refuge in the will of God, that is, the sanctuary of ignorance.

We ought to succumb to neither the confidence in current scientific speculation nor the philosophical reasoning for design. As we have seen, we have little grip on the nature of consciousness. It is no doubt grounded in neural structures, but it does not follow that it could not be grounded in radically different ways. Even if that criticism is dismissed, we may challenge the surprise at this Universe's possession of conscious life. The surprise relies on the assumption that it makes sense to speak of physical possibilities, probabilities and necessities concerning the total Universe. Now, with the spin of a fair coin, we have the intuitive *a priori* conception of there being two equally likely possible outcomes; further, we have empirical evidence of how spins turn out. But such considerations cannot apply to the Universe – for we know only of the single case.

Let us, though, pretend that we can make sense of an infinite number of possible universes as being logically possible, and let us assume that they are equally likely. Now, whichever particular universe existed would have been incredibly unlikely and would have generated surprise had conscious beings been present within. A universe consisting of an infinite number of unknown molecules of the same type, or one that was much like ours but with only amoeba life, or one of chaos, would be (so to speak) distinctive to the molecules, the amoebae, the chaos. Metaphorically, the molecules, the amoebae, the chaos could propose cosmic designers or artists: some minimalist in preference, akin to a Barnett Newman or Mark Rothko; some more chaotic, akin to a Jackson Pollock.

Even if we still accept the move to a designer or designers for this Universe, what may we conclude? As David Hume quipped, if we work on analogy, then, as numerous human contrivances are designed by committees, so maybe a committee of gods designed the Universe, or perhaps this Universe is the first botched attempt of an infant deity. Really, nothing can be deduced about the designer or designers. Paradoxically, the design argument recognizes that explanations must come to an end: its defenders do not push further, asking why the designer exists. Recognizing the need for an end, the arguers should realize that the evidence leads to nothing beyond the Universe. There is no explanatory value in plucking a designer for the Universe out of the hat, if the design and designer are mysteries. Explanations must come to an end.

This is what we do

We turn to the less grand; we turn to our everyday language. When words are unambiguous, there must be something in common between the items so termed. Tables must have something in common to be termed 'tables', trees to be 'trees' and green items to be 'green'. Well, that is a common thought, once linguistic reflection commences. Yet that too may be pushing too far – just as the design argument pushes too far. An influential example, from Wittgenstein, is the following.

> Consider for example the proceedings that we call 'games'. I mean board-games, card-games, ball-games, Olympic games, and so on. What is common to them all? Don't say: 'There must be something common, or they would not be called "games"' but look and see whether there is anything common to all.

When we consider the different games, we encounter a complicated network of similarities overlapping and criss-crossing. Wittgenstein suggests that the items in question have family resemblances, just as there may be various resemblances between members of a family: build, features, colour of eyes, gait, temperament. To insist that there must always be something in common between all the items, something that is necessary and sufficient for those items to be classified as such, is unjustified. It pushes too far.

343

With language in mind, here is another mistaken push. Consider our use of the word 'green' when used with a fixed meaning. In order to explain the consistency in use, speakers must know what they mean; but what is it that they know? What constitutes their meaning one thing rather than another? Those questions have led to what some perceive as a deep philosophical problem, one most recently developed by Saul Kripke in his interpretation of Wittgenstein. The puzzle is sometimes spoken of as Kripkenstein's.

'And so on, in the same way'

Suppose a child seems to learn odd numbers: she is given the examples of 1, 3, 5, 7 all the way to 99. She is asked to continue the series in the same way. She may think that 'the same way' is shown by repeating the numbers 1, 3, 5, 7 rather than by continuing with 101, 103 *and so on*. Suppose a different case: the child has gone through all the odd numbers up to 1,000 – even 1 million – recognizing them correctly as odd. 'I now know what an odd number is,' she says. Yet how does what she knows fix what she counts as odd numbers when given numbers previously unmet? What determines carrying on 'in the same way' – for what strikes one person as 'the same way' may not strike another as the same. What determines that I shall apply the word 'green' tomorrow to grass and to the traffic lights at 'go'?

Our use of any term so far does not seem to fix what we mean to do in the future. The mantras 'and so on' and 'in the same way' on their own leave things open. Maybe we feel that there should be railway tracks stretching out into the future to keep us true to the meanings, or to enable us to recognize when we have gone off the rails, into some new meanings. Yet those rails do not exist. Some may turn to mental images present now that determine our future use, but as Chapter 12, *How to turn noise into meaning*, showed, any such images would be open to interpretation. Arguably, the paradox arises because we may quest for explanations when none could conceivably be given. The quest is for something more than the fact that, when we behave in a certain way in the future – spotting odd numbers, describing items as green – we usually can recognize that that is what we intended. Explanations must come to an end. Of course, that does not rule out other related questions, such as what constitutes our making mistakes in applying terms in the future.

The problems, so far, have been inductive in spirit, concerning how we manage to move from what is present to what is not. But surely deduction is different. Valid deductive reasoning is safe: if the premises are true, then the conclusion is true. And that is so; but the question then arises: what explains some deductions being valid, others not? Any attempt at justifying good deductive practices will doubtless deploy deduction. Here, Wittgenstein merits quotation again:

If I have exhausted the justifications I have reached bedrock, and my spade is turned. Then I am inclined to say: 'This is simply what I do.'

Let us introduce the moral, courtesy of an approach by Lewis Carroll over 100 years ago. We use Lewis as the challenger to the logician, Logs.

A deductive demand too far

Logs puts forward a very simple argument for Lewis to assess:

> Premise One: All men are mortal.
> Conclusion C: Socrates is mortal.

Lewis rightly points out that the conclusion does not follow from the premise. He is right to expect something more: and Logs is happy to accommodate, by adding the following:

> Premise Two: Socrates is a man.

Logs, fine logician that he is, insists that Lewis must now accept the conclusion; but Lewis frowns. 'Yes, I accept the premises, but I am unsure. Must I accept the conclusion?' 'If all men are mortal and if Socrates is a man,' replies Logs, 'then it follows that he is mortal.' Lewis's eyes light up. 'I see – but that is surely another premise – so please add to the argument.'

> Premise Three: If Premises One and
>   Two, then C.

'Right! Now you must accept the conclusion,' says Logs beamingly, but Lewis resists, replying, 'I am still not absolutely certain.' 'You're not very quick,' smirks Logs. 'Look, if you accept Premises One, Two and Three, then C must follow.' Lewis sighs. 'I fancy that is another premise which is needed for the conclusion. Please write it down as Premise Four.' And so the tale continues. Logs is on an endless and ever irritating path once he tries to justify deduction by adding further 'if . . ., then . . .' premises. Following the rule of 'First add a corresponding "If . . ., then . . ." conditional as an additional premise in whatever latest argument is proposed' in order validly to reach a sought conclusion ensures no conclusion is validly reached.

A valid deductive argument, here of the *modus ponens* form, cannot be further justified by adding further premises. It is also no help to say that the argument is valid because it follows the rule of *modus ponens*. Lewis may then set Logs off on an endless task of justifying that rule. To dissolve the problem, we need to accept that at some stages nothing more can be said. True, sometimes an argument casually given, which looks invalid, may be enthymematic: that is, there is a suppressed premise assumed to be accepted. We saw this when Logs revealed Premise Two. But nothing more can be said to justify the argument. It is valid.

A ship on the open sea

Descartes supposed a basket of apples containing some rotten ones. Not wanting the rest to go bad, we should empty out all the apples and select only good ones to place back into the basket. So too, with our beliefs. The apple metaphor may harmonize with the thought that there is a rock bottom of justifications, of explanations – for, of course, Descartes cannot doubt all his beliefs: for example, his belief that contradictions should be rejected. Maybe the basket framework could represent such basic beliefs; but a better metaphor for the nature of our search for knowledge comes from Otto Neurath: 'We are like sailors who must rebuild their ship on the open sea, never able to dismantle it in dry-dock and to reconstruct it there out of the best materials.' To revise some beliefs, we must hold firm to others to keep afloat.

Arguably, the moral of this chapter is that 'in the end' we must accept that we behave in certain ways, and that we have certain tools with which to assess our beliefs, with which to repair the ship. 'Tools' is perhaps a more apt term for what we may otherwise think of as 'basic beliefs' concerning what constitutes good explanations and valid deductions. About such basic beliefs – such tools – nothing more can be said, unless and until we awake tomorrow with new perspectives and new ways of doing.

CHAPTER 35

How to bring meaning to life . . .
and not roll boulders pointlessly

In the myth of Sisyphus, the gods have condemned Sisyphus to roll a huge and heavy boulder to the top of a hill. The boulder always rolls back down, the result being that Sisyphus must start his labours again. His task is, it seems, pointless. We may ourselves suffer feelings of Sisyphean futility. Even when we secure boulders to the top, we struggle with yet more tasks in life; and we know that when we are gone, others will struggle and then, one day, all will be gone. Even when not struggling, when sitting contentedly, what is the point of that?

Eternity solves nothing

'What's the point?' The question hits virtually all of us at some time or other. Of course, we can give points – purposes, aims – *within* our lives. The point of studying is to achieve the degree, to secure the desired job, to enable a better home, to have fast cars, children and holidays abroad, and to have more than just another drink. The point of his life may be her life and the point of her life may be his; but that is circular, providing no answer for the point of their lives together. So, how are lives in total meaningful? Once faced with the 'meaning' questions we may feel that, for life to be satisfactory, there must be answers. Some turn to God, believing that we are part of a greater plan; yet that alone may be no comfort. On the 'glorious twelfth' the shooting of grouse commences: the grouse are part of a greater plan, but a plan that ultimately benefits the grouse not at all.

If it is legitimate always to ask, 'What's the point?', we may ask for the point of God's plan — and the point of any afterlife eternal living. As Wittgenstein wrote, 'Is a riddle solved by the fact that I survive for ever? Is this eternal life not as enigmatic as our present one?'

Assuming no afterlife, our tasks, in contrast to Sisyphus's, are not endless, but when, through death, we finish the daily round of work, home, family and rest, the baton is passed to the children, and then the grandchildren. Yet that our lives stand in relationship to others does not afford meaning to our lives unless the lives of those others are meaningful — but then we are simply passing the 'meaning creation' buck.

King of kings

Shelley's sonnet 'Ozymandias' tells of a traveller from an antique land uncovering some broken pillars and a shattered visage:

And on the pedestal these words appear:
'My name is Ozymandias, king of kings:
Look on my works, ye Mighty, and despair!'
Nothing beside remains. Round the decay
Of that colossal wreck, boundless and bare
The lone and level sands stretch far away.

So much for the attempt by the king of kings to immortalize his fame; yet even had he succeeded, we may still have asked how that immortal fame produced meaningfulness. After all, our lives, and not mere fame, even if eternal, fail to overcome the threat of meaninglessness. Our nature appears to create the threat. Schopenhauer, the philosopher of pessimism, despite (as Nietzsche quipped) after-dinner flute playing, argues that, when we are striving for something, we are dissatisfied, for we have not yet achieved what we seek. Yet if we achieve what we seek, we are bored; so we move on to more striving, which in turn will lead either to failure or boredom.

How to overcome Schopenhauer's view on life's meaninglessness requires, first, recognition that what is impossible ought not to distress. We are bound to be inconsolable if we think that for a point to be of any ultimate value, it must always have a further point external to it, and that there must be a final point.

Secondly, consider why we do what we do. Some things we do merely as means to an end: they have instrumental value. Other things, the ends, must be desired on their own account, and may be desirable in the sense of being worthy of desire. They form the point of what we do. Indeed, the very variety of our activities, contrasting with the Sisyphean repetition, may possess intrinsic value. As with explanations, points must come to an end. One point of philosophy is that it shows that points can come to an end, without loss of value.

Absurdity

The garden blossoms in summer; at the piano the child plays her first simplified Bach; and Evelyn's dinner, so carefully prepared, goes remarkably well. Yes, the flowers eventually wither, the teenager gives up the piano, and the dinner is eaten. That that is so should undermine neither blossoms, piano playing and Evelyn's dinner, nor the various struggles involved in securing their achievement. Such struggles and outcomes give meaning to life.

Sometimes means to an end possess value solely because of the end; often, though, the means and end are intertwined, with the intertwine enhancing. The value of achieving the examination pass, the sensuous love-making, even merely finishing the book, rests in part on having worked for those outcomes. Simply pressing a button to secure the pass, the orgasm or the book well-read often would fail to give what we seek. Of course, human achievements, seemingly great or small, may appear to vanish into the tiniest specks compared with the size of the Universe. We fret and fume, grow excited and proud, sad and anguished, about aspects of our daily lives, but from a detached perspective, the 'perspective of the Universe', how utterly insignificant, how absurd, how immodest of ourselves to care so! Yet, as the quip goes, size is not everything – and in this matter, nothing at all.

'What is the point of philosophy?' Well, it may bring to the fore what we already know. Earlier it reminded us that activities can be meaningful, 'point-filled', without any further point. It may also bring to the fore that what is meaningful does not thereby have to be permanent, eternal or big. Philosophy's intrinsic value is its reflective activity; and in such reflection we encounter incongruities between the pretence of a universe's perspective and the attached perspective of our very real concerns – whether our hair is looking good, whether our date will turn up, whether it was real champagne.

Sleepwalking through life

The unexamined life is not worth living, said Socrates. Here there is no insistence that examination is vital for meaning; indeed, losing the self in experiences, in art, in love, with no further thought, has value. Reflection, though, also has value; it is preferable to sleepwalking through life, sleepwalking bearing kinship to life on Nozick's Experience Machine of Chapter 33.

With reflection, we may make sense of our lives through integrating the events, attitudes, regrets and hopes. Of course, some may enjoy the serendipity of fragments, kaleidoscopic living with no underlying theme. 'Enjoy?' That smacks of a hedonism of transient pleasures. A fulfilled life is likely not to be dominated by pleasurable tingles, but by what is considered worthwhile. Now, what is worthwhile includes sensual delights, the caress of a loved one, the beauty in the architecture; but it also includes struggles to do the right thing, have regard to others – and thus we may fill our lives and others' with meaning.

Jean-Paul Sartre stressed how we must choose our values, our meaning. He told of a student in 1940s Paris under German occupation. The student anguished between escape to England to join the Free French Forces, and remaining in Paris, looking after his mother. The mother was in despair, her elder son having been killed. The student felt for his mother, yet wanted to avenge his brother's death. Advisers may give conflicting advice, but even if unanimous, the student would still need to choose what to do. 'You are free, therefore choose – that is to say, invent.' Sartre's comment holds even if we live in a deterministic world: the student still had to choose to stay or not stay. The comment holds even if we are an Abraham 'hearing' the voice of an angel, telling us to sacrifice our son. We may still choose to resist; we may, indeed, choose to question the voice's angelic credentials.

Choosing may come by spinning a coin; yet that would make the matters appear trivial, the choices capricious. Just choosing may suggest no scope for reason; yet reflection on options helps to highlight consequences and to view actions in new lights. The student, after reflection, discussion and consulting his heart, may suddenly see his face in the mirror as that of a coward if staying with his mother, a coward fearing the jeers of his friends. Yet he may lift himself and meet such accusations with courage.

We find ourselves with values – some things matter more than others – yet even so, we confront difficult choices and, in choosing, we are making ourselves. Recognition of that is to be authentic; denial is Sartre's bad faith, *mauvaise foi*, met in Chapter 28. Bad faith arises, for example, when we announce that we must do so and so because of our upbringing, the voice of

God or what the authorities ordered – or because of the sort of person we are.

Waiters and the owl

Sartre tells of a certain café waiter:

> *His movement is quick and forward, a little too precise, a little too rapid. He comes towards the patrons with a step a little too quick . . . his voice, his eyes express an interest a little too solicitous for the order of the customer . . . he gives himself the quickness and pitiless rapidity of things . . . the waiter in the café plays with his condition in order to realize it.*

Sartre's waiter need not be in bad faith. His actions may be ironic; he may be laughing within at the roles that he – and all of us – play. When detaching ourselves, taking the viewpoint of the Universe, we encountered the anguish of insignificance; here, though, the detachment helps us through life. Irony and play have value; incongruities can cause a smile and rightly so.

And yet before and after the smile, we may live within melancholy. We know of life's disappointments, of suffering. However much we care, we easily forget the dispossessed as we sit in the bar or engage with the opera.

'Life must be lived forwards, though can only be understood backwards.' Thus wrote Søren Kierkegaard, the 19th-century Danish existentialist. With vision cast forwards, we have to make choices and those choices may cast our lives to date in different lights. How we read the past depends in part on the future. What may currently be seen as bad moves may, in retrospect, have success writ large on their face. Prior to death, we retain scope. We take our lives in new directions, make amends for the past, offer our renderings of what we did. The sting is that once dead we are, in Sartre's bleak words, 'prey to the living' – to the Other. We are impotent as others sum up our lives. Even here before death, we may try to see ourselves as others may do.

> 'What if in reality my whole life has been wrong?' It occurred to him that what had appeared utterly impossible the night before – that he had not lived his life as he should have done – might after all be true.

Those words of Ivan Ilyich, presented by Leo Tolstoy, may take detachment one giant leap too far; yet that we can reflect on our lives, and seek for better, is distinctively human.

Hegel observed, with philosophy as the wise owl in mind:

> The owl of Minerva spreads her wings only when dusk starts to fall.

As death approaches, as our own dusk begins to fall, some may feel that a final understanding arrives. Despite, or because of, philosophical reflection, many of us, though, retain a sense of life's mystery and melancholy: we despair at suffering and death – and also at everyday intrusions, utility bills, chores and mobiles. So, to place matters in perspective, let us turn to David Hume's remedy, when bewildered by perplexing philosophical clouds:

> *Most fortunately it happens, that since reason is incapable of dispelling these clouds, nature herself suffices to that purpose, and cures me of this philosophical melancholy and delirium, either by relaxing this bent of mind, or by some avocation and lively impression of my senses, which obliterate all these chimeras.*

When in despair, we should remind ourselves how our spirits may rise in ravishing music. Mystery, awe and piety may be felt by atheistic humanists, not just by those of religious bent. We may find meaning in daffodils blooming, in a small gift filled with thought, in the entanglements, humour and beauty of speaking the sun down with friends and wine. And when all that is said, we may all the more warm to the words of Ludwig Wittgenstein:

> *Wherefore one cannot speak, thereof one must be silent.*

GLOSSARY

Caveat emptor! Buyer beware! The entries below are merely indicative. Each term has generated hundreds of thousands of words by philosophers.

a posteriori and *a priori*
How may you come to know a truth? *A posteriori* truths are those that can only be known through experience. *A priori* truths are those that can be known independently of experience; they can be worked out by reason alone.

absurdity
A term associated with existentialists who claim that our fundamental choices are absurd, namely, without reason. It is also sometimes used loosely to mean 'contradiction'.

action
An event that is someone's doing something intentionally, often contrasted with movement or behaviour such as a twitch or a blush not under the person's control.

argument
Philosophers' arguments are not physical fights (well, not usually), but consist of premises and conclusions. The premises are the reasons for accepting the conclusions. The arguments may be deductively valid, in which conclusions logically follow from premises. The premises, though, may

offer only some support for the conclusions: they do so, for example, in inductive arguments.

Aristotelianism

In ethics, this is a theory that emphasizes the importance of our character, our 'virtues', in leading flourishing lives. If we have the traits, the dispositions, towards honesty, kindness, fairness, for example, we are more likely to live well. The approach is also known as 'virtue theory' or 'neo-Aristotelianism'.

behaviourism and functionalism

All we have to go on with regard to the psychological states of others is their behaviour. The behaviourist understands psychological states as constituted by behaviour and the disposition to behave in certain ways. Behaviourism developed into functionalism, whereby psychological states just are the causal roles of states upon which behaviour and other psychological states depend.

Cartesian dualism

Descartes argues that there are two types of created substances: material and immaterial. What we take as a single entity, a human being with physical size as well as psychological properties, Descartes views as a twosome: a body and an immaterial mind.

category mistake

A term introduced by Gilbert Ryle who accuses Descartes of mistakenly thinking of the mind as an item belonging to the same general category 'substance' as does a material item, except that a mind is not material and not in space–time.

compatibilism

In the context of free will, this is the position that free will and determinism are compatible; they can coexist. Even if all our actions are causally determined, we may yet act freely.

conditionals

'If..., then ...' gives the typical form of conditional propositions. 'If she turns up, he will be pleased.' The propositions need not relate to the future. If a number is even, then it is the sum of two primes. The first part of a conditional is the 'antecedent'; the second part is the 'consequent'.

consequentialism

A moral theory holding that the rightness of actions is determined solely by the actions' consequences.

contingent truths

Truths that might not have been truths. Contingent truths contrast with necessary truths (see below).

contradictions and contraries

A contradiction exists when two propositions can neither both be true together nor both be false together. Two propositions may be contraries, but not contradictory. This print is blue and this print is yellow are 'contraries'. Both propositions can be false; the print need be neither one nor the other.

conversational implicatures

When a student asks for comments on her essay, the teacher may look embarrassed and say, 'Well, the typing is good'. That does not logically imply that the essay is bad, but it does convey that idea. That is an example of a conversational implicature.

counterfactuals

Conditional propositions – see above – with antecedents that are false. Consideration of them usually concerns those in which the antecedents are believed or known to be false.

deontology

A theory that our moral duties are not dependent on consequences: promises, for example, should be kept, even if the consequences are bad.

deduction

This occurs in an argument where the conclusion is intended logically to follow from the premises. When it does, the argument is deductively valid. If, additionally, the premises are true, the argument is said to be 'sound'.

determinism

At heart, this is the claim that all events are caused. If so, then it may undermine the existence of free will, but see 'compatibilism'.

eliminativism

A theory of mind that considers our concepts of belief, desire, hope and similar psychological states as belonging to a folk psychology; one day it will be replaced by a purely neurological theory.

empirical

Relating to knowledge that is based on experiences of the world, through everyday life, experiments or, for example, listening to the news.

epistemic

Epistemic matters concern knowledge and belief – what we can tell and how we represent the world.

eternalism

The position that the past, present and future all exist and are as real as each other. Past, present and future states are merely different segments of the temporal dimension relative to where we are.

existentialism

An approach to life that emphasizes the importance of the individual, his perspective on the world and his need to make his own choices, his own values.

fallacies

Bad arguments. It is a fallacy to move from if p, then q; q, to concluding that p. If the Queen is smiling, then she is happy. She is happy; therefore she is smiling. No, she may be happy without smiling. Another fallacy is that of *post hoc ergo propter hoc* (after this, therefore because of this). Just because the rain started after I prayed, it does not follow that the rain started because I prayed.

free will
Individuals have free will, it is often claimed, when they could have willed otherwise – in exactly the same surrounding circumstances. If so, free will and determinism would appear to be incompatible.

identity of indiscernibles
Leibniz proposed that if two seemingly different items have all the same properties and relations, then indeed they are not two but one.

identity theory
The theory that psychological states are identical with physical states – roughly, mind is brain.

implication
Starting propositions (premises) or positions imply or entail other propositions when those other propositions necessarily follow from the former. 'Implication' in this sense is a relation between propositions. Henrietta deserves to be punished; that implies that she has done something wrong.

induction
Reasoning from evidence to a conclusion that goes beyond the evidence and that the evidence does not guarantee to be true. All water observed to date has frozen at very low temperatures; inductive reasoning

leads to the conclusion that even unobserved water freezes at very low temperatures.

intension/extension

These (note the 's') are conditions associated with words, relating to their meaning. That which is designated is the extension. The name 'Obama' may now be linked to the condition of being US President: that is its intension. The extension is the flesh-and-blood man.

intentionality

The directedness of psychological states, such as beliefs, hopes and, indeed, intentions. Consider the *belief* that John Maynard Keynes was a great economist. The intentional content of that belief is the proposition that it represents, namely, that Keynes was a great economist; the intentional object is Keynes. Arguably, a few psychological states are not intentional, for example, just being depressed, but depressed about nothing in particular.

logic

The science of good argument. It shows which forms of arguments are such that if the premises are true, then the conclusions must be true (in the case of 'deduction') or at least have some support in their favour (in the case of 'induction').

metaphysics

The study of the ultimate nature of reality. One big element is 'ontology' – what there is. There are people and porcupines, purples, protons and prime numbers. Can they all be understood as grounded in one basic type of being – or may ultimate reality be constituted by two or more different types of item, such as the physical and the psychological?

modus ponens

This is a valid form of deductive argument. If p, then q; p: therefore q. For example: 'If Piers owns this book, then he made a good buy. Piers does own this book. Therefore, he made a good buy.' If the first premise is false, the conclusion may be false.

modus tollens

Another valid form of deductive argument. If p, then q; not-q: therefore not-p: 'If Piers owns this book, then he made a good buy. Piers did not make a good buy. Therefore, he does not own this book.'

necessary and sufficient conditions

The conditions that are necessary for a concept to apply and which, taken together, are sufficient for it to apply. Consider whether Higgs is a murderer. A necessary condition is that there be a death. Additional necessary conditions are that Higgs caused the death, did so intentionally – and that it be against the law. Jointly, they suffice for a murder.

necessary truths

Truths that cannot be false. There are also necessary falsehoods, known as 'contradictions'. Necessarily, the number nine is greater than the number seven. Definitions usually give necessary truths by stipulation: a vixen is a female fox.

objectivity and subjectivity
Objective truths are true, independently of what people think or feel about them. Subjective truths depend on what people think or feel about them.

paradox
A paradox arises when we apparently reason well to a conclusion that seems blatantly false. Zeno of Elea thus reasoned that all motion is illusion.

person
Philosophers often use the term to apply to individuals who possess a sense of the self continuing into the future. Some non-human animals, maybe chimps, maybe dolphins, are persons; and some humans are not persons, for example, those in persistent vegetative states.

physicalism
The theory that what exists is what physics, once properly completed, says there is. In particular, it is the theory that psychological states are nothing but neurological states. When science understood the world around us in terms of material atoms, the theory was then known as 'materialism'.

presentism
A metaphysical doctrine that only the present exists. It contrasts with eternalism (see above).

relativism
A position that claims that what we take to be objective

moral truths are in fact dependent upon culture, social norms or circumstances.

rights

Within morality, talk of your having a right to X usually flags the existence of a distinctive and strong ground for its being wrong for someone to interfere with your possession, or seeking, of X.

scepticism

A term usually applied when people are doubting the possibility of knowledge in some realm.

self-reference

This occurs when an item refers to itself. It is sometimes seen as the source of many paradoxes. Classically, when someone says, 'I am lying' what is said seems to be referring to itself and seems to lead to a contradiction. 'This sentence is written in English', though, is about itself and poses no problem. Or, is it about itself? What the sentence expresses – the proposition – is about the sentence, but the proposition is not about itself. In such ways, more complexities arise.

teleology

Often we explain events by reference to their causes, the metaphorical pushes. Teleological explanations look to the end, the 'telos', what is being aimed at – the metaphorical pulls.

type/token distinction

How many words in this sentence are indeed words? If your answer is 'nine', you are counting each token. If your answer is 'eight', you are counting types. 'Words' occurs twice in the sentence; so, there are two instances of the same type. Each mental event, each token, may be identical with a physical event, but there may be no identity between the types of mental event and the types of physical event: this may bring out a difference between different types of identity theory.

use/mention distinction

There is a big difference between a 'cat' and a cat. The latter is furry and miaows, unless radically damaged; the former has three letters. We may use words to talk about items in the world. When we mention the words, we are talking about the words.

utilitarianism

A consequentialist moral doctrine. The right action is the one that leads, or is likely to lead, to the greatest happiness of the greatest number, a phrase much promoted by Jeremy Bentham and John Stuart Mill. Of course, a lot hangs on what counts as happiness.

INDEX